# The UNLIKELIEST CHAMPION:

## The Incredible Story of the 2011 UConn Huskies and Their Run to the College Basketball National Championship

# AARON TORRES

**With a Foreword by CBS Sports College Basketball Writer Matt Norlander**

ISBN: 1466363495
ISBN-13: 9781466363496
Library of Congress Control Number: 2011917477

CreateSpace, North Charleston, SC

*To my parents, who- as best I can tell- have absolutely nothing in common…except for an unbelievable amount of love and support for their children.*

*Everyone should be as lucky as I am.*

# Foreword

Having rightfully never been offered to pen a foreword before, I've got to say, this is pretty awkward and my confidence level is rivaling what it was dialed at on the night of my junior prom. Let's hope for less fop sweat and no pathetic rejection. But I'm flattered nonetheless that Aaron asked me to contribute the first words that will appear in his first book.

So what should I do here? How does this work? Asking these kinds of questions—so unsophisticated for a foreword. But I'd rather be honest and upfront with you. Transparency is the best policy, so I've got no issue sharing the fact I looked online for hints in how to write a good foreword, and I come to you filled with shame and predictable pragmatism. I'm clearly under-qualified for this kind of favor.

Forewords are meant to be written by those with Big and Recognizable Names; I don't even think my mailman knows I exist. I met a coach over the summer, a man I'd talked to on the phone three or four times before that, and when I introduced myself he said, "Oh, Matt Orlandor. Nice to finally meet you, man!" Yes. So whatever I, Mr. Orlandor, can do to help Mr. Torres, I'm here and happy to do so.

One site also stated forewords are implanted to boost a book's credibility. Can you feel the credibility of this book soaring above your head and into the mesosphere with each passing sentence? Additionally, forewords are supposed to be about the man or woman writing said foreword, and the relationship they have with the book's author. I'm not one to talk about myself, as you can see, but I can and will wax about Aaron. Yes, the author should get some love in his foreword, so let's do that.

Everyone loves a good how-I-met-them story. You want to know how I came to know of Aaron Torres' existence? It turns out he stalked my fiancée in college. Or maybe something close to that. Or maybe I'm exaggerating. It's a foreword. Dramatic effect and all. It turns out he did attend UConn with her, shared a couple of classes, and that's eventually what led him to me. Romantic, small-world stuff.

Upon graduating, Aaron was diligent in getting to know me better. For this, I have no answers. We finally met, after months of email and Twitter and podcast correspondence, in the aisles of Madison Square Garden in 2010. I haven't seen him since. For all I know, Aaron Torres no longer exists and I've been sucked into writing this as part of an elaborate, long con. The alternative: just as fun.

Here's how I see it: Writing a book about the 2010-11 Connecticut Huskies was paramount to appeasing Connecticut Husky Fan. UConn's fan base is one of the most intense in the country, and the reason that's so is it spans ages 9 to 90. Plenty of great schools have passionate bases, but the heavy lovers range between 18 and 50 years old. It never ceases to amaze me just how many octogenarians attend games in Storrs.

So the book immediately becomes a staple for any worth-his-salt Husky fan. Get it on the shelf immediately, and prepare to share and tell the story of this team years down the road to the youngins who get the Husky hoodies tossed over their shoulders before they can even pronounce "Khalid El-Amin."

The story of UConn's third and most improbable championship run is unparalleled for a few reasons, and with so many facets to the team and the season, cause for a full-blown book was obvious. I credit Aaron for hopping on this project immediately, as he didn't really wait. He chased after the idea once the janitors swept all the confetti off the floor in Houston.

Aaron's a guy who reminds me of myself in a lot of ways, which is a horrific sign. But he's humble, eager, hard-working, generous and grateful, which is crucial to creating a lot of enemies in this business. It also enables him to get to know a lot of subjects.

# FOREWORD

There is no bigger show in Connecticut than the UConn men's team (though the women's team sprints along stride for stride, something no other state can lay claim to). The 2010-11 squad was so fascinating, because in many ways it really wasn't good for stretches during the regular season. Those clichés about playing together, playing as a team, playing well at the right time—they don't fit UConn, either. The already-fabled Big East run, that five-games-in-five-days epic, hadn't ever happened before. And had it not been for Kemba Walker, UConn doesn't make it to Saturday night in Madison Square Garden.

The tournament run is actually less memorable, in my opinion. That title game was hideous. But: fitting. UConn was so unpredictable all season long. You'll be reminded of that—and learn plenty about why—in the chapters that lie ahead for you. But with all that surrounded this team all season long, from controversy with the NCAA to bad losses, shaky play from its best players and more, it all made for the best story college basketball could have gotten to end its 2010-11 season.

I've believed it since the second the team won it all—no Husky is as beloved now, and perhaps forever, as Kemba. What he did will be cherished and celebrated by the fan base as much as anything outside of Calhoun's tenure.

Plenty of books have been written about college basketball's greatest teams. The '10-11 Huskies were not that, but their story of winning a title is a top-five drama in the history of the sport. This book should be considered one of the most vital tangible chapters in the history of Connecticut basketball. Aaron knows more than just the team. He knows and lives the culture of the Nutmeg state; knows how the relationship between program and state is without conditions in its love. And now the school's greatest men's basketball story is laid out for every basketball fan to relive and relearn.

Matt Norlander
CBSSports.com

# Contents

# Prologue

In the eyes and hearts of most every college basketball fan, Kemba Walker will be remembered above all for his tournament play. He became a household name with his epic Maui Invitational performance; a folk hero in leading UConn to five wins in five days in the Big East Tournament; and a champion when the Huskies won six more games to take home the 2011 NCAA title. Maybe the defining tournament of his life came back in 2007 however, not in front of the eyes of the nation, but instead in front of a handful of spectators and scouts in an Arizona gym.

At the time, Walker was coming off a solid junior year in high school at Rice High School in the Bronx, but was hardly yet a star. Quite the opposite actually, as the 2006–2007 season was the first that Kemba had even started for the New York City powerhouse, after he spent his first two years at the school backing up McDonald's All-American Edgar Sosa.

With the chance to get starter's minutes for the first time, Kemba stepped up his game, averaging fourteen points and leading the Raiders to the CHSAA Class AA title. Included in that successful junior year was a January victory over the No. 4 team in the country, Simeon High School in Chicago, in a game which Kemba got the better of the top senior guard in the country, Derrick Rose. For those wondering, yes, that'd be the same Derrick Rose that would later go on to win the NBA MVP award five years later.

So it's safe to say that entering the Arizona tournament, Kemba Walker was an accomplished basketball player. He held college scholarship offers from hometown St. John's and Cincinnati, which was the favorite for his services at the time.

Still, he just wasn't quite *Kemba Walker* yet either.

That all changed when Walker arrived in Arizona with his New York Gauchos AAU teammates at the 2007 Arizona Cactus Classic. Walker was hardly the highest profile player in Arizona, and specifically in 2007, the tournament was chock-full of the top high school talent in the country. Future college and professional stars filled the gym by the dozens, sneakers squeaking, sweat dripping to the floor. Included in the field were DeMar DeRozan and Jrue Holiday, both of whom would go on to be first round NBA Draft picks within two years. Also in attendance was the consensus No. 1 point guard in the country, Brandon Jennings. The lefty from Los Angeles was the apple of every recruiter's eye and one of the top targets of the University of Connecticut.

Yet despite all that big-name cache, it'd be a little guard from the Bronx who'd steal the show. Like he'd do a few years later in Maui, Kemba Walker would enter the tournament a relative unknown, the proverbial "I've heard the name, but can't put a face with it" high school basketball player. And just like Maui, he'd leave as the buzz of the tournament, the name on the tip of everyone's tongues.

Undersized but hardly overmatched, the Gauchos ripped through the early part of the tournament, overwhelming bigger teams with their quickness and New York City grit. After arriving in Arizona with only eight players, and at times playing as many as four guards, the Gauchos won their opening game against the New Mexico Force before winning an amazing five games in a fourteen-hour stretch the following day (and you thought five wins in five days at the Big East Tournament run was impressive!). Their basketball marathon began just after 10:00 a.m. with a 66–48 win over a team named Sporting Chance and concluded with a victory over Pump-N-Run Elite in a 10:44 p.m. tip, with three additional wins in between. Just another day in the life of an AAU basketball player, huh?

The Gauchos had a quick turnaround the next morning with a 9:57 a.m. tip-off against Wisconsin Playground. Not that the lack of sleep mattered as they would go on to win, thanks to Walker's twenty-three points and ten rebounds.

In their semifinal, the Gauchos should've been intimidated when their guard-heavy lineup went against a California Supreme team with a frontline that's as big as they come in AAU ball. In particular, California Supreme featured Tyler Lamb (who'd go on to play at UCLA), Solomon Hill (the same at Arizona), and one of the nation's top rising sophomores Jeremy Tyler. Tyler would later gain infamy for not only skipping his freshman year of college to play professionally overseas, but also his *senior year of high school* as well, before being selected by the Golden State Warriors in the second round of the 2011 NBA Draft. To this day Tyler is the only person to attempt such a feat (and based on his disastrous results, it will likely remain that way).

But again, for whatever the Gauchos lacked in sized, they made up for with overwhelming quickness and suffocating defensive pressure. The sheer bulk of California Supreme was no match for the speed of the kids from New York as the Gauchos cruised to an 88–76 win. Darryl "Truck" Bryant (who later went on to West Virginia) scored twenty-three points, with Kemba held to "only" twenty.

With the win over California Supreme, it set up a championship game showdown with the only other undefeated team in the tournament, the Belmont Stars. The Stars featured DeRozan and Jennings, both of whom would go on to be Top 10 NBA Draft picks within two years.

Now before we go any further, it's important to give some quick context to this story.

Entering the summer of 2007, Jennings was the point guard of everyone's obsession, including UConn's. The lefty was silky smooth with deceptive speed, and as mentioned, listed the Huskies along with USC and Arizona as his schools of choice. Many believed UConn to actually have been the front-runner in the Jennings sweepstakes since he was the cousin of former Huskies guard Marcus Williams, and was coached at times by Marcus's father Kelly Williams.

"The Williams family saw Brandon as a little brother," former UConn assistant coach Tom Moore said. Moore was the primary recruiter of Jennings, and left UConn just weeks prior to the Cactus

Classic. "At the time, we thought we were in great shape, and would end up getting him."

Which put Kemba Walker in an interesting position. Ultimately everything that Walker wanted to be—the No. 1 point guard in the country and the No. 1 recruiting target of the UConn Huskies—Brandon Jennings already was. Jennings was an Internet sensation even before the Arizona tournament, with a hype that preceded him well before he squared with the little-known Walker in Tucson.

"When we got to Arizona, the first thing we did was go to the gym early and watched Brandon Jennings and Belmont," former Gauchos head coach and current Arizona assistant coach Emmanuel "Book" Richardson said. "There was just an aura to him in that tournament. He was a sheer force. Unstoppable. And you better believe it fueled us."

It certainly fueled Kemba Walker.

From the outset of the game, Walker wouldn't be denied; if anything he took it as a challenge to go ahead and knock the crown of the "top point guard in the country" right off Jennings's head. On the Gauchos' first possession, Richardson set up an isolation play for Kemba, and Walker blew by his defender, got to the rim, made a layup, and got fouled.

From there, it was on.

The point guard with the tiny reputation spent the rest of the afternoon outplaying the point guard with the massive one. Walker finished the game with twenty-four points, five rebounds, and four assists, in a 102–96 title game victory. Jennings chipped in twenty-four points himself, but it was to the detriment of his teammates, when he shot just ten for twenty-four from the field and one for nine from three in the loss. With the victory Walker went from national unknown to hot commodity, doing what he'd eventually do quite often in his UConn career: taking home the tournament MVP.

Of course there was one more caveat with the Arizona Cactus Classic that played in Kemba Walker's favor that weekend. The tournament was played during a recruiting dead period, meaning that college coaches weren't allowed in the gym, and hadn't actually seen him play.

While that was certainly a negative for some, it was nothing if not advantageous for Walker. As he spent the weekend going point-for-point and win-for-win with Jennings before eventually knocking him off in the title game, Kemba's legend only continued to grow as college coaches literally refreshed their computers for box score updates on the previously unknown guard. By the end of the weekend, Walker's recruiting buzz was sky-high with both Richardson and Rice High School head coach Moe Hicks receiving phone calls from virtually every college coach in the country. Included in that group were Kentucky, North Carolina, and Walker's self-proclaimed "Dream School," the University of Connecticut.

That's right. Long before the Huskies had any idea who Walker was, the point guard knew exactly who *they* were. A young Kemba watched fellow New York City point guard Taliek Brown lead UConn to the 2004 National Championship and decided right then and there UConn was the school for him.

But until the trip out to Arizona, it looked more and more certain that the dream of playing for UConn would die in favor of a new likely destination, Cincinnati, which had been heavily recruiting Walker since Coach Mick Cronin's hire a year earlier. St. John's was also a possibility. Even after the big tournament out in Arizona, UConn wasn't totally swayed on Kemba and nearly lost him to a new suitor, the North Carolina Tar Heels. Luckily for the Huskies, fate intervened and right as Walker went online to book a plane ticket to visit North Carolina, Hicks got a call from Tar Heels assistant Steve Robinson. Apparently North Carolina had just picked up a commitment from California guard Larry Drew. Just like that the Tar Heels were out of the Kemba Walker sweepstakes.

Finally UConn stepped forward. With Jennings still unsure about his college choice, the Huskies finally moved on Walker, when UConn assistant Andre LaFleur called Richardson and Hicks about Kemba right as the North Carolina fiasco was going down. A few weeks after returning from Arizona, Walker visited the Storrs campus with his mother, Richardson, and Hicks, and a few days later officially announced his intention to go to UConn. "From day one, Kemba always wanted to be a Husky," Richardson said. "It was the easiest recruiting pitch Jim Calhoun ever had to make."

As for Jennings, well his non-committal attitude ended up as one of the biggest breaks in recent UConn basketball history. As things would play out, Jennings committed to Arizona a few weeks after the Cactus Classic but never actually played a single game of college basketball. After high school Jennings bypassed a trip through the NCAAs, instead signing with a team in Rome and playing what would've been his freshman year in Italy. Eventually he entered the 2009 NBA Draft and was selected ninth overall by the Milwaukee Bucks.

But what was Arizona's loss turned into UConn's gain thanks to a big weekend at the Cactus Classic.

"That was *the* tournament that put Kemba on the map," said Richardson. "He went from a four-star to a five-star, from a Top 50 player to a Top 20 player, from a 'good' guard to one of the best in the country."

It was also where UConn got the first piece to their eventual championship puzzle.

Of course no one knew it at the time.

⌘  ⌘  ⌘

I'm Aaron Torres, and I'm a UConn basketball fan. For better or worse. In sickness and in health. Until death do us part.

Actually I take back what I just said.

I'm not a fan. A fan is someone who watches the games and maybe follows in the newspaper but moves on once the score goes final. A fan lives a normal life, isn't consumed by the tiniest details surrounding the team, and always put things in their proper perspective. After all these are just kids. And they are just playing a game.

The problem is that's just not me.

I can't keep things in proper perspective. Nor can I brush off a loss and move on to the next game. I always take things a little *too* personally, as if I had something to do with the actual outcome on the court. Not to mention that I start thinking about next season before this one ends, read dumb message board threads the way a middle-age housewife consumes *US Weekly* at the supermarket, and can name every hotshot recruit two years before he's even eligible to play in college. In some circles I'm what is known as a die-hard. My friends prefer a different name instead. They call me a lunatic. Quite frankly I can't blame them.

Sadly I'm not alone in feeling this way.

Understand that Connecticut isn't just a basketball-mad state: it's a basketball maniacal one. The two UConn basketball teams are covered by a media contingent so large, they're known simply as "The Hoard." Every men's and women's game is broadcast on local TV if it isn't being broadcast nationally. Head Coach Jim Calhoun is literally the highest-paid state employee in Connecticut (after factoring in contract bonuses), and despite what you may think of him, most everyone here agrees: there's no way he should give a dime back.

For most outsiders it'd be easy to say that in Connecticut the Huskies are like the Lakers in Los Angeles or the Yankees in New York. That'd be factually incorrect. Besides the Lakers, Los Angeles has the Dodgers and Kings, and not too far down the road the Angels and Ducks. Hell, the Lakers aren't even the only professional basketball team that plays in their own building. (Depending on if you think the Clippers are a professional team anyway). And New York is no different. The Yankees are important. They also share the airwaves with the Mets, Giants, Jets, Knicks, Islanders, and Rangers.

In New York and Los Angeles, you've got options. You grow up a Dodgers or Angels fan, Yankees or Mets. In Connecticut you have no option. Everyone loves UConn. The Huskies are our professional team (go ahead and insert your own "paying college athletes" joke here), no different than how the Crimson Tide are treated in Alabama, or the Kentucky Wildcats worshipped in the Commonwealth. But even then, Alabama has Auburn as a dividing line within the state's borders, and the same with the University of Louisville to Kentucky. The fan bases at Auburn and Louisville may be a small minority, but they are a minority none the less. UConn has nothing to draw our attention away from...well...UConn.

So it's with that as a background that you can begin to understand just how important UConn's basketball team is it to the state of Connecticut. And it's my hope that you'll eventually begin to appreciate just how important the 2011 UConn Huskies were in specific.

Understand that although UConn won the title in 2011, they were hardly favorites entering the season. Not even close. As they entered the 2011 season, UConn had no expectations from within the state's borders or beyond. None. Zip. If there's something less than zero, that's how most people felt about the UConn Huskies. Not everyone. But most.

Just two years after a Final Four berth in 2009, UConn's men's team was about as low as you could go. They were a disappointing 18–16 in 2010 and truly came to epitomize everything that you never want your team to be. They were passionless. They went through the motions. And most times they seemed to play basketball only because their coach made them, not because they actually wanted to. A lot like a kid choking down unwanted broccoli stems at dinner, actually.

To add to that, the scariest thing was that at the very least, the 2010 team did have talent. They had three seniors who'd played major roles on a Final Four team just a year before. However enigmatic they were, at the very least they were still fundamentally good at the sport of basketball. They knew how to win games in the Big East, even if they didn't necessarily do it very often.

Well, with those seniors gone following the 2010 season, they were replaced with a bunch of recruits that even most die-hards knew little about. Jeremy Lamb hadn't even started for his high school team as a *junior*. Shabazz Napier and Tyler Olander moved up their high school graduations by a year, only after UConn missed out on bigger recruiting targets. Neither was expected to graduate in time to enroll for the 2011 season, yet there they were on UConn's campus as freshmen in late 2010. And really, of all the freshmen, only Roscoe Smith seemed suited for the night-in and night-out wars of the Big East. Beyond him, the rest seemed to be quality role players, but nowhere near ready to play Pittsburgh, Syracuse, Louisville, and Georgetown on an everyday basis.

And all that wasn't even the worst part. Not even close.

Nope, the worst part was that in the midst of this all, looming NCAA sanctions had hung over the program for two years. Entering 2011, the NCAA's accusations had already cost UConn two assistant coaches, a handful of recruits, as well as their national image. And with the NCAA set to release their punishment against the program during the 2011 season, everyone feared the worst. Even if the team overachieved and was in NCAA Tournament contention, all their hard work could be wiped away with one broad stroke if the NCAA deemed fit.

Add all that together and the University of Connecticut's men's basketball program was at rock-bottom entering the 2011 season. Inexperienced, coming off an awful season and with NCAA investigators snooping around like the Hardy Boys, there weren't many people who thought much of the team. They didn't receive a *single vote* in the preseason polls and were picked to finish tenth just in the Big East. Overall the program was down for the count, and there was good reason to believe that they weren't getting up.

Luckily for UConn fans, no one bothered to tell Kemba Walker. Or maybe he just didn't listen.

Either way the constant questioning of doubters was nothing new for the six-foot guard from the Bronx; he'd been dealing with it since his pre-teen years. Those doubters told him he didn't have the skill to play at New York City powerhouse Rice High School. He proved them wrong. They said he was just a scorer and not a real point guard. Wrong again. Walker's own AAU coach Book Richardson told him he wasn't good enough to play at UConn. Kemba practically lived at the gym until he proved Richardson wrong too. And now they were telling him that his team had nothing to play for, that their season would be over before it'd even begun. It was time for Kemba to go work and let his basketball do the talking.

And over the course of the next seven or so months and forty-one games, that's exactly what he did.

From the first day of practice in October, Kemba Walker put his teammates, a downtrodden program, and an entire state on his back, and refused to let them stay down. He took a bunch of young kids and made them believe, and showed an old coach the fountain of youth. He did it all with a huge smile, and flair, skill, and substance, and heart that was significantly bigger than his six-foot frame. And it ended with a wild ride which culminated in one of the most unexpected championship runs in college basketball history. Through some of my own previously written articles, as well as plenty of new information, I've tried my best to capture it all.

From unranked in November, to forgotten in February, and kings of college in early April, there has never been a college basketball team quite like the 2011 UConn Huskies. All they needed was for someone to tell their story. This is it.

And to think: it all started in a hot gym in Arizona a few summers before.

# Chapter 1

## Prelude to a Championship: UConn's Disastrous 2010 Season

Like any great story, the tale of the 2011 UConn Huskies needed a great opening act. One was provided the previous season, by one of the most disappointing and tough-to-watch teams in school history.

Of course entering the 2009-2010 season, there was little reason to believe that one of college basketball's most successful programs was in for anything but another banner year. The UConn Huskies were coming off a Final Four run the previous March, had plenty of returning talent, and were again led into a season by Hall of Fame head coach Jim Calhoun, his twenty-fourth at the school. UConn was ranked in the Top 15 of both major national polls, and the Big East coaches picked them to finish third in the always tough conference.

And when looking at the roster, the reasons for optimism spread further, the primary reason being that UConn would open the season with the rarest of commodities in today's college basketball world: a trio of well-respected and highly experienced seniors. Jerome Dyson, Stanley Robinson, and Gavin Edwards had seen it and done it all in their three years at the school, and the logical thought process was that they could fill in the talent and leadership void left by departed seniors A. J. Price and Jeff Adrien, and junior Hasheem Thabeet, who had entered the NBA Draft.

Dyson was expected to lead the way on both ends of the court as the team's top scorer and one of the best perimeter defenders anywhere in the country. The six-foot-four guard didn't quite have the handle to play point and probably wasn't big enough to play shooting guard at the next level. But in Jim Calhoun's system at UConn, he was the perfect hybrid two-guard. During the previous year, Dyson had been the Huskies' leading scorer before his season ended abruptly with a knee injury in February. Many experts believed that had he stayed healthy, Dyson's talent might have been enough for UConn to seriously challenge North Carolina for the National Championship. Still, after averaging at least twelve points a game in each of his first three years, he was considered to be one of the better guards in college basketball's toughest conference.

Then there was Edwards. Entering his senior year, Edwards had never been the type of player who stood out during his first three years at UConn, but was the kind of do-it-all big man that every team needs to be successful. Fundamentally sound, but lacking elite athleticism, Edwards played a key role the previous year, backing up Thabeet and Adrien in the front court as the first big man off the bench. The 2010 season would be the first time the senior would get the chance to be a regular starter.

And finally there was Robinson, a crowd favorite and player who Calhoun had a soft spot for, who'd been equal parts frustrating and amazing in his three years in Storrs.

Robinson had arrived at UConn in the fall of 2006 as the heir apparent to NBA lottery pick Rudy Gay, and at six-foot-nine, he had a package of skills that most NBA small forwards would kill for. Robinson could rebound in the paint just as easily as hit threes from beyond the arc. He had the defensive instinct to guard point guards on the perimeter (which he would against John Wall later in the year) or block shots guarding seven-footers. And he had jumping ability that had to be seen to be believed.

The problem of course was that at times, Robinson also had a two-cent head. Calhoun even went so far as to suspend him for the beginning of his junior year, even though Robinson's academics were in check and he hadn't had any trouble with the law. Simply put, the coach believed his twenty-one-year-old small forward needed to grow up. And to a degree Robinson did, working in a scrap metal yard until December, when he was allowed to rejoin the team. The tough love seemed to work as Robinson went on to become one of the Huskies' most important players in their Final Four run. (One of the funniest side stories of the Robinson era was when he once interrupted a Calhoun press conference to hand his coach a Christmas gift. Essentially that was the Stanley Robinson era in a nutshell: nice kid, great talent, yet definitely a bit of an overall enigma.)

And after factoring in those three with a handful of talented underclassmen, including lightning-quick point guard Kemba Walker and bruising freshman forward Alex Oriahki, there was no reason to think that UConn couldn't make a second straight deep NCAA Tournament run. While a second straight Final Four didn't seem likely, it wasn't totally out of the question either.

But to all the experts who say that championships aren't won on paper, there has never been a better case study to explain that than the 2009–2010 UConn Huskies.

Loaded with talent but with puzzle pieces that never seemed to fit, the team struggled from day one, lacking every characteristic of a Jim Calhoun coached team. They were neither mentally nor physically tough, and at the same time, carried an incredibly low basketball IQ. On the court they were outworked, out-hustled, and out-willed by teams with less size and skill. And by the end of the season, they'd quit on both themselves and their coach, in a season which Calhoun would call one of the most frustrating in his forty-plus years of coaching. By the middle of the season Calhoun would take an indefinite leave of absence and his future with the program all together would be questioned. And it didn't help that in the midst of it all was a swirling NCAA investigation surrounding the recruitment of a former player named Nate Miles. Most importantly the 2010 season ended with one of college basketball's elite programs at rock-bottom with significantly more questions going forward than answers.

Of course it didn't start like that. Instead it began with a ho-hum 75–66 win over William & Mary on a Friday night, a victory that neither had the fans thrilled, nor left the head coach shaking his head in confusion either. Beyond that first win though, the concerns almost immediately began to creep in, starting when Colgate came to town for the second game of the season.

Looking at the final score, the Huskies' 77–63 victory left little doubt to who the better team was. UConn finished the game shooting an impressive 55 percent from the field with all five starters scoring in double figures. But dig a bit deeper and a big concern was there: despite Colgate not starting a single player over six-foot-six, UConn was out-rebounded 23–22. Understand that of all things in basketball, rebounding is effort as much as anything else, and with a frontline that was at least six-foot-nine across the board, the effort was definitely lacking that night. Only Oriahki grabbed more than five boards. Afterward Calhoun even told reporters, "This Connecticut team has to start playing like a Connecticut team," before following up with, "It's got to get tougher."[1] Unfortunately that message meant nothing. The next night, UConn followed up with a sloppy 76–67 win over Hofstra, in which they were again out-rebounded.

Still, with the two victories, UConn advanced to the semifinals of the NIT Season Tip-Off and earned a date with LSU at Madison Square Garden. For the first time all season, UConn looked like the team that everyone had expected in the preseason, lighting up the Tigers 81–55. Dyson and Walker each scored twenty points. Finally, their coach was able to breathe a sigh of relief.

"We are thrilled because it's been a funny few weeks for us, where we haven't played the type of basketball we know we're capable of,"[2] Calhoun told the assembled media after the win.

That wouldn't be the last time Calhoun uttered similar words, starting a few nights later when the Huskies played the eventual National Champion Duke Blue Devils in the NIT Season Tip-Off Final. It would go down as one of the strangest games in all of college basketball during the 2009-2010 season. Billed as an epic matchup of Hall of Fame coaches, the game (which was played the day after Thanksgiving) left both coaches with an uneasy feeling in their stomachs. And it had little to do with all the turkey and stuffing they'd consumed a day before. Instead it was a game marred by sloppiness on each side that Duke would go on to win 68–59. The Blue Devils finished the game shooting an almost unheard of 28 percent (it was actually the first time since *1950* they'd won a game shooting under 30 percent) but countered by controlling the paint and out-rebounding the Huskies 56–43. That included a staggering twenty-five offensive rebounds for the Blue Devils. Again it seemed like only Oriahki (thirteen boards) was interested in mixing it up in the paint.

"I'm appalled at the lack of rebounding on this team," an infuriated Calhoun said of his team following the game.

It was back to the drawing board. But after a dominating win over Boston University in their next game, UConn's struggles would continue against, of all teams, Harvard. Yep, that Harvard. Home of no athletic scholarships and the Winklevoss twins. The Crimson had UConn on the ropes all afternoon and actually cut the Huskies' lead to four with just seconds to go before UConn eventually held on for an uninspired 79–73 win. Still, a win is a win, and with the victory, the Huskies improved to 6–1 on the year as they got set to go back to Madison Square Garden for the toughest test of their early season. UConn would play America's most polarizing team, the Kentucky Wildcats.

Entering the game, the Huskies knew they'd need their best effort to beat perhaps the most talented team in all of college basketball. John Calipari had put together a literal college All-Star team in his first season in Lexington, with five players that would eventually go on to become first round NBA Draft picks. Kentucky was skilled and strong with size in the paint, quickness on the perimeter, and athleticism all over. Of course they also featured college basketball's most talented player, point guard John Wall.

And when the two teams got together for an epic mid-week showdown, the matchup of Top 15 teams lived up to the hype. The game had the intensity and tenacity of a Final Four, despite the calendar not yet reading Christmas.

Here is part of a column that I wrote the following day, after attending that game:

> And once the first game did finish (St. John's and Georgia had played earlier that night), the intensity only rose as the

*whole Garden became entrenched in one of those "hiss's," that you hear before a big World Cup soccer match. Sure some fans were cheering and some fans were booing. But honestly, I'm not quite sure most knew exactly what to yell, just that they had to yell something. Especially since 18,000 semi-inebriated people around them were doing the same.*

*When the ball was finally tipped about 20 minutes later, the crowd went from electric, to some kind of word that either hasn't been invented yet, or I'm not clever enough to think of.*

*It defied explanation, it really did. This was a mid-December game, sandwiched between Thanksgiving and Christmas, on a WEDNESDAY night, and yet you couldn't find a seat in the entire place. Not one. People were hanging over railings, and sitting in the aisles. Again, for a mid-week...non-conference game...in December.*

*And when Kentucky jumped out to a 12-0 lead, well, I've never heard the Garden as loud as it was right then. Never.*

*To the thousands of Kentucky fans who made the trip up north (Yes thousands. If you told me the entire state of Kentucky was in the arena Wednesday, I'd believe you), you could tell it'd been awhile. Like an overzealous 16-year-old guy in the backseat of his car with a girl for the first time, there was no holding back. When UConn called their second time-out, Wildcats fans jumped and hugged, creating a massive, almost overwhelming sea of blue. It was honestly like watching a bad crowd shot from a sports movie, everyone erupting in unison, almost like a director was yelling, "And action!" Only it was real life.*

*But to UConn's credit, they handled the initial blow, held firm and fought their way back into the game. Before you knew it, the score was 12–12, then 16–12 UConn.*

*From there, the game turned into a bloodbath and a street fight. I really don't know how the game looked on TV (my guess is maybe a little sloppy), but in person, it was the most physical college basketball game I've ever seen, and it's not even close. Elbows flew, bodies flopped, and every rebound was a war, with six, seven, eight oversized human beings abusing their bodies to get to every loose ball. I don't care what the ages of these players were, this was a Man's game.*

*On the sidelines and in the stands, the game turned into an NCAA Tournament game in December. John Calipari stamped his feet like a little kid being forced to eat their vegetables. Jim Calhoun barked out of the side of his mouth, like I've seen him do a million times in my life. And both coaches subbed players in and out with the friskiness and urgency of a Final Four match-up.*

*Which is exactly what it felt like in the stands, a Final Four. The crowd swayed on every loose ball (OK, some of that was the booze, but still), with one half of the area cheering every time a foul was called, before the other side's boos quickly made them inaudible.*

*And that's how the game stayed until the very end.*

Unfortunately in the end, the game came down to one simple thing: Kentucky had John Wall, and UConn didn't. The freshman point guard gashed the Huskies for twenty-five points, including a layup and foul shot with just over thirty seconds left and the Wildcats trailing 60–59. It gave Kentucky a lead they'd never relinquish as they held on to win 63–61. Like so many games in the 2009–2010 season, UConn would go toe-to-toe, blow-for-blow with a team as talented as any in the country. And they'd come up short.

There was some good news on the horizon though, when, following the Kentucky game, forward Ater Majok became eligible for the Huskies. A highly touted six-foot-ten big man from the Sudan, who later moved to Australia, Majok had gotten attention from nearly every major college in the country during his recruitment before he eventually picked UConn over Kansas, Kentucky, and others. But after arriving in Storrs in the fall of 2008, it took him over eighteen months before the NCAA cleared him to play. He'd finally get to suit up for the first time in a UConn uniform following the Kentucky game, when the team returned to the court at the end of the first semester.

But much like everything else for the Huskies during the 2010 season, the excitement would be fleeting. In Majok's first game against Central Florida, he finished with just one point and three rebounds, a performance that was largely overshadowed by another lousy game from his new teammates. Despite having a new big body in their rotation, UConn still was again out-rebounded 33–31, this time in a sloppy 60–51 win. As much as things change, they stay the same, huh? (On an interesting side note, Central Florida was led in scoring that day by a freshman named Marcus Jordan. For those of you scoring at home, yes that'd be Michael's son.).

Following the Central Florida game, UConn would rack up two more wins before hitting the skies for their first true road game and first conference game of the season against Cincinnati. It would go down as the first of many nails in the coffin of their season.

As had been the case for most of the early part of the year, UConn sleepwalked through roughly the first thirty minutes against the Bearcats, with their play best described as somewhere between "disinterested" and "apathetic." But trailing 59–47 with just over nine minutes to go, the lightbulb finally went on over the Huskies' heads. It started with a Jerome Dyson two-pointer followed by a Stanley Robinson three and a Kemba Walker layup before Cincinnati coach Mick Cronin finally called a time-out. From there the Huskies spent the rest of the half chipping away at the lead before finally, improbably tying the game up at 69 when Walker hit a three with just thirteen seconds to go. The Huskies had all the momentum, and if they could only force overtime, might possibly steal their most surprising win of the season.

Except it didn't happen.

Cincinnati's freshman superstar Lance Stephenson got the ball at the top of the key, and pounded it into the hardwood, until finally making his move to the basket with just a few seconds to play. When Stephenson finally got into the lane and released the ball, Alex Oriahki arrived out of nowhere to block shot, as the crowd let out an audible gasp, and the game seemed headed for overtime.

But there was a catch. With the 2010 UConn Huskies, there was always a catch.

At the same time as Oriahki's block, not only did the horn sound, but a whistle also came from across the court. Gavin Edwards had been called for a foul in the paint. Whether it was actually a foul or not would be disputed by the announcers that night and by fans for days, but ultimately it didn't matter. Seven tenths of a second would be added to the clock, and Stephenson calmly made both free throws, giving Cincinnati the 71–69 win.

The loss proved to be eerily symbolic of what would come the rest of the season as strange things kept happening at the worst possible times for UConn. Truly, 2010 would become one of "those" years. To put things in their eventual perspective, UConn had arrived in Cincinnati with a respectable 9–2 record. They'd go just 9–14 the rest of the season.

But while the disappointing end to season was still a long way away, the crushing losses continued almost immediately. Just a few games following Cincinnati was maybe the worst of all.

After wins over Notre Dame and Seton Hall, UConn appeared to finally be turning a corner when they traveled down to Washington, DC, to take on Georgetown.

To say the Huskies were dominant early in that game would be an understatement; they literally could do no wrong. In front of a national TV audience, UConn sliced and diced through the Hoyas' defense, taking a 40–25 lead into the locker room and silencing the fifteen-thousand-plus fans in the Verizon Center. Against the No. 12 team in the country, finally it seemed as though UConn would get their signature win.

Only once again, it didn't happen.

How the Huskies lost that massive lead isn't easy to say, but their breakdowns on both ends of the court didn't help. Defensively UConn lost every ounce of focus and intensity, allowing the Hoyas to rip off forty-seven points after intermission, including twenty-eight in the second half alone from Austin Freeman. (To put that into perspective Freeman had never scored more than twenty-one in an *entire game* for Georgetown entering that afternoon). And when the Huskies went ice cold down the stretch and didn't make a field goal in the final three-and-a-half minutes, the writing on the wall went permanent in ink.

Georgetown 72. UConn 69.

"It's the most heartbreaking loss of the year," a befuddled Calhoun told reporters following the loss. "It's not even close."[5]

Really, what was even more concerning about the loss was that every problem UConn had dealt with the entire season had come to light in that one afternoon in Washington.

Understand it wasn't just that UConn blew a lead, but *how* they did. The Huskies proved to have next to no basketball IQ with fifteen turnovers in the game, including five each by Walker and Dyson, the latter playing in front of a large contingent of family and friends in the D.C. metro area that day. In addition, UConn shot a woeful 33 percent from three-point land (four of twelve) and 53 percent from the foul line (nine of seventeen). While those numbers might be enough to beat Iona or Central Florida, they simply weren't going to get it done against a talented team like Georgetown. Or really, anyone left on the schedule.

Beyond just raw statistics, was something even more concerning though. The Georgetown game proved beyond a reasonable doubt that the 2009-2010 UConn Huskies simply had no leadership.

And really, that was the dirty little secret of this specific UConn team.

Yes, the Huskies were heavy on experienced players, but they were also woefully short on leadership. It wasn't really any of the senior's faults, since over the previous three years all of the barking in the huddle, all of the keeping people in line, all of the, well, leading, had been done by A.J. Price and Jeff Adrien. Both had graduated the previous spring, and each had left a big leadership void because of it. For all their talent, Dyson, Edwards and Robinson had never been asked to actually take charge, or be accountable for anything more than their own play.

And by the time the 2010 season rolled around, the three, now seniors were failing miserably in that role. To his credit, sophomore point guard Kemba Walker tried to take on that responsibility himself, but as such a young player with so many veterans around him, it was always a slippery slope, and it appeared that (understandably), he didn't want to step on the older players toes. Regardless, that dynamic was never more evident than when the lead started slipping away against Georgetown, and everybody began looking to someone else for answers. Again, for all the talent the team had, they just had no leadership. Even as great of a coach as Jim Calhoun is, that's a trait you simply can't teach.

The problems continued in back-to-back losses that followed the disastrous finish in D.C. The first was against a young Pittsburgh team in Hartford the following game when the Huskies took a 47–46 lead with under ten minutes to go, only to be outscored 19–9 down the stretch in the loss. It got worse a few days later at Michigan when UConn lost their third in a row, this time to a team which was just 9–7 at the time. With the defeat in Ann Arbor, UConn fell to just 11–6 on the season and out of the Top 25 for the first time in more than two calendar years.

However, upon returning from Michigan, UConn was faced with something much more serious than just wins and losses on the court. It was the health of their head coach Jim Calhoun, who announced that he'd take an indefinite leave of absence from the team.

Now understand that the sixty-seven-year-old head coach had dealt with health problems before and had always come out on top. In total he'd missed twenty-one games over the course of his career, including five after undergoing surgery for prostate cancer in 2003, a handful more in 2008 for exhaustion, and even the opener of the 2009 NCAA Tournament. So while the leave wasn't totally surprising, it was still a bit unexpected.

Still this leave seemed different from those in the past, in the sense that no one would publicly discuss the problem. After the announcement, Calhoun's doctors simply told the media that the coach wasn't taking the leave because of a recurrence of cancer or any problems with his heart. Instead everyone was left to speculate, with much of that speculation turning to whether this strangely eclectic UConn team had simply worn the coach out. It wasn't surprising when his former point guard A. J. Price told reporters after the announcement was made, "There's no sugarcoating it, he [Calhoun] doesn't take losing well."[6]

Of course in the typical way in which the 2009–2010 Huskies handled things, with everyone doubting them, UConn opened the post-Calhoun era (if you could call it that) with a dominating win over St. John's. Robinson, Dyson, and Walker combined for forty-six points in the victory.

But after beating the Red Storm, the fun would seemingly be over. UConn's second game without Calhoun would come that weekend when the No. 1 team in the country, the Texas Longhorns, came to town. Despite having lost their previous game, Texas still entered the game at 17–1 on the season with three players in their starting lineup that would be selected in the next NBA Draft.

And in UConn's most surprising result of the season, those poor Longhorns never stood a chance.

After a back-and-forth first half that saw Texas take a 42–34 lead, UConn proceeded to put together their best twenty minutes of the season after intermission. Behind thirty-two points from Jerome Dyson (During the game, announcer Clark Kellogg called him "Eel like in his ability to get to the rim." Whatever that means.), UConn blitzed Texas 54–32 in the second half to run away with a victory.

The game of course served as an emotional high for the season. Moments after they returned to the locker room, the players called head coach who had watched the game from his home a few miles away.

"We've got to play for him," Jerome Dyson told reporters following the victory. "We know these wins will help him get better."[7]

Incredibly, it took nearly three full months and nineteen games for one of the most talented teams in the country to get their first signature win of the year. But it did finally come.

Unfortunately the good times didn't last.

Riding high off the win over the No. 1 team in the country, UConn next hit the road to play helpless Providence College, a Big East bottom-feeder which has made just two NCAA Tournament appearances in the previous thirteen years. The Friars had lost to Marquette by thirty just a few days prior to hosting UConn.

And as you might have guessed by now, the Huskies lost.

After their best win of the year, the Huskies submitted a stink bomb in Providence that could be smelled all the way back in Storrs.

They shot just 38 percent from the field, shot four of eighteen from three, and committed nineteen turnovers in an 81–66 loss. Beyond that, there was one more stat that told the story of that specific game above all others. With the win, Providence would improve its record to 12-8 on the year. They'd finish the season at 12-19, not winning a single game after they played the Huskies. If that doesn't describe the 2010 UConn Huskies in a nutshell, nothing does.

Yet, incredibly, it only got worse from there for UConn.

The following Saturday, UConn hosted a struggling but tough Marquette club, a team having problems winning games themselves. The Golden Eagles were just 3–5 in conference play to that point, with those five losses coming by a combined eleven points. Luckily for them they were practically handed a win on a silver platter by UConn.

It didn't look that way though for most of the game. With just under a minute to go, Marquette got the ball back, trailing by three. Simply getting the game to overtime would've been seen as a monumental success for the Golden Eagles.

What no one expected was that the Huskies were about to have worst breakdown yet. First, Dyson committed the most unforgivable of sins, fouling Marquette guard Darius Johnson-Odom while he was shooting a three-pointer. The junior went to the line and made all three free throws and UConn's seemingly comfortable lead had all but disappeared.

From there, it only got worse.

On the next possession, UConn in-bounded the ball to Walker who—rather than running out the clock, and holding for a late shot—put up a jumper with twenty-five seconds left in the game and nineteen seconds left on the shot clock. Had Walker simply held the ball and not done anything, the game would've likely gone to overtime. Instead, Marquette got the ball back with one last chance, and took advantage. Jimmy Butler hit a jumper with three seconds to go, giving Marquette an improbable 70-68 victory.

Incredibly, UConn had lost another game, and this time found a newer and dumber way to do it. On this afternoon, it wasn't poor free throw shooting or turnovers that cost the Huskies. Nor was it misses from the three-point line, or a lack of effort on the glass. Nope, on this given day UConn had lost because of plain stupidity. It was that simple.

Now at 13–8, and dropping to 3–5 in Big East play, UConn hit the road for what would prove to be a make-or-break game. They were playing the Louisville Cardinals, a club sporting a 14–7 record and struggling in their own right. Many experts saw it as an early NCAA Tournament elimination game with the loser in deep trouble going forward.

The Huskies traveled down to Louisville on a Monday night, but when forty minutes of basketball were done in Freedom Hall, they wouldn't have the win they craved.

A bad season would finally become unraveled.

# Chapter 2

## The UConn Huskies Hit Rock Bottom (Published at AaronTorres-Sports.com, February 1, 2010)

They say you've got to hit rock bottom before you can start the climb back to the top. Well if UConn's loss to Louisville Monday night wasn't rock bottom, it's hard to say what might be.

Through their first twenty-one games and eight losses, this team has been frustrating at times and downright unwatchable at others, but has never given their fans a reason to entirely end all hope. Sure there were missed free throws against Kentucky, a lack of leadership in the loss to Pitt, and no mental toughness at Michigan. But still, there were always just enough little flashes to keep bringing us back every time they played.

Well, Monday night the train officially came off the tracks. Every single thing that'd gone wrong through twenty-one games reared its ugly head last night in forty of the most painful minutes of basketball I've watched in a long time (well, except for when President Obama did some play-by-play in the Georgetown-Duke game last week).

The staples of UConn basketball 2010 were all there: reckless guard play; a non-existent half-court offense; defensive indifference; poor shot selection; bad outside shooting; intensity that can be best compared to that of a *CVS* clerk working the midnight shift; turnovers (not to be dramatic, but, oh the turnovers!); and just an overall lack of basic, simple, basketball intelligence. (Honestly, how many times can these guards continue to drive aimlessly at the rim and get met by four defenders before they realize, "Hey, this might not be working?" Five thousand times? Ten thousand? Does anyone have an answer?)

The result of it all Monday night was a group that looked like a hastily thrown together intramural team. Only sadly, they've been playing together for close to four months now.

About the only bright spot of the abysmal trip to Louisville was the foul shooting, with the Huskies going 19–21 in the first half. Of course that "highlight" undermines the fact that UConn got way more calls in the first half than the Cardinals and that the 42–28 halftime score should have been a lot worse than it actually was.

(Random note: The refs eventually evened things out in the second half in what can only be described as one of the worst officiated games I've ever seen.)

But back to UConn.

After the first half free throw derby Monday night, the Huskies limped to the finish, the final score 82–69. But since Louisville took a nineteen-point lead with fourteen minutes to go and hit cruise control, isn't that a misnomer too? An 82–69 score doesn't entirely tell the story of how one-sided this game was for about thirty-two of the total forty minutes.

With the loss, another loss, UConn stands at 13–9 overall and 3–6 in the Big East. Only St. Johns, DePaul, and Rutgers trail them in the conference standings.

Go ahead, read that again. St. Johns, DePaul, and Rutgers are the only Big East teams worse than UConn right now. And even that is in record only since Rutgers beat Notre Dame Saturday, and DePaul nearly did the same against Syracuse.

It also leaves the Huskies 5 ½ games out of place in the Big East and a game behind South Florida and Providence, both of which were expected to be two of the worst teams in this conference in 2010. All for a UConn team that has as much (if not more) NBA talent than anyone in the conference.

The saddest part is, I'm not sure anyone knows how we got here. After the game last night, my friend texted me asking what I thought was wrong with this team. My response? "Nothing and everything. I really have no idea."

This group doesn't show any of the "can't miss" signs of underachieving basketball teams. Having been around most of these guys personally, I can say they're nice kids. They seem to enjoy each other's company.

Unlike in 2007, when these seniors went 18–14 as freshman, this group doesn't lack experience. The 2007 team didn't have a single senior or junior on their *entire* roster. This team plays three seniors over thirty minutes a game. Sure Stanley Robinson and Jerome Dyson may both be relatively *young* seniors because injury and suspension slowed their development. And yes, Gavin Edwards doesn't have a ton of starting experience. But all three have played over one hundred games in their careers. Shouldn't they be progressing instead of regressing?

Also, although I thought this team might resemble a young 2005 team, clearly that isn't true anymore either. That group was a bunch of role players on the 2004 National Championship team that came into their own late the following season. This team's two stars, Dyson and Robinson, weren't role players last year. One was leading the team in scoring before an injury, the other averaged a double-double in the midst of an NCAA Tournament run to the Final Four.

While some have asked me about the loss of Coach Jim Calhoun, I can't blame that either. I'm sure it's a little emotionally unsettling on a day-to-day basis—it has to be. But with Calhoun on the sidelines, what was this team's best win? Notre Dame? Seton Hall? Without Calhoun, they beat the No. 1 team in the country less than two weeks ago.

Finally, with so many players on this team with NBA futures, you'd think they might be gunning for their own stats, right? Wrong. With the exception of Kemba Walker, this team plays hot potato with the basketball late in games like it's made of plutonium. If anything, they seem to shy away from the ball late in games.

*Which*, believe it or not, may be the biggest problem with this team: these guys aren't selfish enough.

Last Saturday, Lazar Hayward, Marquette's best low post player (and I use that term loosely since he's six foot five), fouled out late in their game against UConn. The Golden Eagles didn't have a single player bigger than six foot six on the court. Nobody. *Which* obviously would have been a perfect time for the six-foot-nine Robinson to post up his six-foot-four defender. Unfortunately, not only did Robinson not post up his defender, not only did he not attempt any shots in crunch-time, he didn't even once touch the ball in the closing minutes in a position to score. Like so many others, that game ended in loss.

Again, that's UConn's biggest problem. Robinson and Dyson are good kids, nice kids. But they are almost always passive to a fault. They don't want the ball. They don't command it.

Which underlies the biggest problem of all: an absolute dearth of leadership.

When these seniors got to campus in the fall of 2006, sophomores A. J. Price and Jeff Adrien had already established themselves as the leaders of this team. Not so much organically as much out of necessity.

It's not that Robinson, Dyson, and Edwards haven't had big games or made big shots over the past three years, because they have. But ultimately, no matter what they did, praise and blame always fell on the shoulders of Price or Adrien. It led to a dismal 2007 season, an improved 2008, and a 2009 team with two of the best leaders in the country. Now those two are gone and twenty-two games in, nobody has adjusted. These seniors aren't bad guys or players, just inexperienced leaders.

Looking back on this entire season, I can only remember one time where I saw a senior yelling in the huddle, which, needless to say, is a problem. That one time? It was two weeks ago against Texas when Dyson was barking at his teammates like he'd seen Price do so many times before. And you know what? UConn beat the No. 1 ranked team in the country that day.

Which is what makes this season so frustrating because, again, the talent is there.

Just a week ago UConn had six losses, four of them to top twenty teams. And in every single one of those games, they were in it until the end. Then they beat Texas, and UConn fans collectively looked at each other and said, "You know what? We can make a run at this." Unfortunately the players may have thought the same thing.

Since that win, they've gone 0–3, with losses coming to Providence, Marquette, and last night against Louisville. And with three games against the top seven teams in the country (at No. 2 Villanova, at No. 3 Syracuse, and No. 7 West Virginia at home) and a bunch more against other frisky, hungry, middle of the pack Big East teams (at Notre Dame and Cincinnati and Louisville again at home), this season has gone from promising, straight to life support in the blink of an eye.

While I'm not giving up, the writing is clearly on the wall.

It seems like just yesterday this team was a sleeper to make a deep run in the NCAA Tournament. Now a trip to the NIT seems more likely, if there's any postseason berth at all.

It's hard to believe, but it's true. The mighty fall pretty fast.

In this case, to the bottom.

# Chapter 3

## Sometimes the Best Expectations Are No Expectations at All In the end, the Louisville loss didn't end up as rock-bottom. But it was pretty close.

At 13–9, UConn followed the Louisville game with an ugly win over a helpless DePaul club. While the victory was nice, it also needed to be put in its proper context; DePaul would finish the regular season at 1–17 in Big East play. Next was another disappointing loss, this time to Syracuse, when a bizarre whistle gave the Orange an extra possession at a crucial part of a tie game. The Orange would go on to eventually win 72–67, proving once again that it really had become one of "those" years. It was also the third loss for UConn to a team which would eventually go on to earn a No. 1 seed in the NCAA Tournament.

Following the Syracuse loss, UConn did get a quick energy boost. Head Coach Jim Calhoun returned to the sidelines after sitting out the previous seven games. The team had gone 3–4 without him.

Unfortunately his return did little to rally the troops in an early Saturday afternoon tip against Cincinnati. Playing the same Bearcats squad that started the Big East slide back in December, the Huskies lost 60–48 in a game which was twice as ugly as the final score might have indicated and nowhere near as close. UConn—which again had four guys in their starting lineup (including Majok) who would be selected in the next two NBA Drafts—scored an embarrassing thirty-six points through the first thirty-seven minutes of play before a late run made the final score somewhat respectable. In a game which truly was the microcosm of their season, UConn finished shooting 34 percent from the field, 20 percent from behind the three point arc, and 50 percent from the free throw line, with nearly twice as many turnovers (fifteen) as assists (nine). Welcome back, Coach!

Yet incredibly, after their worst loss of the year, Calhoun—as he's done so many times in his Hall of Fame career—once again rallied the troops in a last ditch effort to sneak into the NCAA Tournament.

After the Cincinnati loss dropped them to 14–11, UConn hit the road for a Big Monday showdown with the No. 3 ranked Villanova Wildcats in a game that next to no one gave them a chance in. But much like the Texas game a few weeks before, the Huskies proved they could beat anyone in the sport, dominating from start to finish in an 84–75 win. The win was as shocking as it was well-timed, and when UConn beat Rutgers and then No. 7 ranked West Virginia for a late season three-game win streak, their dim NCAA Tournament outlook brightened a bit. With a 17–11 record, UConn had plenty of losses on their resume. But with wins over three teams ranked in the Top 10, few teams had more impressive wins either.

Unfortunately, as was the story all season, the good times just wouldn't last.

Riding that three-game win streak, UConn next hosted Louisville, and—as they'd done so many times during the season—stole defeat from the jaws of victory. The Huskies blew a five-point halftime lead with the final nail coming as Edgar Sosa drove the lane for an uncontested layup with just eight seconds to play. That one bucket gave Louisville a 78–76 lead they wouldn't relinquish and UConn a loss they would never recover from. The Huskies closed out the regular season with losses to Notre Dame and South Florida.

Still, despite it all, despite the 17–14 end to the regular season, UConn had the chance to make a run at the NCAAs if they could get a couple wins at the Big East Tournament. Granted, the Huskies had a next to impossible task: they needed five wins in five days to guarantee a trip to the NCAA Tournament. But with wins over Villanova and West Virginia and a hard fought loss to Syracuse on their resume, it wasn't inconceivable that UConn could steal a few wins against top ranked teams and maybe throw their name back in the NCAA Tournament discussion even if they didn't win the tournament outright.

Instead, they rolled over.

Playing in the same building where they lost an epic six-overtime thriller against Syracuse just a year earlier, UConn simply quit in their opener against St. John's. The Huskies fell behind 8–2 by the first TV time-out, trailed 35–22 at halftime, and ended up losing by twenty-two as Calhoun—college basketball's ultimate fighter—put his head in his hands and gave up with about ten minutes to play. The season finally ended two games later in an NIT loss to Virginia Tech, concluding one of the most puzzling seasons in UConn history.

With the loss, the careers of Stanley Robinson, Jerome Dyson, and Gavin Edwards had come to an end.

Many thought the same to be true of UConn's time on top of the college basketball world.

⌘　⌘　⌘

Upon the completion of what he called one of the most frustrating seasons in his entire coaching career, Jim Calhoun immediately put to rest any speculation about his future with the school. Within days he announced that he'd be back at UConn for the 2011 season, and by mid-May he finalized a contract that would keep him there through the 2013–2014 season.

The question next became what the parts around him would look like.

The first major puzzle piece came shortly after the season when Kemba Walker announced that he'd bypass the NBA Draft and come back to school for his junior year. After averaging nearly fifteen points and over five assists per game as a sophomore, it was clear that Walker had the talent to play at the next level. But after averaging over three turnovers a game too, it was also clear that he had a lot to improve on.

It was assumed that Walker would be joined by up-and-coming sophomores Alex Oriahki and Ater Majok along with seniors Donnell Beverly and Charles Okwandu to make up the core of the 2011 squad. Unfortunately those plans had a wrinkle to them because Majok departed the school just a few days before the fall semester was about to begin in late August. The highly recruited forward that UConn had spent a year getting eligible, left after just twenty-six games, taking his modest 2.3 points and three rebounds per game with him. Still, Majok's departure was seen as a crippling loss for a young team that was thin up front. It proved to be just another kick in the teeth for a UConn team which simply didn't need any more bad news.

Then there was a modestly ranked freshman class that was set to join the upperclassmen in the fall. None other than Roscoe Smith was considered elite. The rest were believed by outsiders to either be an afterthought, a role player or simply a fill-in, after UConn had missed out on a handful of elite players late in the spring recruiting season.

Along with Smith, the player who seemed most likely to make an impact was Jeremy Lamb, a wing from Georgia who shot up the recruiting rankings after a huge AAU season the summer before. Of course at the same time, Lamb hadn't even started for his high school until his senior year, a seemingly ominous sign if ever there was one. Shabazz Napier and Tyler Olander weren't even supposed to graduate high school until the *following* spring, with each passing up an expected post-graduate year to come to Storrs ahead of schedule for the 2010-2011 season. And rounding out the seven-man class were two unknowns from Germany, Niels Giffey and Enosch Wolf, and a project big man form Tennessee named Michael Bradley. It was hardly the freshman class most fans envisioned when Brandon Knight, C. J. Leslie, Josh Selby, and other top recruits entered the spring signing period with UConn on their final lists. But with each selecting another school, the seven who signed would have to do.

Yet with all the scholarship roulette taking place, it was actually the coaching staff which would see the most change. None of it was for a good reason.

Their story had started nearly two years before when Yahoo Sports released a report alleging UConn's coaching staff of recruiting improprieties, involving the recruitment of ex-player Nate Miles. While we'll get to the important details of the situation later on, the crux of the Yahoo report described Miles's relationship with a former UConn student-manager turned NBA agent Josh Nochimson, who provided a litany of illegal benefits to the recruit, including food, transportation, and lodging. And while those allegations were bad enough, what made things worse was that not only did Nochimson have a background as an agent (he's since been decertified), but that as a former UConn manager, the NCAA considered him a "representative of UConn's athletics interests,"[1] which is essentially a fancy way of calling him a booster. The fact that UConn's coaching staff had heavy contact with Nochimson during Miles's recruitment made a bad situation even messier.

Well, with the Yahoo report released in March of 2009 and the NCAA launching an investigation after that, the official Notice of Allegations came to UConn in May 2010, just before Memorial Day weekend. Yet even before the report was released, UConn's program was rocked when it was announced that both Assistant Coach Patrick Sellers and Director of Basketball Operations Beau Archibald had resigned their positions within the program. Those resignations made more sense a day later when the NCAA's Notice of Allegations came out and each had been charged with "Providing false and misleading information"[2] in a report to the school. Those were just two of eight major violations the program was cited for, proving to be just another black eye for UConn basketball in a year full of them.

But while it would be another eight months before the NCAA officially handed out the final verdict on UConn, the two open positions on the coaching staff allowed Calhoun his first chance to right the wrongs of the 2010. He acted quickly and aggressively.

His first hire was nothing short of a home run when he tabbed former UConn point guard Kevin Ollie to fill Sellers's spot as an assistant. Simply put, Ollie was the foundation of everything that Calhoun had built the UConn program on and everything that was lacking with the 2010 team. As a player, Ollie was a mentally tough guard from Los Angeles who shined as the Huskies floor-leader alongside Ray Allen, Donyell Marshall, and others from 1991–1995. After leaving Storrs, Ollie would continue to prove the doubters wrong, going from undrafted free agent to the Continental Basketball Association and eventually ending with a fifteen-year NBA veteran.

In that NBA career, Ollie was never more than a bit player, but did serve almost as basketball's Forrest Gump: a bystander and background participant in some of the league's most important events. Amongst the many credits on Ollie's resume were a supporting role alongside Allen Iverson during the Philadelphia 76ers' run to the 2001 NBA Finals, a spot on the Cleveland Cavaliers roster during LeBron James's rookie year, and as a wily veteran at the end of the bench when the Oklahoma City Thunder made their first trip to the NBA Playoffs in the Kevin Durant/Russell Westbrook era. With his family already stationed in Connecticut, Ollie called it quits after the 2010 NBA season, filed his retirement papers, and returned home to UConn, accepting a position on the staff in June. After mentoring the NBA's best young players for a decade and a half, Ollie would take on a vital role in Storrs, coaching one of college basketball's youngest backcourts in 2011.

Then there was Archibald's director of basketball operations position which needed to be filled as well.

Understand that in the world of big-time college basketball coaching, the director of basketball operations spot is almost exclusively reserved for young people trying to break into the business. The job is short on pay and long on hours and doesn't carry the kind of responsibilities one might immediately think. Simply put, the director of basketball operations handles all the myopic things that the rest of the coaching staff just doesn't have time for, like travel logistics, setting up practice schedules, and things of that nature. At the same time, the job does limit actual basketball coaching and recruiting—one of the biggest reasons Archibald was forced to resign from his post. Under NCAA rules, he wasn't allowed to have contact with Nochimson or Miles during the high school player's recruitment.

With that as a background, it would seem to make sense that Calhoun would replace Archibald with another young up-and-comer willing to get to the office early, stay late, and act as the coaching staff's whipping boy, right? Wrong.

Instead Calhoun went out and grabbed one of his former players and assistants, Glen Miller, who'd spent the previous ten years as a Division I head coach at both Brown and Penn. With Miller having been fired as coach of the Quakers, he bounced back at UConn under the newly appointed role of "Director of Basketball Administration." He would handle a lot of the same roles as his predecessor while also adding additional responsibility in areas of compliance and administration. Understand that for Calhoun to land anyone with head coaching experience for the position would be considered a home run. But for him to get someone who'd been a head man at a Division I school for a decade would be akin to a five-star chef showing up to work at a high school cafeteria. Miller wasn't just the right fit for the position, he was as overqualified as overqualified gets.

With the two changes on the coaching staff, the page had been officially turned on the 2010 season once and for all.

But with a bunch of freshmen replacing three seniors and Majok, would the team be any better?

⌘　⌘　⌘

The answer of course yes, although no one knew it at the time. And interestingly the run to the title in April 2011 started with some phone calls in the spring of 2010.

With the 18–16 season officially complete, new co-captain Kemba Walker called each of the new freshmen individually and made his expectations clear: they were to get to Storrs in the summer and needed to come ready to work. All obliged on the first part with the exception of Wolf, who would come from Germany later on and needed to enroll in prep school for the first semester to clear up some academics.

But despite the team getting to know each other on and off the court and the countless hours put in playing pickup ball, it meant little when college basketball's prognosticators started putting together their projections for the 2011 season. UConn didn't just have low expectations. They had none at all.

When the national polls first came in late fall, one of college basketball's elite programs was nowhere to be found. UConn wasn't ranked in the Associated Press Poll.

"Not only did I not vote them in the Top 25, I didn't know if they'd even make the NCAA Tournament to be honest," CBS Sports college basketball writer and AP Poll voter Jeff Goodman said of the 2011 Huskies. "They'd been such a train-wreck the previous season, nobody could've predicted how good they would be."

And apparently those who voted in the USA Today Coaches' Poll agreed with the sentiment of Goodman and the AP. The Huskies didn't receive a *single vote* from the thirty-one coaches polled, while schools like NC State, Cal, and Murray State (none of which would make the NCAA Tournament) all received at least a handful. The snub was a direct indictment on the team's talent as opposed to their previous year's record since North Carolina was ranked in the Top 10, although like UConn, they too had missed the 2010 NCAA Tournament. Things weren't much better when the Big East coaches got together and picked the Huskies to finish tenth—in their own conference.

Yet there was one surprising voice who actually agreed with the doubters. That man was Jim Calhoun who stated at Big East media day in October, "We're Connecticut, we don't belong here," the coach said of his team's low preseason ranking. He then added, "But I would've taken 12th based on the factual information."[3]

His star point guard didn't disagree. At the same time, Kemba Walker also let everyone in attendance know that 18–16 was a thing of the past, not something that would become a regularity.

"It only motivates us," Walker told reporters the same day. "It lets us know how hard we have to work."[4]

That work started right away and showed in the Huskies' very first game of the season against Stony Brook.

Understand that while a 79–52 win over the Seawolves was nice, it wasn't the victory alone that set the tone for the season. Instead it was just that for at least one night every problem from the previous year disappeared. The Huskies controlled the boards, out-rebounding Stony Brook 56–30 (including a career-high eighteen from Oriahki). They made eight three-pointers, including four from Shabazz Napier, playing his first career college game. And they converted fifteen of twenty free throw attempts. Most importantly the Huskies gained a halftime lead and maintained it, something the previous year's team never seemed to do. Sure it was only Stony Brook, but it was a start.

What really stood out though was something that couldn't be found on the stat-sheet and instead could only be seen by those who'd sat through all the miserable losses the season before. It was an entirely new attitude and body language, and it was night and day compared to the 2010 club.

Whatever entitlement or egotism that the previous year's team had was gone that night and replaced by the scrappiness and hustle of a bunch of freshmen just trying to earn their keep. Guys dove on the floor and hustled after loose balls. They high-fived each other after big plays. And as cliché as it sounds, everyone seemed to play for the name on the front of the jersey instead of the one on the back. Sappy, yes. But definitely a change from before.

Yet it was the second game of the year that would best describe the early part of the 2011 UConn Huskies season. A win over Vermont turned into the Kemba Walker Show.

Again it was no secret that the six-foot-one guard from the Bronx had as much talent as anyone in the sport. He'd averaged 14.6 points and 5.1 assists as a sophomore and established himself as an emerging star while playing with a group of college All-Stars against Kevin Durant, Derrick Rose, and the United States National Team as they prepared to go to the World Championships. As Calhoun told reporters in the preseason, "Kemba is clearly above everyone else. We can't stop him. Hopefully no one else will either."[5]But even more than talent, Walker needed to improve his leadership the most. With the seniors gone and so many freshmen in place, there was no doubt that Walker was in charge of the team now. And while he might have been hesitant to get in someone's face the year before, the success of the Huskies in 2011 depended on it.

That leadership started with the phone calls in May, continued through the workouts in the summer, and appeared first in the Huskies' opener with eighteen points against Stony Brook. But at no point were the fusion of talent and leadership and the dynamic of "Kemba and Company" more evident than in the Huskies' second game of the year. Against Vermont, with his teammates not totally focused after the team's opening night victory, it was Walker who had to make up for their sloppiness. He did it all, gashing through the Vermont defense for a career-high forty-two points.

But while a star was born with Walker's performance against Vermont, it hardly made the college basketball world take notice. With the win, no one immediately put the Huskies in the same breath as Duke, Kentucky and Kansas, and instead saw the Vermont game as nothing more than a great player on a lousy team lighting up inferior competition. With the Huskies set to go to the Maui Invitational and play against some of the nation's best teams, it was hard to see the perception of the team changing much.

Only it did.

It was time for college basketball to get to know the new UConn Huskies.

It was time to get to know Kemba Walker.

# Chapter 4
## Getting to Know Kemba Walker

Plain and simple, New York City has a love affair with basketball. It dates back to the days of CCNY and NYU as college basketball super-powers in the early 1950's, through the last great Knicks teams of the 1970's, and into the 1980's and beyond with Lou Carnesecca's St. John's clubs. In the process, dozens of future NBA superstars honed their craft on the city's courts, becoming local celebrities long before they became international ones in the NBA.

There are many names that have become synonymous with New York City basketball over the years, people like Lew Alcindor, Kenny Anderson, and Red Holzman, not to mention Stephon Marbury, Connie Hawkins, and countless others. But of all the names you do know, one that you might not is that of Moe Hicks. Over the last two decades, few have had as much of an impact on the city and its basketball tradition as Hicks has.

From 1994-2010 Hicks was the head coach at New York City super-power Rice High School in the Bronx, amassing a record that would've made just about any coach, anywhere in the country jealous. He went 352-86 in his 16 years at the school, winning an insane 80 percent of his games in the New York Catholic League, one of the toughest collections of high school teams in the country. In the process, Hicks sent countless players to colleges nationwide, including (but certainly not limited to) Andre Barrett, Russell Robinson and Edgar Sosa, all point guards and all of whom went on to become McDonald's All-American high school players. Hicks is now the director of basketball operations at St. John's, taking a position on the staff when Steve Lavin came to town in the spring of 2010.

With a resume like the one he has, there's no doubt that Hicks knows basketball talent. But sometimes even the best coaches need to get lucky. That was certainly the case when Hicks saw a young seventh-grader in the spring of 2003.

"The first time I saw Kemba Walker, he was actually playing in a tournament against my son," Hicks said. "I wasn't there to scout or anything. I had no idea who he was, and kept saying to myself 'Who's that kid with the braids?'"

That kid was Kemba Walker, and within a few weeks the player and coach connected, and the seeds were planted for the next great point guard to go to Rice. Like UConn years later, Walker decided he wanted to attend the school, and after Hicks sent his assistants to watch Kemba play as an eighth-grader, the decision was made: Kemba would become a Rice Raider. He arrived at the high school the following fall, but did so with little fanfare. At the time, Hicks was one of the few people in the city who saw potential in the kid with the braids. Actually, what he saw in Kemba Walker was what the college basketball world would see some six years later.

"As soon as he decided to go to Rice, people tried to talk him out of it," Hicks said. "They told him he wasn't good enough, that he'd never play. But I never believed it. The first time I saw him I said to myself 'That kid is a Rice Raider.' He was a little erratic at times, but tough. And he had a huge heart."

Obviously, that wouldn't be the last time someone noticed Kemba Walker's heart.

However, at a powerhouse like Rice, you've got to earn your keep no matter who you are, and Walker was certainly no exception. He spent his first high school season on the junior varsity team, and even as a sophomore was relegated to the bench where he learned behind Sosa, a McDonald's All-American who'd eventually end up at Louisville. Also on that team was a center named Curtis Kelly, who'd spend two years at UConn before transferring out and finishing his career at Kansas State.

With a veteran lineup, Walker didn't play much in his sophomore year, but when he was called upon, Walker delivered. The most memorable moment for Hicks was a game in the state championships of Kemba's sophomore year, when Sosa got in foul trouble and Walker was forced to play big minutes. Not surprisingly, Kemba stepped in and helped his team to victory. It was the first time others saw in Kemba, what Hicks had seen all those years earlier.

"After that game, I had scouts come up to me and ask, 'Moe, who is No. 15?'" Hicks said. "I told them, 'That's Kemba,' and they told me 'Moe, that kid is a pro.'"

Still, not everyone was sold.

With Sosa gone the following fall, Rice was unquestionably Kemba's team entering his junior year. Hicks moved him to the point, where Walker, along with several of his Gauchos teammates he helped Rice to a Catholic High School Athletic Association division title. That winter was also the first time that Walker's name crossed the radar of the University of Connecticut's coaching staff. It only came by accident and only after another hard sell by Hicks.

"I was at this tournament up at Baruch College in New York," former UConn assistant coach and current Quinnipiac University head coach Tom Moore said. "It was an all-day event, and I was there to see a bunch of players. As I'm walking out of the gym I see Moe Hicks, and he's really pushing Kemba on me. I trust Moe, he's had a lot of great players. But I really didn't know."

No one did. And that wouldn't change until a few months later at the Arizona Cactus Classic, a tournament you hopefully remember from the beginning of this book.

At the time, the Cactus Classic was considered by many evaluators to be the premiere event in the country. Run by Arizona businessman Jim Storey, the Cactus Classic wasn't a sanctioned AAU tournament, meaning that Storey had the opportunity to handpick the teams he wanted at the invitation only event. Included on his wish list was one of the most successful teams on the East Coast, the New York Gauchos.

"They used to call us 'Tiger Woods' back then," former Gauchos head coach Book Richardson said. "Because we won all the majors."

Winning aside, there was one problem with the Gauchos committing to an event all the way across the country: money. As much as Richardson wanted his guys to get the opportunity to play the nation's best, it wasn't cheap to fly a bunch of teenagers out to Arizona, especially with several other tournaments already booked for that summer. As we now know, Kemba Walker's national coming out party was at the Arizona Cactus Classic. But he and his Gauchos teammates almost missed the opportunity because of simple dollars and cents.

"Since it wasn't a scheduled trip, we really didn't have the funds," Richardson said. "We only brought eight kids with us, and everybody was sharing hotel rooms, including the coaches."

Whatever the Gauchos accommodations in Arizona were, once they arrived their presence was felt. Three days and eight wins later, they had beaten the nation's talented teams, with Walker getting the best of virtually every elite high school guard in the country. He was named tournament MVP, beat Brandon Jennings head-to-head, and within hours of the tournament final his recruitment had taken on a whole new life. By the time Walker returned to Rice for his senior year, he had committed to play basketball for the UConn Huskies.

Moe Hicks never had to vouch for Kemba Walker again.

⌘ ⌘ ⌘

Following his hot summer in Arizona and with college future settled, Walker returned for his senior year at Rice with a newfound sense of confidence. Along with Gauchos teammate Durand Scott, Walker's Rice High School entered the 2007–2008 season as one of the top teams in the New York City metro area and ranked by Rivals. com as the No. 13 team in the country nationally. More importantly the kid from the Bronx who few knew a couple months earlier was now a national name with recruiting analysts everywhere. Walker entered his senior year ranked by Rivals as the No. 2 point guard in the country and one of the top twenty players regardless of position.

And the self-assurance that Walker had the previous summer transitioned well to the courts in his hometown of New York as the Rice Raiders jumped out to a 10–0 start.

"As good as he'd been as a junior, he was even better that senior year," Hicks said. "He just got better and better every year."

With Walker leading them, Rice had plenty of highlights that season, and on the court, Kemba's best moment likely came when he put up a career best thirty-nine points in a win city rival St. Raymond's in February, a team which prominently featured his Gauchos teammate Truck Bryant. Still, the biggest moment of his senior year actually came away from the hardwood, when on February 19 he was given the biggest honor a high school basketball player can get. On that day, Kemba followed in the footsteps of so many great Rice guards before him, and was one of twenty-four players named to the 2008 McDonald's All-American Game.

Back on the court, Kemba's final year at Rice wouldn't quite have the same cheesy-Disney-movie ending that his last season at UConn did. After cruising through the first few games of the CHSAA Intersectional Championships, the Raiders ran into a Holy Cross team from Flushing, which hadn't quite lived up to expectations but had plenty of talent of their own. Included was one of Walker's McDonald's All-American teammates Sylven Landesberg, who'd be heading to the University of Virginia in the fall.

And unfortunately for Walker and Rice, it was Landesberg who played like the All-American that night. With Walker plagued by foul trouble, Landesberg scored twenty first-half points and thirty for the game in leading Holy Cross to a shocking 64–62 upset. The Crusaders would go on to shock Christ the King in the championship game, giving them their first title in forty years.

As for Walker, his career at Rice was over.

⌘　⌘　⌘

But before Walker headed off to scenic Storrs (well, scenic until around Halloween anyway, at which point Storrs essentially turns into the North Pole), there was still plenty more basketball to be played.

It started a few weeks after Kemba's Rice career ended when he went to Milwaukee for the previously mentioned McDonald's All-American Game.

Now for those of you who aren't college basketball fans (to which I must say, shame on you!) being named to the McDonald's All-American Game isn't just an honor for a high school basketball player, it's *the honor*. Name a famous basketball player that has graduated high school since 1977 (when the game started) and chances are all but certain that he was named to the team. There's Magic Johnson. And LeBron James. Dwight Howard. Isaiah Thomas. Kobe Bryant. Chris Paul. Shaquille O'Neal. And yes, even Ron Artest. Not to mention that some guy named Michael Jordan held the McDonald's All-American Game scoring record for close to twenty years before a Mississippi high schooler named Jonathan Bender broke it in 1999.

But back to 2008 where it's safe to say that Walker was in some rare company when he took the floor at the Bradley Center on March 27 with twenty-three other elite high school stars. Starting for the East side, Walker poured in thirteen points with six rebounds and three assists, helping lead the East to a 107–102 victory. Later in the spring he played in another All-Star game, this one the Jordan Brand Classic at Madison Square Garden.

In addition, Kemba would make one final stop before heading to Storrs, spending the middle of July in—of all places—Formosa, Argentina.

Why Formosa? Well if you're thinking he needed a pit stop on his way to campus for a glass of red wine and a good steak, you're mistaken. I think. Instead Walker and a group of high school superstars traveled to Formosa to represent the United States in the FIBA Americas Under-18 Championship. The club was coached by Bob McKillop (who'd become a college basketball celebrity just a few months earlier when he led Stephen Curry and Davidson of the tiny Southern Conference to the NCAA Tournament's Elite Eight) with players such as JaMychal Green of Alabama and future UCLA Bruin Malcolm Lee joining Kemba on the court.

And in the least surprising storyline maybe ever, Kemba Walker quickly became the star and leader of the team.

Kemba averaged 13.4 points, five assists, and 4.6 rebounds per game in the tournament, leading the United States to three straight wins in pool play and an 82–66 semifinal win over Canada. And although the United States would lose the championship game to the Argentines, Kemba was hardly to blame. He scored twenty-one points and added seven rebounds with three assists and two blocks in the final. In a situation that is rarely seen in sports, Walker was named tournament MVP, even though his team didn't actually didn't win the tournament.

After spending the previous twelve months dominating the high school courts of New York and the AAU scene nationwide, for the first time the Kemba Walker Show had gone international.

Now it was time to go home.

⌘　⌘　⌘

Upon arriving in Storrs, Connecticut, in the fall of 2008, Kemba Walker was put into a role he hadn't held in quite some time: that of an ancillary player. With seniors A. J. Price and Jeff Adrien as well as juniors Hasheem Thabeet, Stanley Robinson, and Jerome Dyson, the 2008-2009 UConn Huskies were a veteran club built to win a title that year. Kemba's role would simply be to provide some offense off the bench and spell the All-Big East point guard Price when he needed a breather, and otherwise just stay the hell out of everyone's way and not do anything stupid. For the first time in a long time, Walker was hardly the star of the show.

But instead of doing like a lot of superstar hotshot recruits would've in that situation (namely, sulking), Walker instead followed Price around like a puppy dog would a new owner and soaked up everything the fifth-year senior had to say.

Speaking of Price, Walker told Mike Anthony of the *Hartford Courant* in November of his freshman year, "He's great and he's definitely a leader. He got me through this practice. He spoke to me a lot. Every time I messed up, he tapped me on the shoulder and told me what to do. I'm definitely looking forward to playing with him."[1]

Interestingly, as history played out, Shabazz Napier would speak about Walker in the same reverential tone two years later. But that of course, was still a long way away.

Once the games started, Walker played about the way you'd expect a freshman to: good, but a little erratic. Walker wasn't great and wasn't terrible and made just enough good plays to keep him on the court. He also made just enough bad ones to give every fan heartburn and make them yell, "What the heck is he *doing!*" at their TV at least once a game.

Offensively Walker most certainly had his moments.

There was the twenty-one-point outburst in his second game of the season against the University of Hartford and a season-high twenty-three points four days later against LaSalle in the first round of the Paradise Jam preseason tournament in the Virgin Islands.

But of course there were also the bad with the Kemba Walker freshman experience, mainly the turnovers. Four in twenty-six minutes in the season opener. Seven against Wisconsin in the Paradise Jam Final. Four in the Huskies' first loss of the year in the Big East opener. Just as easily as Kemba Walker could put the ball in the basket his first year in Storrs, he could give it away too—which is not the way to endear yourself to any coach, especially a no-nonsense Hall of Famer like Jim Calhoun.

However, despite the ebbs and flows, peaks and valleys of the first few months of his career, Walker's role with the team would forever change on February 9, 2009. In an otherwise mundane 63–49 win over Syracuse in Storrs, the Huskies' season would be altered drastically when Jerome Dyson, their leading scorer at the time, left the game in the first half with a knee injury. Although the injury wasn't originally diagnosed as serious, that all changed a few days later when Dyson was informed he'd torn his meniscus. He'd need surgery and wouldn't play another minute for the Huskies that season. Senior Craig Austrie moved into his spot in the starting lineup with Walker seeing increased minutes as well.

Not that it mattered much. At least at the beginning.

The 2009 Huskies had been Price's team from day one, and that was even more the case without Dyson. After he went down, Price scored double figures in every game but one the rest of the season, including a career-high thirty-six in a thrilling 93–82 win at Marquette in late February. That game would also become a milestone for another reason: it was the eight-hundredth win in Jim Calhoun's legendary career.

As for Walker, he had some big games after Dyson's season was lost, most notably with the anomaly of all box scores against Syracuse in the Big East Tournament. You may of course remember that game for becoming one of the all-time classics, a six overtime bloodbath that went down as the second longest game in NCAA history. On the court, Walker played fifty-two minutes that night (after not playing more than thirty-one in a game all season), scoring eight points with eleven rebounds.

(Meanwhile yours truly will always remember that night for one thing: I almost missed the last train back to Connecticut from Grand Central Terminal.

That's right, despite there being probably fifty thousand people who claim they were in Madison Square Garden the night of the six overtime Syracuse-UConn classic, I was actually one of them. I even have the ticket stub to prove it. And although I'm not sure at exactly what time I arrived at the arena, I know that I left right before 1:30 a.m. when the last train leaves Grand Central to go back to Connecticut. Let's just say that if that game had gone into a seventh overtime, I might still be sleeping in the train station right now.

As it was, I got to the train station sweating and jumped on it as the door was closing. My head finally hit the pillow sometime around when most people were getting up for work.)

Anyway, back to basketball.

After the Syracuse loss, UConn had some extra time off before starting NCAA Tournament play as the No. 1 seed in the West Region. The Huskies cruised through the first two rounds, beating UT-Chattanooga (which last had made the NCAA Tournament in 1997 when a loud-mouthed walk-on named Terrell Owens was on the roster) and Texas A&M by a combined eighty-two points. Kemba had a total of eighteen points in the opening weekend wins as the Huskies were led by their usual cast of Price, Jeff Adrien, Hasheem Thabeet, and Stanley Robinson.

With the two wins, the Huskies advanced to the West Regional finals in Glendale, Arizona, where they were met by an unwanted guest—a report by Yahoo! Sports with alleged recruiting improprieties involving Walker's former roommate Nate Miles. Miles had moved onto campus late in the previous summer but never played a game for the Huskies that season as he was suspended before the season started and then expelled for violating a restraining order against a female student. Regardless, the Yahoo report was pretty damning, and will be explained in much more detail later in the book.

To the Huskies' credit though, they at least publicly brushed off the allegations when they returned to the court Thursday. UConn beat a scrappy Purdue team 72–60 in a Sweet Sixteen matchup—a game that was much tougher than final score might indicate. It set up a Saturday showdown with the Missouri Tigers and a trip to the Final Four on the line.

Speaking of the Tigers, if there was ever a team for Walker to flash his immense speed, skill, and New York flair against during his freshman year, Missouri seemed to be it. The Tigers were coached by Mike Anderson, a disciple of former Arkansas coach Nolan Richardson and the legendary "Forty Minutes of Hell" style that allowed the Razorbacks to go to three Final Fours under Richardson and take home the 1994 NCAA title.

Anderson brought the fast-paced, pressing and trapping "Forty Minutes of Hell" with him to Missouri after a stint at UAB, and the 2009 club was far and away his best yet. They were one of the great surprises in college basketball that season, going 31–6 and winning their first conference tournament title in sixteen years just a few weeks prior to their Elite Eight showdown with UConn. Missouri's up-and-down pace produced 81.1 points per game, which was the eighth best total in the country that year.

Unfortunately that pace also played right into the hands of a true freshman at UConn who'd had an otherwise quiet first year on campus: Kemba Walker.

While the senior Price had eighteen points that afternoon, his freshman teammate stole the show. The same flair that had made Kemba Walker a household name in an Arizona gym almost two years prior had come out again that day in the same state as Walker led the Huskies with twenty-three points, five assists, and five steals. They'd go on to win 82–75 and advance to the Final Four, thanks in large part to the play of one of the youngest players on the roster.

As Price mentioned to reporters about his freshman teammate, "I told him, he grew up. He played like a man today," Price said.[6]

Walker's response? "I can't lie to you," he said. "After the game, I actually did cry[2]

⌘   ⌘   ⌘

A solid freshman year for Walker ended on the first Saturday of April 2009 at the Final Four in Detroit, Michigan. The Huskies lost to Michigan State 83–73, ending the careers of Price, Adrien, and Thabeet, the latter of which left college a year early for the NBA Draft. The team would need to take on a new shape the following year. But in large part they'd take their cues from their new point guard, Kemba Walker.

Entering the 2009–2010 season, the Huskies were a great paradox of team (having already been discussed at length in previous chapters). They were a talented and experienced bunch that just happened to have next to no leadership. Dyson, Robinson, and Gavin Edwards were all seniors and had always been comfortable putting up stats on good teams. At the same time, they never seemed nearly as comfortable taking charge of a huddle as Price and Adrien, who had always handled that aspect of things for the first three years of their careers. And by choice or not, that responsibility now fell on Kemba Walker.

Walker started the year out hot (averaging sixteen points in the first four games), but when the Huskies played eventual National Champion Duke at Madison Square Garden in the fifth game of the season, Walker would get exposed for exactly what he was: young with a long way to go. He finished the game with nine points and nine assists, but also had six turnovers and would eventually foul out in a 68–59 loss.

Unfortunately for the Huskies, that'd be the story of the season: they'd get close against the big boys. They just rarely pulled out wins.

There was a loss a few weeks later at the Garden to John Wall and the Kentucky Wildcats when the Huskies led 61–60 with under forty seconds to go and ended up losing the game 64–61. Later was the Big East opening loss at Cincinnati by two and the crippling defeat at Georgetown when the Huskies led by fifteen at halftime and still found a way to lose. Ultimately, UConn never did recover from that Georgetown game. They entered the game at 11–3 and would go on to finish the year 18–16.

And through it all, the man who received the most blame was Walker. When it came to the UConn point guard, two differing opinions began to split the Huskies fan base.

The first thought that Walker was immature and out of control, driving recklessly to the basket late in games rather than deferring to his veteran teammates and getting others involved like a good point guard should. That camp pointed to his 40 percent shooting (down from 47 percent the year before), including a meager 33 percent from three. Really though, his 2.9 turnovers a game were what broke the spirit of UConn fans, with many of those turnovers coming at the worst possible times. Understand that it's one thing to lose basketball games. It's quite another to literally give them away.

Of course there was another side to the camp too. Disenchanted and frustrated by the lack of leadership and seeming lack of heart by the seniors (namely Dyson and Robinson), the second camp wasn't crazy about Kemba's play but gave him credit for at least doing *something*. Yes Walker played out of control at times. Sure they'd have preferred to see him limit the turnovers. But at least he wanted the ball with the game on the line. Which is more than some of his teammates could say.

The second camp was actually the one I stood in, and on February 26, 2010, wrote that sentiment in my "40 Most Valuable College Basketball Players" column[4]:

**39. Kemba Walker, UConn:** *Ahh, Kemba Walker, maybe the most controversial player on this list. At least in my mom's house anyway.*

*You see, my mom and I are both alumni of UConn and watch a lot of the games together. And she hates Kemba Walker. I mean hates him. Like right up there with the Ayatollah, Simon Cowell, Fidel Castro, and Lady Gaga. Weird list, I know.*

*And like (Kyle) Singler, I get why she and others have grown weary of Walker. He plays most possessions out of control, and some, just downright reckless. He forces too many shots and not enough passes. He makes bad decisions, lots of them.*

*But in Kemba's defense, look at who he's playing with. The other "stars" on UConn are Jerome Dyson and Stanley Robinson, who are nice kids, most of the time probably a little too nice if you know what I mean (Honestly I've seen Mormon kids at frat parties less passive than those two in crunch time). And except for Gavin Edwards, UConn's bigs are young and raw, which is a nice way of saying that at times they're actually just gawky and clumsy.*

*Enter Kemba. He's not perfect, I get it. But when the game is on the line, he wants the ball. And there's no one else on UConn you can say that about. Finally, here are two other reasons why Kemba made this list:*

*1. As I said, he wants the ball in crunch time. And I don't care how pretty or ugly he is when he gets the ball, the guy gets to the foul line and makes his shots. Do not underestimate how important this will be if UConn makes the tournament.*

*2. Speaking of the tournament, as bad as UConn has been for parts of this season, they can still get there. But it couldn't happen if not for wins against Villanova and West Virginia in the last two weeks. And in those two wins, Kemba went for a combined fifty points and was the leading scorer in each. I'm just saying.*

Of course that NCAA Tournament I was dreaming about in late February? The Huskies never got there.

After the 17–14 regular season finish, UConn got run out of the Big East Tournament, losing on a quiet Tuesday afternoon to St. John's 73–51. It was undoubtedly their worst effort of the year and a true sign of how bad things had gotten; the Huskies had beaten the same St. John's team by sixteen points two months before.

UConn's season mercifully came to an end two games later in the NIT loss to Virginia Tech. As was the case all year, Walker led the way with eighteen points. He also ended with three turnovers. And just one year after finishing his freshman year a game away from playing for the title, Walker's sophomore season ended in a half-empty arena in Blacksburg, Virginia, in a consolation tournament. Probably not quite the way he'd pictured things when committing to the school back in August of 2007.

Maybe even more concerning was the future. After such a disastrous season, it was easy to forget that this UConn team had been talented and had been ranked in the Top 20 for the first half of the year. More importantly, as erratic as Robinson, Dyson, and Edwards had been all season, at least they were seniors and had been through the wars of Big East play.

With a group of unheralded freshmen set to take the place of those seniors, there was reason to think that the best UConn teams that Kemba would ever play had already passed through Storrs.

The next time he would take the court in a UConn uniform, Kemba would have to wear many hats: that of a leader and scorer, distributor, and of course, superstar.

And even then, it still might not be enough.

⌘　⌘　⌘

Often times after a student completes either their sophomore or junior year of college, he or she will take a summer internship. For business students it might be at J.P. Morgan, for those trying to get a job in professional sports, maybe with the marketing department of a minor league baseball team. That's just the way the world works, with everyone trying to gain that leg up on the competition and get real world experience.

To an extent, you could say that after his sophomore year at UConn, Kemba Walker did an internship of his own. Only his didn't include getting coffee for the boss in the morning or delivering the TPS reports every afternoon (*Office Space* anyone?) but instead came on the hardwood. Walker played on the USA Select Team with a group of college All-Stars who scrimmaged against the United States National Team as they prepared for the World Championships in Turkey. The NBA roster included the previous year's NBA scoring champ Kevin Durant as well as future MVP Derrick Rose, a player who Walker had beaten head-to-head when they were both in high school.

Still, entering the camp, no one was quite sure what to expect from any of the college players on the roster, least of all Walker who was coming off a stellar, if not spectacular, sophomore year. That group included Washington head coach and USA Select Team assistant Lorenzo Romar who hadn't seen the guard play in over a year.

"The first time I saw Kemba play was back in his freshman year against Missouri in the NCAA Tournament," Romar said. "At the time, I remember seeing a talented guard, but one who was score first, and pass second. He was a guy who was trying to make the plays for himself, by himself. That's not an insult, just who he was at the time."

But by the time Kemba arrived in Las Vegas, it was clear that he had changed not only as a basketball player but also as a leader on the court. By the end of the camp, Walker was far and away one of the best college players in the camp, someone who was not only an emerging basketball star but also an emerging leader as well.

"He was so much more of a complete guard for us than the last time I'd seen him," Romar said. "It showed in his ability to get others involved, but also take over when he needed to as well. Of all the college players in the camp, Kemba probably had the best combination of confidence, and the ability to actually perform. He took it right at the pros."

After playing well in the pre-trials in Las Vegas in late July, Walker then was one of ten to make the final cut and return to New York for more practices against the NBA superstars.

Playing against the NBA's best, Walker and his teammates got immeasurably better on the court, while also learning valuable lessons off of it. And ultimately they'd all head back to their respective college campuses knowing that whatever beating they took from the pros had paid off. The U.S. National team went on to win the World Championships in August, qualifying the country for the 2012 London Olympics.

As for Walker in specific? Well, he got quite a bit out of the experience personally as well. As he told reporters about the experience later on during UConn's season, "The way those guys guarded me, nobody guarded me like that in my life," Walker said. "Playing those guys made me realize how good I was on this level. It made me see things slower." He also added, "It changed my life."[4]

It would take another couple months, and a trip to the Maui Invitational before the college basketball world saw that change. But when they did there was no doubt.

Kemba Walker was definitely different.

And so too were the UConn Huskies.

# Chapter 5

## UConn's Maui Invitational Win: What a Difference a Year Makes (Published November 25, 2010)

Twelve months. What a difference twelve months makes.

Twelve months ago, chance and circumstance brought me to New York City on December 9, which in turn brought me to Madison Square Garden for the Kentucky-UConn game being played that night. I wasn't planning on attending. But I'm a UConn fan and a UConn graduate, I was in New York, and figured, "Why the hell not?"

Unexpected to everyone in the arena—myself included—that night turned into a classic, one of those games that you'll stumble across a replay of three, four, five years from now and get sucked into watching. It was physical. It was emotional. And when UConn lost, it was a kick in the stomach.

At least for me it was. But as I documented in my column[1] the following day, it was anything but for Kentucky fans. That game wasn't just a win, but *the* win. *The* win that welcomed in the John Calipari era. *The* win that washed away the pain of the Tubby Smith and Billy Gillispie years. *The* win that let the college basketball world know that Kentucky basketball—the team and brand that I'd grown up hearing about but never seeing—was back after an extended disappearance. As I said in the article, for Kentucky fans, that win shouldn't have meant so much. But it did.

Well, twelve months later, here I am. I'm not the one patting Kentucky fans on the back and congratulating them, but instead, it's the opposite. My team is back on top of the college basketball world. Maybe only for a day, a week, or a month, but it feels good none the less. Last night's win in the Maui Invitational, in November, in a time when we have real things to be thankful for (our friends, our family, those protecting us overseas), shouldn't have meant so much. But for this one fan, it did.

You see, that loss to Kentucky last year at Madison Square Garden was the beginning and the end of UConn's season as we knew it. It was one of those games that—as I mentioned—was emotional and physically draining, not only for the guys on the court, but for us in the stands as well.

But at the same time, it was a sign of hope. It was a sign that said, "You know what, we may have lost to a damn good Kentucky team. John Wall may have ripped our hearts out. But when this team finally figures things out…watch out."

The problem was, that team never got things figured out. The 2009–2010 UConn Huskies toed the line between "supremely talented" and "utterly disappointing" for the better part of five months. There were the highest of highs (beating No. 1 Texas) and the lowest of lows (too many to count). There were times when they could do no wrong but, more often than not, when nothing went right.

Most days though, UConn was everything you never want your team to be: arrogant, entitled, and disinterested. Jim Calhoun called last season one of his most frustrating in forty-plus years of coaching. It was certainly my most frustrating in twenty-plus years as a fan. Like Sisyphus in Greek mythology, just as soon as we got the boulder inches from the top of the mountain, it came crashing back down. That Kentucky game was the season in a nutshell. UConn could play with anyone. They just usually didn't beat them.

Which, again, is why Wednesday night was so special. Not necessarily because we beat Kentucky to win the Maui Invitational.

But because it made up for everything that happened a season ago. Reflecting on things, this UConn team really is everything last year's wasn't. This year's team is scrappy. They hustle. They play for another. They're overachieving. They're a team in every sense of the word.

And really that's the biggest thing that's going to get lost in the shuffle as Kemba Walker and Alex Oriahki return to Connecticut as conquering heroes in the coming days: as great as those two guys were all tournament long, the three wins in Maui were a team effort.

Thinking back on the three days, I can't think of one guy who saw that court that didn't contribute in some way.

There was Niels Giffey who scored a couple buckets early to settle things down against Kentucky. Shabazz Napier forced turnovers with his full-court pressure defense. Tyler Olander got key rebounds against bigger, stronger, and older guys. Charles Okwandu won the opening tip against Kentucky (OK, maybe that one's a bit of a stretch). Roscoe Smith hit a handful of big threes, including one that totally changed the momentum of the Wichita State game. And speaking of Wichita State, UConn wouldn't have won that game if the young guys didn't keep things close early. If it weren't for Napier, Smith, and Jeremy Lamb's play in the first half, we would've never seen Kemba Walker take over in the second half. More importantly, UConn might've been playing Virginia in the fifth-place game Wednesday rather than Kentucky in the final. Again, these three wins were a team effort.

Of course those wins couldn't have happened without Walker and Oriahki doing the heavy lifting.

Let's start with Oriahki because, really, what can you say about the guy? I half joked on Twitter_Wednesday night, "Apparently Oriahki wants some big checks of his own next year instead of just mooching off Kemba." No kidding, huh?

Coming into the year, I expected Oriahki to be good, but other than Mama Oriahki herself, I don't think anyone thought we'd see what we have so far. His stat lines would make any low-post player proud. In three games in Maui he had forty-five points and thirty-five rebounds, including a fifteen-point, seventeen-rebound effort against Michigan

State. It's not often someone out-physicals the Spartans, but that's exactly what Oriahki did Tuesday night.

Of course numbers only tell part of the story, and here's something I think that's getting lost in the shuffle: Oriahki's basically doing it by himself in UConn's frontcourt. Remember, Jeff Adrien (whose game I've heard Oriahki compared to) had the luxury of playing alongside Josh Boone, Hilton Armstrong, and Hasheem Thabeet in his four years at UConn. Oriahki has a very limited Onuwaku, an inexperienced Olander, and Smith doing most of his damage from the perimeter. Oriahki has to be the physical and emotional leader down low and basically do it by himself. If Walker was the MVP of this tournament, Oriahki was the runner-up.

Finally you can't talk anything UConn basketball right now without talking about Walker. He's been a star. He's been a superstar. He's been the best player in college basketball. Nobody has worked harder, and nobody has earned it like Kemba has.

And after last year, I thought that Kemba had a bit of a bad rap with some UConn fans. At times he did try to do too much, and he took heat because of it. There were bad turnovers and reckless drives at the basket, often in spite of running a crisp offense or finding the open man.

Still, if you really watched UConn, it was hard to blame Kemba.

He got thrown into a no-win situation last year with a lot of skilled guys around him but no leaders. Believe me, I know Jerome Dyson and Stanley Robinson personally. They're nice guys. They'd be fun to hang out with. They'd talk hoops if you met them at an airport. But they're not guys that you want as faces of your team.

And whenever those two did lead last year, it was only by default. Almost like they looked around the huddle, waited for someone to say something, waited some more, before finally throwing out a haphazard, "Let's go." Again, they're great guys if you only need them to play basketball (like in 2009). But ask them to bark at their teammates or get on someone's case, and it ain't happening. That's just not their personality.

Well that's the situation Kemba was thrust into last season. In 2009 this was A. J. Price and Adrien's team, and in 2010 the logical progression would've been for Robinson and Dyson to take over. It just never happened. Meanwhile, Kemba had to do the following things: try to run the offense; be a distributor; lead by example; and take big shots when no one else wanted them. Not to mention he had to do it all without stepping on anyone else's toes in a season where, because of illness, UConn basically had two coaches. Talk about multitasking.

But after all those struggles, I thought it would make this UConn team, and Walker in particular, better than many expected. I even wrote it last week.[2] With Dyson and Robinson now gone, this would be Kemba's team. No stepping on anyone's toes. No faux leadership. It's Kemba and Co. with all the young pups falling in line behind him.

Of course I'd be lying if I said I thought he'd be this good.

Really his development is staggering. He still plays at the same speed but is doing it under more control and without forcing things. Which is maybe the most incredible part of Kemba's season so far, that he's averaging thirty points a game and doing it all within the flow of the offense. Crazy but true. Last year he shot just 40 percent from the field. He's at 52 percent so far this year. Not to mention that his three-point shot is better, he's figured out a floater in the lane and still picks off errant passes on defense. As I joked with a friend last night, if the pride I feel in watching Kemba mature is anything like having a kid, then I may have to reconsider my stance on children.

And really the difference in the tournament was the difference in Walker. There was no common denominator about his three performances in Maui other than that the opposition never had an answer for him. Kemba was a cold-blooded assassin against Wichita State, more of a facilitator against Kentucky, and somewhere in the middle when UConn played Michigan State. But he was the best player on the court all three nights. As I said after last year's UConn-Kentucky game, the difference between the two teams was that "Kentucky had John Wall." It was no different with UConn and Kemba Walker Wednesday night.

Going forward I don't know what the whole Maui experience means. It might be the start of something incredible, a Big East title run, a Final Four run, who knows. Just as likely, the three wins might mean nothing (if only because dopey sportswriters like me are quick to praise the freshmen five games into their careers). More than likely it'll all end somewhere in the middle.

But honestly on this day and this Thanksgiving morning, it doesn't matter.

All that matters is after a season of head-scratching, teeth-clenching, remote-control-throwing losses, I've got my team back. Maybe not as a title contender, but as one that plays hard and, more importantly, seems to enjoy each other. As I said before, I didn't expect UConn to win Wednesday night, and they might not have if Terrence Jones hadn't gotten into foul trouble. But ultimately it doesn't matter. Because had they won or lost, I'd already derived more pleasure out of watching their first two games in Maui than I had all thirty-five games last year.

What a difference twelve months makes, huh?

A year ago I was talking to Kentucky fans about how one win so early in the year shouldn't mean so much. And now a year later I know exactly how they felt that night.

One win shouldn't mean so much, but it does.

It's good to have my team back.

# Chapter 6

## Getting to Know Alex Oriahki and Jamal Coombs-McDaniel

If UConn fans felt like they'd known Alex Oriahki for his entire life by the time he'd enrolled as a freshman, they really wouldn't have been all that far off. The six-foot-nine power forward who'd go on to be the Huskies' best post player in 2011 had committed to the program in 2006…a full thirty-six months before he'd even be eligible to attend the school. Along with AAU and high school teammate Jamal Coombs-McDaniel, they became the youngest players to ever give Jim Calhoun a verbal commitment, doing so after their *freshmen* years in high school.

But unlike most of his eventual teammates, Oriahki wasn't an under-the-radar or underappreciated recruit. After averaging just under thirteen points and eleven rebounds a game as a freshman at the Brooks School outside of Boston, Oriahki blew up the following summer playing alongside Coombs-McDaniel for the city's esteemed AAU program, BABC. By the end of the summer, Oriahki would widely be considered as amongst the best players in his age group in the country.

Now for those that don't follow the AAU basketball scene with a fine-tooth comb, understand that BABC is amongst the finest programs in the country. Started in 1977 by a young local named Leo Papile, BABC has been a staple at national AAU tournaments for more than three decades now. They play a competitive and exhaustive schedule that includes upwards of eighty games a summer both domestically and abroad, and in the process, have taken home multiple National Championships in multiple age groups. In addition, they have also sent countless players to colleges on scholarships and even a handful to the NBA (Dana Barros, Chris Herren, and some guy named Patrick Ewing among them). The 2012 season will mark Papile's thirty-fifth year running the program, and in the last seven, he has taken on an additional role outside the program with the Boston Celtics as the senior director of basketball operations. Yep, *those* Boston Celtics.

Simply put, Papile knows basketball. And in the summer of 2006, Papile had his next great low-post star in Oriahki.

"As soon as Alex walked into the gym, he had an NFL body," Papile said of his low-post star, who first played with BABC as a thirteen-year-old in 2004. "But besides being strong, he also had a competitive nature, which in my experience—regardless of size—is something you can teach. You're just born with it."

Along with Coombs-McDaniel, Oriahki and BABC would score their first big title together in the summer of 2006, securing the fifteen-and-under AAU National Championship. However it was a tournament a week later that caught the attention of the UConn coaching staff.

Just one weekend after winning a National Championship, BABC flew down to Orlando and won another tournament known as the Super Showcase; and they did it with a catch. The Super Showcase was a sixteen-and-under event, meaning that BABC had won a tournament full of teams whose rosters were comprised almost entirely of players a year older than their own. Boston's best fifteen-year-olds had beaten the best sixteen-year-olds anywhere in the country.

Apparently, the tournament win was enough to impress the UConn coaches. They invited Oriahki, Coombs-McDaniel, their families and BABC assistant coach Chris Driscoll up to campus for an unofficial visit. By the end of the day, Calhoun and his assistant coaches had commitments from the two youngest Huskies in program history.

"We were in contact with Chris, and he's really the one who kind of hatched the idea," former UConn assistant and current Quinnipiac University head coach Tom Moore said. "He told us, 'They're young, but they'd commit to you guys if you offered.' At the time we were winning championships, sending guys to the NBA, and were close to home for them. From their perspective it was kind of those 'what's not love' deals. By the end of the visit, they'd committed."

From there the pair stayed together throughout the remainder of their time in high school and beyond, first as sophomores at the Winchendon School in Winchendon, Mass., before eventually transferring to the Tilton School in New Hampshire for their final two years of high school ball.

Of course before enrolling at Tilton, there was AAU basketball to be played, and the pair wore the BABC jersey proudly again in the summer of 2007, a year after they'd first made names for themselves and caught the attention of UConn. Oriahki and Coombs-McDaniel were a large part of BABC's success at another major AAU tournament, this one the Boo Williams in Virginia, where the boys from Boston took home another title. This time they beat a team from New Jersey in the championship game.

Later on that same summer, Oriahki and Coombs-McDaniel would also make an appearance at their future digs at UConn, attending the Connecticut Elite Camp in August; a camp hosted by the school for some of the top high school players in the country. Amongst others who were on campus for the three-day event included future North Carolina Tar Heel Dexter Strickland, future Florida Gator Allan Chaney and some guy named Kemba Walker as well. Heard of him? The lightning quick point guard from the Bronx had committed to the Huskies just two months before, and the Connecticut Elite Camp proved to be an opportune time to meet his future teammates Oriahki and Coombs-McDaniel. Even if the trio wouldn't be playing together for over three more years.

Back on campus at the Tilton School for their junior years, neither Oriahki nor Coombs-McDaniel seemed to have much problem fitting in at the small New Hampshire school. With their arrival, Tilton immediately became favorites in Class B, and didn't disappoint.

"When those two kids came, they were well known commodities," Tilton coach Marcus O'Neil said. "It put a lot of pressure on us as coaches not to fail. But their attitudes and work ethics made it pretty easy for us."

That's right, within days of their arrival on campus, Tilton's two newest stars became two of the team's hardest workers and leaders. They organized 6:00 a.m. runs, worked hard in the weight room, and were known to hang out in the gym and shoot extra free throws during free periods.

"Jamal took a lot of responsibility early on," McNeil said. "He has a lot of pride, and being an older brother has no problem being a leader. Same with Alex. He's someone who knows what kind of player he is, and leads by example."

On the court, the duo barely missed a beat. Tilton lost a handful of games that season, but ultimately won the ones that counted the most. After splitting with fellow Class B power Marianapolis Prep in the regular season, Tilton would go on to defeat them in the New England Prep School Association (NEPSAC) Class B Finals that spring. Oriahki controlled the paint with fifteen points, fourteen rebounds, and four blocks, with Coombs-McDaniel leading all scorers with twenty-nine points. Like they'd done their entire careers up to that point (and as a true sign of what would come), all Oriahki and Coombs-McDaniel did was win championships. By that point, it was practically commonplace.

Next the pair hit the summer circuit and, much like their prep school run, they'd again shine. For Oriahki in particular, that summer cemented his place amongst the nation's elite high school players.

The summer season started out on a bit of a downer as BABC was unable to defend their Boo Williams age-group title. But from there, they rolled through the competition.

A few weeks after the Boo Williams, BABC would go on to capture the King James Classic championship in Akron, winning three games on Sunday to take home the title. They beat the CAP All Stars, then the CP3 All-Stars (sponsored by who else, but CP3 himself, Chris

Paul) and won the final against the Rising Stars 63–43. Really though, the future UConn pair were the rising stars with Oriahki putting up thirteen points, eleven rebounds, and six blocks in the title game, and Coombs-McDaniel ending up as the leading scorer throughout the tournament. From there BABC would go on to a second place finish at the Peach Jam (where future UConn Husky Jeremy Lamb would explode onto the recruiting scene the next year) and the Final Four at AAU nationals.

"Look at those results," Papile said, reflecting on his time with that particular BABC group. "Every tournament, we won the title, played in the championship game, made the final four. It was an amazing run, and a credit to that whole group.

"With Alex and Jamal, it's a credit to them too. Sometimes when a kid commits [to a college] early they lose their focus. Well I coached those two in close to 250 games through the years, and that was never an issue."

Back on the court, Oriahki would gain the admiring eye of the entire AAU circuit when he was invited back to Akron later that summer for the LeBron James Skills Academy. The Skills Academy takes place every summer, when eighty of the top high school players in the country are invited to LeBron James's hometown for individual positional work and scrimmage play. The Top 20 are next invited to represent the United States in the Nike Global Challenge, an invite which was extended to Oriahki in the summer of 2008. One of his teammates at the event was a skinny small forward named Roscoe Smith, another future UConn Husky.

With the long summer complete, the duo returned to Tilton for their senior years and in the process finally fulfilled a promise that had been three years running. After being extended scholarship offers to the University of Connecticut on August 11, 2006, the pair officially put their allegiance into writing on November 12, 2008, signing letters of intent to attend the school. The youngest players ever verbally to commit to the school were now finally, officially, UConn Huskies.

On the court in their last year at Tilton, Oriahki, and Coombs-McDaniel continued to do the only thing they'd ever done since joining forces, and that's win. They would again beat Marianapolis

Prep to claim the NEPSAC Class B title (the first time in school history that Tilton went back-to-back) and would eventually be the first ever Class B school invited to the Prep School National Championships, an event reserved exclusively for larger, Class A schools. It was there where Tilton had some unfinished business from the year before.

"Because we'd had a few too many losses the previous year, the boys—Jamal especially—were frustrated that we didn't get invited to the National Championships." McNeil said. "After that first season, Jamal said, 'We will go to the National Tournament.'"

Well a year later Tilton did just that, arriving at the National Prep School Championships under little fanfare. They were the No. 5 seed and had been beaten badly by their opening round opponent South Kent earlier that season, when injury and illness plagued the team. Not much was expected from Tilton when the two teams took the court a few months later.

"Right before tip, we actually heard a couple of the South Kent guys say to themselves, 'Why are we playing *these* guys?'" McNeil, said. "That got everyone's attention."

In the end, the surprise was on South Kent as the team they'd played earlier completely different than the one they faced that evening. With Oriahki in foul trouble, Coombs-McDaniel scored forty-two points, in leading them to the upset win.

As surprising as that quarterfinal was however, the true surprise came two games later: Tilton shocked everyone in prep school basketball circles, and won the National Championship. The first ever Class B school to even enter the event won it, with Coombs-McDaniel leading the way with thirty points in the championship game.

"That team will always be special to me," McNeil said. "They were just so damn competitive, and that started with Jamal and Alex. We were practically getting in fights in practice every day, the guys just wanted it so bad."

With his high school career now done, Oriahki—much like future UConn teammate Kemba Walker did the year before—would hit the All-Star game circuit that spring. In February, Oriahki had been named to the prestigious McDonald's All-American team, with the game to be played that April in Miami.

But for whatever interest there was in the basketball on the court, in a lot of ways, the leading story was actually off of it.

With Memphis coach John Calipari weighing an offer from the University of Kentucky, it turned basketball into a side-story, with the recruitment and commitments of many of the game's top players turned upside down. And while Oriahki obviously wasn't affected, a handful of other players were, including Oriahki's top AAU low-post adversary through the years DeMarcus Cousins, as well as Oklahoma forward Xavier Henry who had both already signed letters of intent with Memphis. The Tigers were also recruiting the nation's top player, guard John Wall (who wasn't in town for the game, but was still a name on the tip of everyone's tongues). The domino effect that started in Miami would eventually lead Calipari to Lexington, where along with Wall and Cousins, Kentucky would become the top story of the 2009-2010 season, and at one point, an opponent of the UConn Huskies. On the court in Miami, the East squad would go on to win, with the future Husky Oriahki chipping in five points and four rebounds. He'd have an even better game a few weeks later at the Jordan Brand Classic in New York. Just like what had happened for BABC and at Tilton over the previous three years, Oriahki's team again won, 110-103 in front of a jam-packed Madison Square Garden.

⌘  ⌘  ⌘

After knowing they'd be Huskies for over three years, Alex Oriahki and Jamal Coombs-McDaniel finally arrived on campus in the fall of 2009. And the two former high school superstars couldn't have arrived to roles any more different.

On a veteran team that was coming off a Final Four, minutes would be limited for any newcomers, regardless of position or high school acclaim. In the paint Oriahki seemed destined to see more time, if only because as the old adage goes, "You can't teach size." At six foot nine and with the body of man, Oriahki certainly had plenty of that. Meanwhile things wouldn't be nearly as easy on the wing for Coombs-McDaniel. Seniors Jerome Dyson and Stanley Robinson were starting at shooting guard and small forward respectively, the two places that Coombs-McDaniel seemed most likely to see time. It didn't help that he was sharing those limited minutes with a pair of fellow freshmen who were trying to make names for themselves, Jamaal Trice and Darius Smith.

However, despite what were expected to be limited roles, each got off to a hot start.

For Oriahki, the rebounding prowess he'd shown his entire high school career took all of one game to show up in college. He had ten boards the first time he put on a UConn uniform in a victory over William & Mary. Coombs-McDaniel showed a nice scoring touch in the Huskies' second game that fall, when he scored eleven points with three 3-pointers in a win over Colgate.

Unfortunately the hot play wouldn't continue for either.

With Oriahki, his numbers would plummet as the Huskies entered Big East play in January. The freshman remained in the starting lineup, but with cerebral but efficient senior Gavin Edwards as well as emerging sophomore Ater Majok coming on, there were only so many minutes to go around. And with Oriahki looking like a lost kid in a grocery store on offense and battling foul trouble on defense, most of those minutes didn't go to him. He played thirty-plus minutes in eight of UConn's first sixteen games, but never again for the rest of the season. Oriahki's best performance came in a January 9 loss at Georgetown, a game that was mentioned in Chapter 1 of this book as a turning point in the train wreck that was the 2010 UConn Huskies season.

Oriahki finished that afternoon with eleven points and ten rebounds, but from there on out would score in double figures only once and never again grab more than ten boards. Most importantly, while Oriahki's play didn't leave fans wanting and wishing for more (like most of his teammates), what it did make them was something even worse: totally apathetic. As the Huskies continued to lose games, Oriahki didn't do much to hurt the team but didn't contribute a whole heck of a lot to help either. Mostly he was just lost in the shuffle as the UConn staff tried everything imaginable to get their team back on track. Nothing seemed to work, and little if any of it involved the six-foot-nine freshman with deteriorating confidence.

Interestingly, that Georgetown game would also be the last meaningful game of Coombs-McDaniel's 2009–2010 season as well. He put up eleven points that afternoon but would never again score in double figures. From there his play (much like the rest of his team's) plummeted, with his box scores becoming more barren than UConn's library the first night of Spring Weekend (an inside joke for any former or current UConn student). He played four minutes against DePaul. Eight versus Syracuse. Four against Cincinnati. And so on.

By the time the Huskies' disappointing season ended in the NIT, the duo who'd done nothing but win their entire careers were just about at rock-bottom. They combined to shoot just three for nine in the season-ending loss to Virginia Tech.

Mercifully for UConn fans, the year had come to an end. But for the two that had been a self-proclaimed package duo since they were barely shaving, their Huskies' careers were just beginning to take form. At the time, no one knew that form would take them in opposite directions.

⌘   ⌘   ⌘

With the misery of their freshmen seasons behind them, Alex Oriahki and Jamal Coombs-McDaniel returned to campus with completely different roles as sophomores. With so many new faces on the roster, not only would they need to provide statistical production, but leadership too.

The burden would fall especially hard on Oriahki.

Simply put, the sophomore who was inconsistent, foul prone, and lost on offense his first year, had no margin for error entering his sophomore season. With Edwards and Robinson gone to graduation, Oriahki would be the focus of everything in the paint. His burden only became greater as the season closed in, and Majok, a raw, but long-armed six-foot-eleven center originally from the Sudan, who was expected to complement him in the front court, left UConn under mysterious circumstances. Majok would eventually sign a professional contract in Australia.

With Majok gone and Oriahki now the focus of an all-of-a-sudden razor thin front-line, his role again changed. Not only would he have to be good every night, but quite frankly, exceptional. There could be no foul trouble. No mental lapses on offense. There needed to be 100 percent effort, 100 percent of the time, or his team wouldn't win. It was really that simple. While Kemba Walker was the most talented player on the UConn roster, Husky fans almost universally agreed that Oriahki was their most *important* player. Big difference.

Luckily for UConn fans, Oriahki took his role seriously, dominating the paint from the very first game of the year. The sophomore warrior scored eleven points in the Huskies' season opener, while also ripping down a mind-boggling eighteen rebounds. The tone had been set. Oriahki followed it up a game later with eleven points and seven rebounds in the victory over Vermont in which Kemba Walker had 42 points

Still, it's one thing to put up big numbers against Stony Brook and Vermont, and quite another to do it against the teams UConn would be facing in Maui. Forget the fact that three of those teams were ranked nationally (Michigan State, Kentucky, and Washington), and understand that even the opening game against Wichita State would be no jaunt in the park either. The Shockers had just as much size as any of those ranked teams, with starters Aaron Ellis and Garrett Stutz, as well as key backup J. T. Durley, all standing at least six-foot-eight. UConn may have been the "high major" program on paper, but if you'd lined the two teams up for a shirts and skins game that day, it would've been Wichita State that looked to be the more physically imposing bunch.

That of course is what made what Oriahki did in his three days in Maui all the more special.

(Before we go any further, there is one very important side note that needs to be mentioned here: One of Coach Jim Calhoun's oldest rules, is that when a player picks up two first half fouls, they must sit until halftime. No exceptions. That's just how it's always been.

The rule most famously came into play in the 2004 Final Four when National Player of the Year Emeka Okafor picked up two fouls before the first TV time-out even hit, with over sixteen minutes to play in the first half. To the bench he went as Duke built—at one point—a nine-point lead. The Huskies' All-American sat on and watched in agony from the sidelines.

However as is the case with most of Calhoun's coaching decisions, it ended up working out for the best. Okafor scored all eighteen of his points in the second half, leading UConn on a furious rally and a 79–78 win that would catapult the Huskies to their second straight title two nights later. In an interesting twist, UConn made their final run after Duke's Shelden Williams fouled out late in the game, in large part because Duke coach Mike Krzyzewski decided to leave him with two fouls in the first half. He picked up his third before halftime, a whistle that altered the game later on, and potentially swung the National title.

And while it's impossible to say what would've happened if Okafor had stayed in the game after picking up his second foul, or if Williams had been removed at the same point, it did no doubt leave Calhoun looking like the smarter coach that evening. His star player was on the court to close out the most important win to that point in the season, while all Duke's best big man could do was watching from the sideline. For the record, that game is also Reason Number 2,171 why UConn fans are convinced that Coach K is overrated. Just saying.)

Anyway, back to Maui.

With the Huskies playing Wichita in the first afternoon of the tournament, they were dealt a brutal blow when Kemba Walker picked up his second foul less than six minutes into the game. He went to the bench, but unlike Okafor a few years before, his team held strong and took a one point lead into intermission. Oriahki contributed a key five points, four rebounds, and a block in the first half, steadying the team in Kemba's absence. Walker would take care of things from there, scoring twenty-nine of his thirty-one points in the second half as UConn got a thrilling 83–79 to open the tournament. But while Walker went out and won that game in the second half, it's impossible to discount the leadership and poise Oriahki showed when Walker was on the bench. The big power forward finished the game with twelve points and seven rebounds.

A day later UConn would be back on the floor at the Lahaina Civic Center and would face an even stiffer test from the No. 2 team in the country Michigan State. Tom Izzo's club was coming off their second straight Final Four and was a program always known best for their toughness in the paint. That had to be bad news for an undersized UConn team, right? Wrong. Oriahki was once again a rock in the middle, scoring fifteen points and ripping down a game-high seventeen rebounds in the win. Thanks to Oriahki's strong play and another thirty point performance from Kemba Walker, the Huskies advanced to Wednesday's final to take on Kentucky.

And when they did play Kentucky, UConn would again be the team with a major disadvantage in the paint.

John Calipari's club was missing six-foot-eleven Turkish superstar Enes Kanter (who had been ruled ineligible by the NCAA), but still had one of the biggest front-lines UConn would see all year. There was seven-foot center Josh Harrellson. And six-foot-nine superstar freshman Terrence Jones. With six-foot-eleven Eloy Vargas coming off the bench, and six-foot-seven Darius Miller lining up as a "guard."

Apparently that meant little to Oriahki however, as he played arguably the best game of his UConn career that night. Not only did Oriahki score eighteen points and grab eleven boards in thirty-seven minutes while staying out of foul trouble, but what's most important is *how* he got those stats. Oriahki was quicker to every loose ball, soared over the less athletic Harrellson and Vargas for rebounds, and dominated defensively with three blocked shots.

As was predicted in the preseason, Oriahki might not have been the best player on the court that night—that title was given to tournament MVP Kemba Walker.

It was hard not to make the argument Oriahki was the most important, though.

⌘　⌘　⌘

Unfortunately things weren't going nearly as well for the man who'd stood by side-by-side with Oriahki in both success and failure, victory and defeat, Jamal Coombs-McDaniel.

Entering his sophomore year, it seemed like (if only because of default) Coombs-McDaniel's minutes would increase. Dyson and Robinson were gone to graduation and two fellow freshmen the previous year (Jamaal Trice and Darius Smith) had left via transfer. In their place stepped a group of unheralded and highly inexperienced freshmen who were expected to compete along with Coombs-McDaniel for those minutes. Included in that group were Jeremy Lamb, Roscoe Smith, and Niels Giffey, with only Smith considered a signature recruit among the three.

But for Coombs-McDaniel the boon in minutes and stats never happened.

If anything his playing time was down from even a year before when he saw significant minutes in the early portion of his freshman year. With Lamb providing scoring punch at the shooting guard position, Smith athleticism that couldn't be matched at small forward, and Giffey a sort of mental toughness that came from the tutelage of the notoriously tough coaches in his native Germany, someone had to be the odd man out, and again it ended up being Coombs-McDaniel.

Even in Maui there was little to celebrate on a personal level for Coombs-McDaniel. He played just ten minutes against Wichita State, despite there being plenty of playing time to go around with Walker on the bench in the first half with foul trouble. Two days later Coombs-McDaniel played twenty-one minutes against Kentucky, but even that number was a bit misleading. With UConn gaining a twenty-one-point halftime lead and cruising to victory, it allowed for a handful of players to see minutes they normally wouldn't.

Once the team returned to the mainland, things, incredibly, only got worse. There were just fourteen minutes to be played in a win over Maryland Baltimore-County. Just seventeen against Fairleigh Dickinson. Eighteen against Coppin State. Nine against Harvard— yes, that Harvard. By the time Big East play opened, things didn't get better. Coombs-McDaniel played a combined twenty-three minutes in games against Pittsburgh and South Florida to open conference play.

It seemed like no matter what Coombs-McDaniel did, he couldn't get off the pine, even in the early season when Jim Calhoun notoriously expands his playing rotation.

"Jamal is just one of those kids that wants to play forty minutes a night," said Tom Moore, the coach who helped recruit him to UConn. "That's not a knock on him at all. But where some kids might be ok playing fifteen minutes, averaging six or seven points, that's just not who he is."

Eventually it would lead to a frustrated Coombs-McDaniel and one of the few off-the-court conflicts that the otherwise notoriously harmonious UConn Huskies would face.

# Chapter 7

## Hope Springs Eternal: The Start of Big East Play

**W**ith the Maui Invitational win, the college basketball world was put on notice: You could go ahead and forget everything you *thought* you knew about UConn. This was a new team, with a new attitude, summed up best by their star player after the tournament. "We're just so close," Kemba Walker told reporters before departing Maui as college basketball's newest superstar. "We want to win so bad, everyone is willing to do whatever it takes."[1]

And after some early season waffling by both coaches and the press, there was no denying that the perception of the team had changed by the time they returned from the sunny shores of Hawaii. Between the end of the Kentucky game and their next one, UConn had gone from unranked to No. 9 in the Coaches' Poll and to No. 7 according to the Associated Press. It was the second biggest jump ever in the Associated Press Poll, with the Huskies just narrowly edged by the 1989 Kansas Jayhawks who had gone from unranked to No. 4 after a similar early season run.

But, as is so often the case (especially with young teams), the Huskies had a bit of a letdown when they faced New Hampshire a few days after returning from Maui. UConn trailed 24–23 at halftime and got next to no contribution from anyone other than Shabazz Napier and of course Kemba Walker, who went off for thirty points. The Huskies eventually pulled away simply because of more talent, but the narrow victory left a bitter taste in the mouths of both the coach and the star player.

"It's the first time I've seen this team—whether it be in practice, exhibition or the regular season—that we haven't done the extra things needed to win," Jim Calhoun said following the victory.[7]

Kemba Walker added, "The intensity wasn't where it needed to be."[2]

That intensity certainly returned the next game when the Huskies blitzed Maryland-Baltimore County 94–61 in front of a mostly quiet and half-empty XL Center in Hartford. Still, those who did show up were privy to some history courtesy of the usual duo of Walker and Calhoun. The player finished with twenty-four points, thirteen rebounds and ten assists, and in the process became just the eighth player in UConn's storied basketball history to record a triple-double.

As for the coach? Well, the win was the 830th of his career, tying him with legendary Mt. St. Mary's coach Jim Phelan for sixth most on the all-time Division I coaches list. Calhoun would move into sixth place by himself a few days later when the Huskies beat Fairleigh Dickinson in another home victory.

And while the win over Fairleigh Dickinson was a small reason for Calhoun to celebrate, there was real reason for the players to be excited following that 78–54 victory over the Knights. Following the win, UConn got their first real break from basketball in months. The first semester had come to a close, finals had to be taken, and it would be twelve days before they again took the court.

When they did return from break, the Huskies welcomed a new player to the team for a second year in a row. A season after Ater Majok first gained eligibility, another raw, foreign, big man did the same when Enosch Wolf finally arrived in Storrs. The seven-foot-one German had spent the first four months of the school year at prep school finishing his high school requirements and came to campus just in time for the Huskies' December 20 game against Coppin State. Wolf finished with four points in that first game; incidentally, a total that eventually ended as his season high.

As for the rest of his new teammates, well frankly, they looked a lot like a team which hadn't played in twelve days. Against Coppin State, UConn jumped out to a 38–21 halftime lead but took their foot off the pedal from there, holding on to win by a final score of 76–64.

To their credit, the team did look better a few days later when they played Harvard and won going away 81–51. Unlike a season before when the Crimson almost upset the Huskies under similar circumstances, UConn left nothing to chance and jumped out to an 11–0 lead before cruising to victory. With the win, UConn improved to a surprising 10–0 heading into Christmas.

Even with the strong start and a holiday upon them, there was little time to celebrate, though. Just two days after Christmas, UConn's real season was about to begin; they'd open conference play with their first true road game of the season in maybe the Big East's toughest road venue. The Husky pups were headed to the Petersen Events Center to take on the No. 6 ranked Pittsburgh Panthers.

To fully understand what the Huskies were up against as they went to Pitt that evening, let's give a little background on the opponent.

Entering the game, Pitt was 12-1, and off to another red hot start under head coach Jamie Dixon, who has turned a good Pitt Panthers program into a national powerhouse upon taking over in the summer of 2003. With eight seasons at the school now complete, incredibly, Dixon has never won fewer than twenty games, and 2011 would mark the sixth in a row in which they won at least twenty-five. Elite programs like UConn, North Carolina, Duke, Kentucky and UCLA can't say the same.

And in combining Dixon's coaching acumen with a tough grit that is the backbone of the Steel City, the Panthers have been practically unbeatable at the Petersen Events Center since it opened in 2002. When the Huskies tipped off for their Big East opener with Pitt on December 27, 2011, the Panthers had won a staggering 92 percent of their games in the building. At the time, their record stood at 141-11.

So when you factor in that particular team in that particular arena, with the jitters of a conference opener on the road for a young team, you can probably guess how the game turned out. UConn got beat. Badly.

From the opening tap, the undefeated UConn Huskies were beaten like a drum. Pitt scored the first basket of the game, and from there the Huskies would play catch-up the rest of the night; UConn never once had a lead the entire game. Instead they were outworked, out-hustled, and simply outplayed on both ends of the court as Pitt finished the game shooting 52 percent from the field and held UConn to only 32 percent on the other end.

Even Kemba Walker—as great as he'd been all year—played his worst game of the season at Pittsburgh. He finished a miserable eight of twenty-seven from the field with just about the ugliest thirty-one point performance you'll ever see. Not that it mattered much, since collectively his teammates disappeared like a scared dog during a thunderstorm. No one besides Walker had more than nine points that night, with an especially disappointing eight-point, one-rebound effort from the big man who'd done it for the Huskies all season, Alex Oriahki.

"I'm not sure if he's better playing or sitting," a frustrated Jim Calhoun said after the game. "He's not playing like the player he's capable of being."[3]

In the end, the loss was as disappointing as it was humbling for a team which did little wrong their first ten games of the season. To make matters worse, it'd be awhile before they got their mojo back.

Following the loss at Pittsburgh, UConn played a game twice as ugly against South Florida a few nights later. Thankfully, with a 6:00 p.m. tip-off on New Year's Eve, few people were in front of the TV or in the stands as the Huskies fell behind 46–37 with eleven minutes to go before a furious rally forced overtime, where they'd eventually win by five. Of course the simple fact that the Bulls even forced the extra period showed how much work had to be done for the Huskies. South Florida came to the XL Center with a 6–9 record that night and finished the season with a disappointing 10–23 mark. Yet they still almost beat the Huskies, who at that point were a Top 10 team in name recognition only.

With the sloppy win, UConn was back to .500 in the conference, but it meant little as the team got set to hit the road again to play another highly ranked team. This time it was No. 15 Notre Dame in their tough home court venue, Purcell Pavilion. And while the final result wasn't pretty, the Huskies did show a bit of improvement from their first trip on the road.

Against a team that was even more experienced than Pittsburgh (Notre Dame started four players that night who were in their fourth or fifth years of college), the Huskies again fell down early and headed to the locker room trailing 38–30 at halftime.

But unlike their first Big East road game, the Huskies didn't get run out of the gym but instead battled back. The eight-point halftime deficit became two within minutes, before Notre Dame again seized control and took another eight-point lead into the final four minutes of the game. The Huskies continued to battle and used their superior quickness and athleticism to repeatedly get to the foul line where Shabazz Napier and Walker combined to make seven straight in the final two minutes. But in the end the lead was too big to overcome, and Notre Dame made enough free throws of their own to hold on and win. The loss was the Huskies' second in three games after the 10–0 start.

Yet for those who watched the game closely, this loss had a completely different feel than the one a week before at Pittsburgh. In the first game, a young UConn team seemed to be overwhelmed on the court, overwhelmed by the moment, and never mentally into the game. But at Notre Dame? Against a team that would eventually finish second in the Big East, UConn held their ground after a tough start and rallied before coming up just a bit short.

To the keen observer, what was most important was how the Huskies made their run though, as they essentially did it without much help from their two best players. From the start Notre Dame's defense suffocated Walker, in the process ending his eleven-game streak of at least twenty points scored; the star guard settled for nineteen on just eight of twenty-three shooting. As for Oriahki, he was again bad—worse than at Pittsburgh, actually—and fouled out in just nineteen minutes of play. He didn't score a single point that night.

But in the absence of their superstars, UConn's young guys had held strong, a feat especially impressive since they were going against players that in some cases were three to four years older than them. Napier finished with eighteen points off the bench, Roscoe Smith scored eleven, and Coombs-McDaniel had nine. No it wasn't a win. But it was still progress.

Well, it was progress in the eyes of some, anyway. But to others-the national pundits and writers in specific- the loss was just one more sign that the Maui dream had been replaced by the reality of the Big East. And with a trip to play Texas coming up, few gave the Huskies a chance. In the previous few weeks, the Longhorns had beaten Michigan State and North Carolina, cementing themselves as one of the early season favorites in college basketball.

As they did six weeks before in Maui though, UConn would head to Austin with a chip on their shoulders. And they'd prove the doubters wrong.

In a back-and-forth battle, the two teams exchanged the lead like heavyweight fighters sharing body blows. UConn trailed by five at halftime, but thanks to another big day from Walker (twenty-two points) and a "Hey don't forget about me, I'm pretty good too," eleven-point, twenty-one-rebound statement effort from Oriahki, UConn was able to battle back and force overtime on the road. To a large degree, the Huskies got lucky to force the extra period after a late game gaffe by Roscoe Smith. At the end of regulation, he threw up a wild, length-of-the-court shot with eleven seconds left, after he mistakenly thought the clock said "one second" instead of 11. It gave Texas an extra, unexpected possession, but luckily for UConn the Longhorns were unable to capitalize. Oh, freshmen.

In overtime the resolve that would be the trademark of this UConn team was on full display. The key play came with the game tied at 77, when Walker hit maybe the wackiest shot in a season full of them. Caught at the top of the key with the shot clock running down, Walker passed the ball to Roscoe Smith, who immediately tipped it right back to him. Kemba took two dribbles to create just the tiniest bit space, and without looking at the basket, blindly tossed the ball up off one foot. As was the case for most of the season, everything Walker touched turned to gold, as the ball swished through the net. The shot silenced everyone in Austin that day, with the exception of the UConn bench, and ESPN TV analyst Dick Vitale.

"OHH…OHH…OHH…OHH…Are you SERIOUS?!?" Vitale yelled into his microphone, in the loud, abrasive and excited way that only he can.

Still, the shot only gave the Huskies a brief 80–77 lead that was immediately erased after two straight Texas buckets gave it back to the Longhorns. But Walker again ended up as the hero, nailing a tough jumper over the hand of defender Dogus Balbay to give the Huskies a lead they wouldn't relinquish. Texas got one last look, but Cory Joseph's shot was no good, giving UConn- the team that the college basketball world had *again* given up on - a surprising 82-81 win.

"I told my kids very simply, that was our biggest win of the year," an ecstatic Jim Calhoun told reporters after the game.[4]

To that point, it certainly was. And with their confidence back at "post Maui" level following the thriller in Austin, and an understanding of what it took to play quality competition night in and night out and win, UConn went ahead and wiped the floor with their next two opponents. Poor Rutgers and DePaul never stood a chance. The Huskies beat each by double-digits.

What was most interesting about those wins though, was that the Huskies continued to change the label which so many had pinned on them" that of a "one man team."

Granted, Walker was spectacular in each of the subsequent wins following Texas (including a thirty-one-point outburst against DePaul), but really, everyone else's ability to step up was the difference between mere victories and absolute domination. Following his epic output at Texas, Oriahki returned with a seventeen-point, twelve-rebound, four-block performance against Rutgers; and against DePaul, Jeremy Lamb added thirteen points of his own.

"Kemba can score any time he wants," the freshman told reporters after the win in Chicago. "But I think we're doing a great job of getting everyone else involved."[5]

Of course that didn't necessarily mean that UConn forgot where their bread was buttered. Nope. Everything still started and finished with Kemba Walker, and that was never more evident in the following game against Villanova.

Entering the showdown between the two in Storrs, the ESPN executives who'd planned the game months in advance for the afternoon of Martin Luther King Day couldn't have been happier. Both teams entered the afternoon ranked in the Top 10, with UConn up to No. 8 with three straight wins, and Villanova at No. 7.

Once the game tipped off, the narrative of the game took the tone of UConn's other recent wins. With Villanova focused on shutting down Walker, others stepped up. Oriahki dominated the paint with fourteen points and twelve rebounds, while Lamb added fourteen more points of his own.

But in the end, the game once again turned into the Kemba Walker Show.

After Walker hit a crucial three with just over a minute to go, he came through again with the game on the line, a theme which was becoming quite common to that point in the season. Tied at 59 with just seconds to go, Napier handed the ball to Walker, and the star did the rest.

"We wanted to double him, but he's just so fast,"[6] Villanova coach Jay Wright would later say of the final possession in which Walker grabbed the ball from Napier and, with a quick dribble, beat his defender into the lane.

Once there, Walker put up a high-arching floater which seemed to touch the roof of Gampel Pavilion before effortlessly falling through the hoop with just 2.5 seconds to go. Wright furiously called a time-out, but it was to no avail. UConn held on to win another thriller, 61–59. The team which hadn't received a single vote in the preseason poll improved to 14–2 with the win, including their fourth over a Top 15 team.

And it was again because of college basketball's newest superstar, the man who by that point in the season only needed to be referred to by one name: Kemba.

"Of course I wanted the ball in my hands," a confident Walker would say to a room full of reporters in the post-game press conference. "Being the leader of this team, I wanted it to be in my hands."[6]

After Villanova, UConn's next game was their final out-of-conference matchup of the season, against the University of Tennessee. And if the matchup with Villanova was the most exciting of the season, the game against the Volunteers proved to be the most unique. It served as both a brief hello and goodbye to embattled Head Coach Bruce Pearl.

Pearl's story was one that proved to be one of the most dominant of the 2010–2011 college basketball season. It started in September when the NCAA discovered a photo of former recruit named Aaron Craft (who ended up at Ohio State) with the coach at a barbeque at Pearl's house. Because Craft was just a junior in high school at the time, his presence was considered an NCAA violation, and when the NCAA asked Pearl about it, he looked investigators in the eye and lied to them, point-blank.

After he later got caught with his hand in the cookie jar and admitted the truth, SEC Commissioner Mike Slive was proactive and suspended the coach for the first eight conference games of the 2010–2011 season. But with the UConn game an out-of-conference affair, Pearl was allowed to coach in Hartford, which he did, smack dab in the middle of that suspension. At the time he had served four games of his punishment, with four more to come, but at the XL Center, he was allowed to patrol the sidelines like any other coach at any other school. It was truly one of the more bizarre sights of the season.

(Pearl—one of the most successful coaches in Tennessee history—was eventually fired following the 2011 season, ultimately because of the lie to NCAA investigators, not because of the original indiscretion with Craft itself.

Let this be a lesson to any young Division I coach out there: The cover-up always gets you in more trouble than the crime. Don't ever, ever forget that.)

Once the game did tip-off, it was clear that Pearl had made the edict to his team clear: don't let Kemba Walker beat us. In that regard, the Volunteers were actually successful, holding Walker to just sixteen points on six of eighteen shooting from the field.

What the embattled coach didn't plan on however, was that Walker's teammates would step up and play well beside him.

In a game which Jim Calhoun would later call "Far and away the best team effort"[7] of the season, UConn slowly pulled away from Tennessee in the second half, winning 72–61. The Huskies finished the out of non-conference portion of their schedule at 12–0 (incredible given the teams they played) with four starters scoring in double figures against the Volunteers. Simply put, the mantra of UConn as a one-man team was dead.

Above all, it was becoming clearer by the game that Jeremy Lamb would be a legitimate second scoring option for the team. The young wing scored in double figures in back-to-back games entering the Tennessee contest and finished with sixteen against the Vols, tying Walker for the team lead. And by the time Lamb finished the next game against Marquette with a career-high twenty-four points, there was no doubt that a star had been born.

It was something that no one could've guessed just two years before when Lamb couldn't even crack the starting lineup of his own high school team.

# Chapter 8
## Getting to Know Jeremy Lamb

When a little known guard from Norcross, Georgia, committed to UConn in September 2009, most UConn fans reacted the same way a woman in her mid-twenties might describe a bland first date to her girlfriends. Essentially they let out a big, collective, "Ehh." Even after a strong summer playing for his Georgia Stars AAU team and having earned the praise of coaches nationwide, most fans saw Lamb as no more than a complementary player and stopgap. Someone who might give good minutes off the bench, and maybe—just maybe—earn a starting spot by his junior or senior year. Nothing more, and quite possibly a bit less.

Then again, you couldn't totally blame UConn fans for feeling that way either. When Lamb committed, it came just weeks before UConn entered the 2009–2010 season with a top-heavy veteran roster that would need to be replaced the following fall. And with all due respect to Lamb, there were simply bigger fish to fry in the recruiting market that summer. UConn was after many of the country's top high school players, and at least to the fans, Lamb was believed to be an afterthought.

Looking across the national landscape, there were a handful of players UConn fans would've preferred instead of Lamb. There was combo-guard Josh Selby from Baltimore who de-committed from

Bruce Pearl and Tennessee in July and had UConn on his short list. So too did Doron Lamb of Oak Hill Academy and Cory Joseph, a Canadian born import, playing his final year of high school basketball at Findlay Prep School in Nevada. And of course there was Brandon Knight of Florida who was quite literally everybody's All-American. The six-foot-three point guard had been named the Gatorade National Player of the Year as a junior the previous season, and along with LeBron James and Greg Oden, would go on to be only the third person ever to take home the award twice the following spring. Knight also had UConn listed amongst his favorites and would eventually make an official visit to the school just a short time after Jeremy Lamb committed. As history would show it, all four of those players would go on to be named McDonald's All-Americans and none would commit to the Huskies. History would also show it to be a blessing in disguise.

But in the fall of 2009, they were all out on the market, so to a degree, one might understand the general apathy surrounding Lamb's commitment to the Huskies. One might truly understand the apathy around Lamb after further examining the guard's resume following his junior year of high school. It had less meat on it than a Victoria's Secret model.

Unlike so many of his peers in the AAU-fueled, grassroots basketball world, Lamb didn't start his run to college basketball superstardom playing in showcase events across the country as a young teen, but instead working on the fundamentals of the sport in the driveway of his Georgia home with his father and brothers. To call Lamb a "young high school superstar" would be factually incorrect, since not only was he not a superstar, but technically didn't even attend a high school, let alone play basketball. Lamb was home-schooled until the end of his freshman year, and even when he arrived as a sophomore, spent most of his time on the junior varsity, watching a varsity team led by future NBA lottery pick Al-Farouq Aminu make a run deep into the Georgia state playoffs.

Even when Lamb moved up to varsity in his junior year, it was in a back-up role on a roster full of seniors, including his own brother Zach. That winter, the younger Lamb had a productive season…at least relative to the little time he was playing, averaging a respectable

12.5 points in 14 minutes a game. But while that 12.5 point average is a phenomenal mark in just 14 minutes of play, it's not exactly the stuff high school All-Americans are generally made of. And it's especially not the production that a recruit who has just committed to a school the caliber of UConn is expected to put up. Not when his competition for open scholarships- most notably Knight and Selby- had been household names since their freshman years of high school, anyway.

So you can understand the frustration from some circles when Jim Calhoun and his staff offered a scholarship to Lamb so early in the recruiting process. Most fans took the same attitude, with many wondering, "Wait, shouldn't we be saving our scholarships for the big-name guys, rather than handing them out to someone who couldn't even start as a junior in high school?!?!" Lamb's commitment made some even question if Calhoun had lost his recruiting touch altogether. Little did the critics know that they were not only wrong, but that Calhoun and his staff had one of their best recruiting finds ever.

That's because after his relatively quiet junior year, Lamb did nothing short of explode on the AAU circuit that summer. Playing his first summer of AAU ball for the Georgia Stars, his recruiting interest not only intensified, but rose quicker than the temperature in Atlanta's hot summer months.

"When we got Jeremy that summer, our biggest thing was instilling confidence in him," Georgia Stars coach Norman Parker said of his new recruit. "We kept telling him, 'Jeremy you've got the green light. Just shoot!'"

Jeremy's father, former NBA player Rolando Lamb shared similar sentiments.

"Early on that summer his shot wasn't falling, and you could tell he was getting frustrated," Rolando Lamb said of his son. "So I told him, 'work on your mid-range game. Slash to the basket. Put the ball on the floor. Become a *complete* player.'"

Lamb did exactly that, and as the summer continued to progress, his confidence level increased as well. By the time he arrived at the Peach Jam Tournament in South Carolina, Lamb's mid-range game was as strong as it had ever been, and he had re-discovered his previously absent shooting stroke. It proved to be the most opportune of times for Lamb's game to come together – Peach Jam is the biggest AAU event on the summer calendar.

At the time, nobody knew to be on the look-out for an unknown guard from Georgia.

"Quite frankly, I had actually never heard of him," CBS Sports college basketball recruiting expert Jeff Borzello said of Lamb prior to that summer. "Nobody had."

It wouldn't stay that way for long though, with the four days at Peach Jam doubling as Lamb's personal coming out party. During his time in South Carolina, he went head-to-head with the nation's best players, and more often than not, got the better of them. Lamb finished as one of the tournament's top scorers, leaving both coaches and talent evaluators in the crowd shaking their heads and clamoring for more information. By the end of the four days in South Carolina, the 17-year-old who hadn't even started for his high school team just months before, was the only player anyone wanted to talk about.

"Peach Jam is maybe the biggest tournament all summer," Borzello said. "It's the best of the best. So to go there and do what he did was incredible. We were literally searching around, asking 'Who is this guy?' Afterward, Lamb was the talk of the rest of the summer."

And it wasn't just the scouting services who took notice. The quiet kid from Georgia who only small-time interest from colleges, and one scholarship offer before Memorial Day, all of a sudden could pick any school he pleased by the start of August. Kentucky assistant coach Orlando Antigua called Lamb's high school coach Jesse McMillan within days of the Peach Jam. So too did local schools Georgia and Georgia Tech. And national power Texas, as well. In total, more than thirty schools were looking for Lamb's services and extended scholarship offers, mere weeks after UNC-Greensboro was his only suitor.

However, it was after a visit from an old family friend that Lamb finally figured out where he wanted to attend college. In early September of 2009, just weeks before he was set to take on his first starting role in a high school jersey, Jeremy Lamb committed to UConn.

⌘   ⌘   ⌘

So who was that family friend who visited the Lambs and swayed Jeremy into becoming a Husky? It was Jim Calhoun, of course. In a story that could only be conceived in the tight-knit world of high-level basketball, the connection between Calhoun and the Lamb family ran deeper than anyone could've ever imagined.

The story starts in Boston, Massachusetts, where Calhoun began his college coaching career at Northeastern University in 1972. After a couple tough seasons at the onset, the young coach had the program humming by the early 1980s. The Huskies (Northeastern had the same nickname as UConn) made the NCAA Tournament in 1981 and 1982, advancing to the second round in each of those two years. But by 1984 Calhoun had his best team thanks in large part to a freshman named Reggie Lewis, who averaged just under eighteen points per game that year (After being selected in the first round of the 1987 NBA Draft, Lewis would tragically die of a heart attack prior to the 1993–94 season. He was twenty-seven). Northeastern entered the NCAA Tournament 27–4, and had been undefeated in league play.

And with the Huskies drawing an overmatched VCU squad in the opener of the NCAA Tournament, it looked like the school—and its up-and-coming coach—would advance to the second round of the tournament for the third time in four years. With a lead and just two seconds left on the clock, all Northeastern had to do was stop VCU for one possession, and they would move on.

It wasn't to happen.

The Rams inbounded the ball and hit a shot at the buzzer to win a 70–69 shocker, in a game that Northeastern had all but wrapped up just a few seconds prior.

As for the player who hit that shot? He was a young kid by the name of Rolando Lamb, who'd later have four kids of his own, including a son named Jeremy. The younger Lamb committed to the Huskies after a meeting between the Hall of Fame head coach, his family, and Norcross coach Jesse McMillan.

"A lot of places sent down assistants to talk to Jeremy, but Coach Calhoun was one of the few head coaches who came down himself," McMillan would say of the visit of the Hall of Fame coach. "When he got here, I was a little hesitant. But coach laid out the plan he had in mind and you could tell how serious he was, how bad he wanted Jeremy."

Rolando Lamb agreed.

"When each coach called, I always made sure to ask them one specific question, 'Is Jeremy your priority,'" the elder Lamb said. "When I asked Coach Calhoun, he gave us his word, and told us 'We won't sign anyone else at his position until Jeremy makes up his mind.' Calhoun was a man of his word."

Eventually the younger Lamb did end up at UConn, and during his freshman year Calhoun took a lighthearted approach to the whole unique recruitment. He joked with reporters that upon calling the Lamb household for the first time, he told Rolando, the man who had tormented him all those years ago, "You owe me."[1]

Laughing about the call months later, Rolando replied, "Oh, it didn't really happen that way. That's all an exaggeration!"

And whether it was true that Rolando Lamb felt obligated or not, only he knows. But he did deliver.

⌘　⌘　⌘

By the time Jeremy Lamb did arrive in Storrs for his freshman year in the fall of 2009, the fans' stance on him had softened quite a bit. Getting starter's minutes for the first time his senior year, Lamb had excelled in leading his team to a 27–3 record and an Elite Eight appearance in the Georgia AAAAA State Tournament. In the process he was named the *Atlanta Journal Constitution*'s AAAAA All-State team and named All-Metro Player of the Year as well.

"Jeremy did just about everything for us that year," said McMillan. "He rebounded. He played great defense. He made all the big shots."

Apparently Calhoun and his staff had again proven the doubters wrong and stolen a hidden gem out of the South.

Meanwhile, regardless of their trepidation during the recruiting process, Lamb endeared himself to UConn fans the second he took the court for the first time. Standing six-foot-four and generously listed at 185 pounds (85 pounds might be a bit more appropriate) with a silky smooth jumper, Lamb immediately reminded many Huskies fans of former UConn All-American Richard "Rip" Hamilton. Sure Lamb might have been an inch or two taller with arms a little longer, but with the same easy shooting motion and cool demeanor, the resemblance was most certainly there (Hamilton of course was the star of the Huskies first National Championship team in 1999).

And while Lamb clearly wasn't quite at Hamilton's skill level once the games started, he did share the UConn legend's fearless offensive approach in the opener against Stony Brook on November 12. Lamb attempted fourteen shots (second in the game to only Kemba Walker), and although he was only one for seven from behind the three-point arc, it was an impressive display for a player wearing a UConn jersey for the first time. While the stats could've been better, most everyone seemed pleased that a player so young was willing to take that kind of offensive responsibility so early on in his career—especially after the previous year's team could be described as anything but "aggressive" on the offensive end.

After the opening two games, Lamb did show quite a few of those freshman jitters on the team's trip to Maui. He played a season-high thirty-seven minutes against Wichita State (thanks in large part to Walker's first half foul trouble) but scored just seven points. From there he was limited to just thirteen minutes against Michigan State and twelve versus Kentucky. If anything, Calhoun seemed to prefer the physical nature of Niels Giffey and athleticism of Roscoe Smith in addition to an advantageous two-point guard lineup when Shabazz Napier playing alongside Walker. Like Jamal Coombs-McDaniel, Lamb proved to be one of the odd men out.

Two games after returning from Hawaii though, Lamb started to show flashes of what would eventually make him an All-Big East freshman and All-Big East Tournament team member. He even scored double digits in four games straight, helping UConn to a 10–0 mark at the Christmas break. Most importantly with Lamb's emergence as a consistent scoring threat, it seemed like the Huskies had finally shut up the national critics who, since their win in Maui, had been calling the

Huskies "Kemba Walker and a bunch of other guys." Finally UConn had their second scorer.

Unfortunately that wouldn't last, at least not for the time being.

With Lamb slumping, the Huskies lost the two games to Pittsburgh and Notre Dame when in either case—especially against Notre Dame—one more scorer could've propelled the Huskies to a victory. Napier and Smith at least played well against the Irish, but getting little contribution from the starting shooting guard didn't help. Lamb combined for just seventeen points in those two games.

Slowly though he began to gain his sea legs, and earn his title as "Kemba Walker's wing man." And it all started innocently with a text exchange between the young freshman and his father.

Since his retirement as a basketball player, Rolando Lamb has worn many hats in the professional world, most recently as a highly sought-after motivational speaker, and someone nicknamed by his peers as "America's Character Coach." And in mid-January of 2011, Rolando Lamb challenged the character of his son, not only to overcome adversity on the basketball court, but to face a life obstacle head-on.

"It was the middle of the year, and he was really struggling," Rolando Lamb said. "So one night I texted him and said, I want you to write down a list of your goals and send them to me."

What arrived in Rolando Lamb's inbox at one the following morning, were four goals, written by his son and transported to father via the miracle of modern technology. Rolando Lamb looked them over the following morning, and texted his son back, asking him to add one more goal, one more belief, to his list.

"I am a big-time scorer," the words read on the son's cell the next morning.

"For Jeremy, we all knew he could be a big-time scorer. I knew it. Kemba knew it. Coach Calhoun knew it. It was about making sure *Jeremy* knew it though," Rolando Lamb said.

Eventually Jeremy Lamb came to know it too. His belief started to take shape on an otherwise quiet Saturday afternoon against DePaul.

Now to give you a bit of a quick history lesson, just understand that anything that happens against DePaul needs to be taken with a major grain of salt. The Blue Demons have been a literal punching bag since joining the Big East back in 2005 and have been nothing short of an atrocity in recent years. Since the beginning of the 2008–2009 season, DePaul had gone an almost unbelievable 2–52 in league play, including an 0–18 mark in the 2010 season that cost Coach Jerry Wainwright his job. In 2011 things were just slightly better. The Blue Demons would improve to 6–6 on December 22 before losing eighteen of their next nineteen games to finish the season. They did however go 1–17 in Big East play, a one game improvement from the year before. At DePaul, that's considered progress.

So it's with that as context that you need to understand that no one was throwing a ticker-tape parade when Lamb scored thirteen points in UConn's 82–62 win in Rosemont on January 15. Then again, it might've been hard to notice Lamb's strong performance as Kemba Walker again stole the show with thirty-one points.

But with that big output against DePaul, high-scoring games from Lamb started to become a trend. He scored fourteen points the next game in the epic Martin Luther King Day win over Villanova. And put in sixteen a few days later in the win over Tennessee in front of a national TV audience. Along with Walker, Lamb led the way, helping the Huskies finish up non-league play at 12–0.

Really though, it wasn't just that Lamb was scoring points, but more importantly *how* he was doing it. The once timid freshman was expanding his game and learning what it took to play at the college level. All of a sudden Lamb wasn't just limiting himself to jump shots but instead taking people off the dribble, hitting a soft little floater in the lane, and finishing dunks with athleticism that no one knew he had. Jeremy Lamb was no longer just a shooter. He was now a *scorer* instead. It was something that one of college basketball's top analysts, ESPN's Jay Bilas, acknowledged as a key to the Huskies late season success: "I don't know if you can point to one moment, or one game when the light went off for Jeremy Lamb. But by late in the year, he was a real asset for the team. It was no longer just Kemba," Bilas said.

Never was that more apparent than in a mid-week game against Marquette at the end of February. With the Golden Eagles blanketing

Walker and daring someone else to score, it was Lamb who took them up on that challenge. He finished with a career-high twenty-four points, including three 3-pointers from downtown. Lamb had officially arrived as a commodity on the college basketball landscape.

But just as the freshman was hitting his groove in Storrs, the dynamic of UConn's whole season would begin to change. It started on the following Saturday when Lamb was again phenomenal against Louisville. Unlike his big games against DePaul, Tennessee, and Marquette, this game wouldn't end in victory but instead in a double-overtime defeat.

This loss, however, would be different from the others. And it would take weeks for UConn to recover from.

# Chapter 9
## Caught Up in the Big East Meat Grinder

Thanks to Lamb's strong play against Marquette, UConn improved to 17–2 on the season as they continued their narrative as one of the most surprising, compelling, and fun storylines of the 2011 college basketball season. Little did anyone know that within a few days—and fifty minutes of basketball—their season would change forever.

Next up on the schedule was a Louisville club who, quite frankly, was having a season strikingly parallel to UConn's. The Cardinals had been picked along with Marquette to finish one spot ahead of UConn in the Big East preseason at No. 8, and taking all things into account, that ranking was probably a bit generous. Louisville had lost four starters off a disappointing team the season before, a team which finished 20–13 and had gotten crushed in the first round of the NCAA Tournament by Cal. To make matters worse, Louisville's sole returning starter (wing Jared Swopshire) ended up missing all of 2011 with injury. If UConn had no expectations at all entering the 2011, Louisville's weren't significantly better.

When dissecting things further, it was hard not to see additional parallels.

While Calhoun had the awful 2010 season and a looming NCAA investigation hanging over his head, things weren't much better for legendary Louisville coach Rick Pitino. Pitino had spent the summer prior to the 2011 season in a very messy and public extortion case involving a woman with whom he'd been caught in an embarrassing extramarital affair with a few years prior. While the woman was eventually found guilty of extortion, Pitino's reputation off the court had been called into question, similar to Calhoun's, but obviously for different reasons. Factoring that in with the struggles of the 2010 team and the emergence of Louisville's biggest rival (the University of Kentucky) as a new college basketball superpower, many of the same questions people had about Calhoun they had about Pitino too. Like UConn, Louisville had been on top of the college basketball world just two years before as a No. 1 seed in the 2009 NCAA Tournament. But by 2011 many wondered, was Pitino's best coaching already behind him?

And it's that context which made the Cardinals matchup with the Huskies on January 29, 2011, all the more surprising. Like UConn, Louisville came to Storrs ranked in the Top 20 with a 16–4 record, and like the Huskies, they were having success with a group of players who'd been virtually unknown just a few months before. The 2011 Louisville Cardinals were a team whose sum was significantly greater than their parts, no different than their opponents on the last Saturday in January.

Still, when the two teams actually tipped off, it seemed like for most of the afternoon that UConn would again notch another win over a Top 20 team. Led by Lamb's fourteen first-half points and Shabazz Napier picking up the slack early in the second half (ten points in the first twelve minutes), the Huskies looked to be on their way to victory.

Instead it was the Cardinals who would pull the rug out from under the Huskies. In the process they'd expose a handful of flaws in UConn's game that would take weeks for the team to resolve.

Behind the strong play of point guard Peyton Siva and a matchup zone that left the Huskies helpless on offense, the Cardinals clawed their way back into the game. After UConn blew the lead and re-took it with a Kemba Walker three, it would be Siva who'd take over from there. He'd hit a jumper to force overtime, another to send the game into a second overtime, and score the last four points of the game, helping the Cardinals overcome a nine-point deficit late in the second half to steal a wild 79–78 double-overtime win. For the first time all season, UConn's dynamic defensive duo of Walker and Napier had met their match in a guard with the ability to beat them off the dribble and get to the rim at will. Simply put, Siva was the best player on the court that day. It was something no other UConn opponent could've said up to that point in the season.

But dig deeper, and a more serious problem seemed to be brewing.

Not unlike Tennessee and Marquette before them, Louisville's game plan from the start was clear: make someone besides Kemba Walker beat them. And to the Huskies' credit, the rest of the roster did their part. The lead that UConn carried late into the second half had as much to do with Lamb, Napier, Alex Oriahki, and Roscoe Smith as it did Walker. Unfortunately the Huskies went away from what had made them successful late in the game and, to their own detriment, almost deferred too much to their star.

"We weren't running it efficient [offense] and that ended up killing us at the end of the game," Napier would tell reporters of the Huskies' stagnant offense late in the game. "We just sat out there like robots."[1]

Understand that the quote was in no way blaming Walker for the loss; Napier made sure to follow up and say the team wanted the ball in Kemba's hands late. But it did seem like Walker might not have been the best option for the Huskies down the stretch. Other guys had carried UConn early in the game, and Walker tried to do too much late, forcing a handful of shots that allowed the Cardinals to creep back into the game and eventually win it. For the first time all year, Walker was a part of the team's failures as much as their success.

Going forward, things only got worse for both the player and the team in their next game against Syracuse. The Orange entered the game on a four-game losing streak, but thanks to a similar zone defense which had given the Huskies problems just a few days before, they limited UConn offensively, winning 66–58. It was a game that wasn't nearly as close as the final score might've indicated.

For UConn it was just about their worst performance of the year. After the Huskies jumped out to a 23–14 lead late in the first half, Syracuse controlled every aspect of the game from there, with the Orange outscoring UConn 52–35 over the final twenty-four minutes of play. UConn finished the game shooting a woeful 36 percent from the field and got crushed on the glass, getting out-rebounded 42–32. As for Walker, he was no better, finishing the game with just eight points, on three of fourteen shooting from the field. It was the first time all season that he hadn't scored in double figures.

With the loss to Syracuse, UConn was officially someplace they hadn't been to that point in the season: in the midst of a losing streak. But luckily, after playing five straight games against teams who would eventually make the NCAA Tournament, the Huskies finally got a schedule reprieve against the 10–13 Seton Hall Pirates.

Or at least that's the way it seemed. Instead, Seton Hall employed the same 2-3 zone that had given UConn problems the previous few games and nearly pulled a shocking upset.

After trailing early, Seton Hall took a 37–32 lead into halftime and only widened the margin after intermission. They led by fourteen with fourteen minutes left and by ten at the under eight TV time-out. And it was at that point that Head Coach Jim Calhoun had finally had enough. The lack of effort and overall malaise that had plagued his team over the previous couple games would no longer be acceptable.

"I said if there's one damn excuse—I didn't use that word exactly—I will put you on the bench so hard that you'll be here when we come back next year," Calhoun told reporters about his impassioned time-out speech following the victory. He then told them, "This game is winnable."[2]

Whether it was because of inspiration or simple fear, the Huskies rallied, starting when Walker made a layup off an offensive rebound and an ensuing free throw after being fouled. From there UConn played suffocating defense of their own and didn't allow the Pirates a field goal for nearly the rest of the game until they finally put in a harmless layup at the buzzer. Thanks to a final eight minutes when the Huskies played their best basketball on both ends of the court in weeks, they held on for a narrow 61–59 victory.

Unfortunately that win proved to be little more than a bandage for UConn's problems. The Huskies next went to play a resurgent St. John's squad in a game which would show just how far they'd fallen since the beginning of the season.

Even before the game, it needs to be understood that UConn was entering a proverbial snake pit; simply put, St. John's was much more dangerous than their 13–9 record might have indicated. The Red Storm had a deceptively experienced and desperate team as a roster full of seniors was running out of time to turn the season around and qualify for the first ever NCAA Tournament of their careers. Prior to the Huskies' arrival at Madison Square Garden, the Red Storm had already beaten both Notre Dame and Duke (both ranked in the Top 15) at home. They would also beat Pittsburgh at Madison Square Garden later in the season.

To their credit, the Huskies knew how dangerous the opponent was, took nothing for granted, and it appeared that they'd go into halftime trailing by just one point. It wasn't a great effort. But it certainly could've been worse.

Then all hell broke loose.

It started on the Huskies' final possession of the half when Roscoe Smith had the ball stripped by Malik Boothe. Boothe proceeded to take a couple dribbles, and with the clock down to a mere few seconds, tossed up a desperate half-court heave that somehow, improbably went in. All of a sudden a one-point deficit became a 35–31 deficit as the two teams walked to the locker room.

But before they could even get there, a dissatisfied Calhoun had some choice words for the officials, words which resulted in a technical foul. St. John's was awarded two foul shots to start the second half (which they made) and the ball (a possession which they converted). Within a few seconds on the game clock, a one-point deficit became seven. And from there the rout was on. St. John's cruised to an 89–72 win.

Really though, it wasn't so much that UConn lost, but how their attitude changed after Boothe's shot. They no longer seemed to be the jolly, happy-go-lucky, glad-to-be-there team that had played the first 60 percent of the season. Instead their demeanor was different.

Their body language changed. I wrote about it the following day in a column on college basketball's national championship, "Contenders and Pretenders." In it, I said:

> The problem is that not only did UConn get beat by St. John's on Thursday night, they got beat so badly that it completely made me re-evaluate how I feel about them. Yes, they'd lost in the past, but they'd never been run off the court. They'd never been embarrassed. They'd never quit. All three things happened Thursday night. And that's my biggest point of contention with this team. You can fix struggles on offense. You can't fix struggles with effort (And yes, I just pulled out my "Cliché Coach Speak Handbook." How'd I do?)
>
> Anyway, this list is about fairness and reality, and I can't give anyone a pass, not even my own team.
>
> Yesterday I listed the "Pretenders," and today the "Contenders." And right now UConn is the former, not the latter.[3]

The loss, which was UConn's third in four games, also marked another disappointing effort for Kemba Walker. Whether it was mental fatigue, physical exhaustion, or familiar Big East opponents slowing him down, there was no doubt that Walker was struggling. The St. John's loss was another disappointing effort as he finished just four of sixteen from the field, the seventh straight game he made less than half his shots. And even with improved play from Lamb and others, UConn clearly needed a boost. They got it from one of the most surprising places: sophomore Jamal Coombs-McDaniel.

Up until the St. John's game, Coombs-McDaniel was in the midst of a relatively quiet season following a quiet freshman year in its own right. The kid who'd had so much success playing AAU and high school ball with Alex Oriahki was averaging just 4.5 points a game following the St. John's loss.

Really though, Coombs-McDaniel's struggles came much more so because of his attitude than anything which happened on the court. On a team that had next to no character issues, and an overall harmony that would've made the Brady Bunch jealous by comparison,

Coombs-McDaniel was just about the only player who caused any problems on the 2011 UConn Huskies. There was a shouting match with Jim Calhoun in Maui (a situation which was quickly resolved) and an ominous post on Facebook about playing time later in the season. The most disappointing thing was that by all accounts Coombs-McDaniel wasn't a bad kid, just one who happened to have the same quick temper as his head coach Jim Calhoun. And unfortunately for Coombs-McDaniel, when it comes to an argument between a Hall of Fame coach and little used bench player, the coach is going to win twelve times out of ten.

"Knowing Jamal and knowing Jim [Calhoun] they're just both so competitive, and so head-strong," said Leo Papile, Coombs-McDaniel's AAU coach, and long-time friend of Calhoun. "Both think they're right all the time, and truthfully, both usually are. But if you're a player, you're never going to win against the coach."

But with UConn struggling on offense, Calhoun was looking for answers and turned to Coombs-McDaniel when the Huskies next took the court against Providence College. And surprisingly he delivered. The sophomore wing provided the spark that the team so desperately needed, pouring in twenty-five points while Kemba Walker looked like "Kemba Walker" for the first time in a long time. He finished with twenty-two points on an efficient seven of ten shooting, while also adding six rebounds and seven assists.

After the game though, the only thing the star wanted to do, was praise his newest wing man.

"He's been through a lot," Walker told the assembled press of Coombs-McDaniel. "He and coach have had some differences, and coach always tells him he believes in him."[3]

And it was the same dynamic duo of Walker and Coombs-McDaniel which led the Huskies to another victory the next time they took the court against Georgetown. The bench player scored twenty-three points while Walker was again dominant with thirty-one points and ten assists as UConn beat the No. 8 ranked Georgetown Hoyas. Georgetown had entered the game as the hottest team in the Big East with eight straight wins.

But as good as things seemed to be, they wouldn't last. Not on the court or off of it.

Two nights later was another game with Louisville and another loss to a team which the Huskies couldn't quite seem to figure to out. The same combination of Siva (nineteen points and *six* steals) and the Cardinals defense (UConn shot just 37 percent from the field), proved to be too much for the Huskies. Things even got so bad that Kemba Walker (a player who'd spent more time smiling during the 2011 season than a Miss America contestant) was charged with a technical foul.

Still, if were only about wins and losses, it'd be one thing. Instead Jim Calhoun had much bigger problems on his hands.

After almost two full years of investigating the program, NCAA officials were ready to release their findings to the school just a few days later. Sanctions of some kind seemed certain; the question became how bad would they be? It didn't seem likely, but in a worst case scenario, a postseason ban was even possible.

Despite UConn's recent struggles, they were still light years ahead of where most had thought they'd be at that point in the season. Barring a monumental collapse, a trip to the NCAA Tournament seemed like a certainty.

But with one written statement from the NCAA, all the hard work the team had put in, the wins in Maui, the shocker over Texas, everything could be erased. It could all be turned into a historical footnote. It could all have been for nothing.

For the UConn Huskies basketball program, it was time to face the music.

# Chapter 10
## Getting to Know Shabazz Napier

If UConn fans were disenchanted when Jeremy Lamb committed in the fall of 2009, well, they were nothing short of apoplectic when Shabazz Napier did the same in the spring of 2010. Coming off a disastrous 18–16 season and in desperate need of a talent infusion, Huskies fans were already nervous about the next season to begin with. And signing a five-foot-ten point guard who wasn't even supposed to graduate high school until the *following* spring certainly didn't help the anxiety. Especially with a handful of bigger named recruits still in the process of making college decisions.

You remember those recruits, don't you? Well with the 2010 season in the books and plenty of talent still on the board, everyone scratched their head at the commitment of Napier on April 4. Why him? Why now? Where the hell did *that* come from?

In large part it came from several top recruits saying, "Thanks, but no thanks." With the 18–16 record fresh on everyone's mind and an NCAA investigation still pending, when the recruiting dominoes began to fall that spring, not many fell in UConn's direction.

Brandon Knight—the two-time National Player of the Year, and guy everyone dreamed of adding to their roster—finished the recruiting process with UConn in his final two. But after seeing John Wall depart Kentucky for the NBA, Knight chose to become the next great guard to play in John Calipari's dribble, drive, motion offense. He signed to play at Kentucky on April 14.

At the Jordan Brand Classic the following week, two more big names came off the board. Doron Lamb decided against joining his high school teammate Roscoe Smith in Storrs and instead chose to follow Knight to Kentucky. Later that night Baltimore guard Josh Selby decided to play his college ball at Kansas; although truthfully by that point, most UConn fans had already given up on him ever becoming a Husky. The nation's No. 1 ranked player had a trip planned to visit the school in February but cancelled and never rescheduled. And when Cory Joseph committed to Texas a week after that, UConn had officially gone 0–4 on their "big-name" guard targets in the spring recruiting period.

Or so everyone thought.

Because everything that Shabazz Napier wasn't (namely a highly ranked recruit) made him what he was. And what he was, was a street smart, mentally tough kid who believed in his own basketball skill more than any recruiting service or All-American game committee ever could. And really, just in getting himself to UConn, Napier showed more resolve than most people show in a lifetime.

Napier grew up the youngest of Carmen Velasquez's three children in Dorchester, a neighborhood that might not be the toughest in Boston but is pretty damn close. According to 2010 crime rate statistics, you're four times more likely to get robbed and the murder rate is nearly twice as high in Dorchester than in the average American town. And after two years at neighboring Charlestown High School, Napier was brimming with basketball talent while also lacking maturity. If he didn't shape up, there was a real possibility that he could be engulfed by the neighborhood that surrounded him.

"Shabazz was never a bad kid, but he was a knucklehead," said former Detroit Piston and childhood friend and mentor Will Blalock. "Just the kind of kid who would talk back to teachers, clown around, little stuff."

It was time for some changes, and it started that summer when Napier signed up to play for Coach Mo Vasquez and the Metro Boston AAU program.

Started in 1997, Metro Boston is what Vasquez describes as a "full-scale AAU" program, focusing just as much as what happens off the court, as on it. Simply put, if you don't do your school work, you don't play. If you talk back to coaches, you don't play. If you don't come to practice and work hard, you don't play. And it was that world that Napier walked into in the summer of 2007.

"When Shabazz came to us, it's because no other AAU program wanted him," Vasquez said. "He had a little bit of an attitude, but that experience humbled him really quick. He realized he had nowhere else to go."

But to Vasquez, there was additional weight added to Napier's arrival.

At the time, to say that Napier was struggling academically would be an understatement; he was barely keeping his head above water. Which is why when Vasquez made a promise to Napier's mom that summer, it raised more than a few eyebrows. After placing dozens of kids from Metro Boston at colleges of all levels, Vasquez told Carmen Velasquez, "If Shabazz comes to me, he will get his high school diploma, and earn a college scholarship."

At the time, it seemed like more fantasy than reality.

But after a non-descript summer for Metro Boston that plan— at least from a basketball perspective — began to take shape in Napier's junior year at Charlestown. There he shined as one of the better young players in the Boston area, leading Charlestown to a 20–1 record in the regular season and the No. 1 seed in the Massachusetts Intercollegiate Athletic Association North Division I Tournament. Napier's team would eventually lose to Central Catholic in the quarterfinals, with their star guard chipping in fifteen points.

That following spring, Napier again played for Metro Boston, establishing himself for the first time as a big-time recruit. In particular he lit up the AAU Super Showcase in Orlando, scoring thirty-three points in one game and thirty-eight the next, becoming the buzz of the tournament. The player who'd entered the summer with no scholarship offers all of a sudden had the attention of some of the nation's elite.

Still, there was plenty of work to do. It started in the classroom, and it started by changing addresses. With interest coming in from college coaches all over the Northeast, Napier made the choice to not only change his high school, but more importantly, make some changes to himself.

After three years at Charlestown High School, Napier moved over to Lawrence Academy where he would repeat his junior year, and in all likelihood, need an additional prep year to get fully caught up academically. With Lawrence looking for someone to replace former Metro Boston guard Stevie Mejia, Vasquez recommended Napier, and in the fall of 2008 he was on his way. With the school needing a player and the player needing a structured academic setting that the Boston public schools simply couldn't provide, it was set to be a match made in heaven. Only it wasn't.

"When Shabazz got here, the reality of who he could be, wasn't who he was," said Lawrence coach Kevin Wiercinski. "There were a lot of things weighing on him at Charlestown that any student would've struggled with, and it was only highlighted more because he was an athlete."

On the court, basketball was hardly the problem. It never had been. Starting from day one at Lawrence, Napier was an immediate hit, leading an undersized and— at times—overmatched team to a respectable four loss season. The team would eventually lose in the quarterfinals of the New England Prep School Athletic Council (NEPSAC) Class C, but the burgeoning superstar was hardly to blame.

"He was doing things that no one else in prep school could do," Wiercinski said.

Still, despite his stock rising in the eyes of college coaches, Napier's time at Lawrence wasn't strictly about basketball. And he showed it by making strides off the court that no one fully saw coming when he had enrolled the previous fall.

"Once he got comfortable, and came to trust people, you could see the change in Shabazz," Wiercinski said. "It was the fresh start he needed. A fresh start with his coaches, and his teachers, and his friends. He realized, 'This experience can be whatever I want it to be.'"

His friends at home noticed it too.

"Every time I spoke to 'Bazz that year, he was in study hall, working on school stuff. It was good for him to get away from Boston," said Blalock.

That newfound maturity and confidence resonated again when Napier returned home and laced it up for Metro Boston for the third straight year.

With an extra year of prep school included, Naper was now listed as part of the class of 2011, and used a strong early spring to get invited to the Reebok All-American Camp in Philadelphia where he'd go toe-to-toe with some of the nation's best. However it was back at the AAU Nationals where, to use Vasquez's words, Napier "went nutty" in leading Metro Boston to the Round of 16. Included in those wins were a victory over Texas Elite where Napier out-dueled future Missouri Tiger Phil Pressey and a win a day later over a club called E1T1, which just so happened to feature the No. 1 player in the class of 2011, Florida guard Austin Rivers (Rivers is the son of Boston Celtics head coach and former NBA player Doc Rivers. He started his college career in the fall of 2011 at college basketball powerhouse Duke).

"Once he went head-to-head with Austin Rivers, that's really when I think Shabazz thought he could play with anyone," his AAU coach Mo Vasquez said.

Apparently college coaches agreed. Napier picked up scholarship offers from schools like Providence College, St. John's, and Memphis, with interest from places like UConn and Pittsburgh. Napier also skyrocketed in the eyes of the recruiting services, ending the summer ranked as one of the top 60 players in the class of 2011 by Scout.com (39) Rivals.com (51) and ESPN (56). Of course, within a few months, it'd become clear that if things broke right, the only place Napier would be spending 2011 was on a college campus.

In the fall, Napier returned to Lawrence Academy and, to put it simply, willed his team to win after win.

"Shabazz is just so damn competitive," gushed Wiercinski. "After we'd lost the previous year, you could almost see in his eyes that he wasn't going to let us lose another game, and he didn't."

Playing against teams with—in some cases—as many as three to four future Division I players in their starting lineup, Napier was masterful, averaging twenty-one points, six assists and 4.5 steals in leading Lawrence Academy to the Class C NEPSAC title. He was named tournament MVP and named the Class C Player of the Year by New England Prep Stars. As Wiercinski would say of his star, "There were certain nights where the difference was just that we had Shabazz, and they didn't."

Off the court, Napier's recruiting was picking up steam, but it again came with a twist. After making a visit to UConn in February (coincidentally the same weekend that Josh Selby cancelled), the Huskies coaching staff (along with a handful of other schools) began to wonder if Napier would be interested in reclassifying again. This time he'd move from the Class of 2011 back to 2010 with the intention of getting eligible immediately.

At first Napier seemed to have little interest and appeared content to play another year at Lawrence. But as those whispers began to grow louder, his tune began to change. And by the time he committed to UConn in April, it was an all-out race to get him to Storrs for the fall, as a member of the class of 2010.

Despite the work of a lot of people though, it wasn't easy.

Understand that with five years of high school under his belt and a ton of catch-up work at Lawrence, Napier had done enough to qualify to play college basketball by the NCAA's standards. Not only did he substantially raise his GPA over his two years at Lawrence, but he did it by taking a much tougher course load at the private school.

The problem was that as much progress as he'd made, it still wasn't quite enough to graduate from the more stringent curriculum of Lawrence. Napier had met every requirement to become eligible under the NCAA's guidelines, but was literally just a course or two short of meeting Lawrence's requirements.

"We tried everything we could to work with them," Napier's AAU coach Mo Vasquez said. "We asked if Shabazz could come back in the summer, finish up his requirements then. It was just one or two next level courses we were talking about."

Wiercinski concurred. "We worked hard, but there were certain classes particular to our school, certain deadlines that we couldn't meet," he said.

In the final twist of his wild journey, Napier did in fact graduate high school in 2010. It just wasn't at Lawrence Academy, but instead back at Charlestown. With more than enough credits, Napier went back to where it all began, receiving his high school diploma in the spring of 2010.

While the path was unconventional, it left no ill-will at Lawrence.

"I speak for a lot of people when I say that our only regret is that we didn't get to work with Shabazz another year," said Wiercinski. "After everything he overcame, it's a shame that he couldn't finish with us here."

But while Napier's path to UConn would hardly be considered normal, it did fulfill a promise that had been made to his mother nearly three years before.

Mo Vasquez had kept his word.

Carmen Velasquez's youngest son was going to college.

⌘　⌘　⌘

With his high school saga now in the books, Shabazz Napier made his way down to Storrs, Connecticut, in the summer of 2010. Nobody knew what to expect from the baby-faced point guard, including himself.

"My role isn't really set in stone right now," Napier told the Hartford Courant's Mike Anthony while playing the Hartford Pro-Am with some of his future teammates that July. He followed up, "I'm just here to do whatever is needed."[1]

Really though, for Napier to get a true understanding of how he'd contribute for UConn, all he had to do was browse the vast history books of UConn basketball. Because from the time Jim Calhoun took over in the mid 1980s, players with Napier's particular skill set thrived.

Understand that while the Huskies have become known over the last couple years for big men like Emeka Okafor, Hasheem Thabeet, and Josh Boone, Calhoun built the program on the strength of great guard play. In particular, UConn has had some of its best seasons under Calhoun when employing a two point guard set. They went to the Elite Eight in 1995 with Doron Sheffer and Kevin Ollie (who'd end up as an assistant with the 2011 team) complementing each in the backcourt, and took home their first title in 1999 when Ricky Moore and Khalid El-Amin (two point guards by nature) did the same. To a smaller degree it also happened during UConn's run to the Final Four in 2009 when senior A. J. Price played big minutes alongside a freshman named Kemba Walker.

And now it was time for history to repeat itself. From the time Napier arrived in Connecticut he was side-by-side with Walker, watching and learning, trying to soak up everything the veteran had to offer.

"Kemba is one of the best players I've ever played with, one of the best I'll ever play with in my life," he told Anthony. "Just learning from him how to be a leader is only helping me out and helping UConn in the future."[1]

Once the games did tip off a few months later, it was clear that Napier not only had learned from the player he described as his "older brother," but that Calhoun and his staff had again rolled snake eyes on the recruiting trail. From day one, the point guard who wasn't supposed to play college basketball until 2011 proved that he could fit in just fine in 2010. He even scored twelve points in his UConn debut in early November.

But really, to watch Napier play during his freshman year wasn't to check the box scores and be overwhelmed. The things he did weren't ones that made the *Sportscenter* highlights and often times weren't even noticed by casual basketball fans. While Napier did score big at times (five double figure scoring games in his first ten), his play on the other end of the court set him apart.

Blessed with lightning-quick speed and a seemingly never-ending motor, Napier was at times a one-man full-court press and always a constant nuisance on the defensive end. Most importantly, with Kemba Walker taking on such a heavy offensive load, Napier was often assigned to defend the other team's best guard.

It started in UConn's second game of the season when Napier had five steals against Vermont, and continued in the Maui opener when he added three more in the win over Wichita State.

Speaking of Maui, remember that Brandon Knight guy whose name keeps popping up throughout this book? The one who chose Kentucky over UConn in the recruiting process which—in large part—led to Napier's commitment and expedited his road to Storrs? Remember him? Well in the Maui Invitational championship game, Knight finished just three for fifteen from the field with Napier guarding him for big chunks of the game and making his evening a living, breathing, tropical nightmare. Other than Walker and Oriahki, no one played more minutes in the Huskies' championship run in Hawaii than Napier.

Once the team returned to Connecticut and the season rolled into Big East play, Napier remained one of college basketball's best "glue guys." While his role fluctuated from game to game, it seemed like whatever Jim Calhoun asked for, his young guard delivered.

At times it was offense: Napier had eighteen points in a loss at Notre Dame and followed it up with fifteen in a wild win at Texas. At others it was deep three-point shooting: the guard led UConn with twenty-three points on five three-pointers in the crushing double-overtime loss to Louisville. Sometimes it remained defense (Napier averaged 1.5 steals in conference play despite playing just twenty-three minutes a game in the regular season) and at others just a steady hand. With Kemba Walker asked to do so much offensively, Napier often did the bulk of the ball-handling, ran the offense and, again, often defended the other team's best guard.

Unfortunately though, when the Big East grind began to wear down the Huskies in late January, Napier fell into a trap that a lot of freshmen do: he struggled with turnovers. It had happened to Kemba Walker two years before, A. J. Price two years before that, and incredibly Marcus Williams two years before Price.

Now it was Napier's turn.

"The good thing about Shabazz is that he at times plays for both teams, which I think is a unique ability," Jim Calhoun jokingly told reporters early in the season. "It's kind of unusual. It keeps everybody entertained, including the coaching staff."[2]

But as the season progressed and losses mounted, those turnovers became no laughing matter. Napier had two crucial ones late in the February loss to Louisville and three more in another loss to Marquette a few days later. Then there were six in a sloppy win over Cincinnati and six more in the final two games of the regular season. To his credit, by the end of the season Napier was handling a bigger scoring burden than most expected for the Huskies, and to some degree he was one of the few players on the team who seemed to be progressing, rather than regressing. At the same time, when you're losing everyone and everything you do comes under a microscope.

Napier was no exception. At times he even reached out to Blalock, who was overseas playing professional ball in Europe.

"Shabazz is one of those kids who thinks he knows everything, and when I would talk him you could tell he was frustrated," Blalock said. "But I told him, everybody hits a lull their freshman year, you'll get through it."

Still, frustration or not, as the calendar turned to late February, the UConn basketball had much bigger problems than a few Napier turnovers. The NCAA had been investigating the program for close to two years, and they were ready to release the findings of that investigation.

After years of watching, waiting, and wondering, they were finally there.

And everyone was holding their breath to find out what was next.

# Chapter 11

## The NCAA Comes Calling

To understand the complete story of the UConn basketball program and the long odds they were facing in the 2011 season, you must first travel back a few years to their previous Final Four run in 2009. At that time a dark storm cloud would form over the program, one which wouldn't clear for close to two years.

With UConn's program cruising that spring and a Sweet 16 date with Purdue set for the last weekend in March, the Huskies arrived in Glendale, Arizona, expecting to focus on some fun, sun, and a run at the program's third Final Four. What they arrived to instead was a shocking report by Yahoo.com that alleged Jim Calhoun and his staff of major recruiting improprieties. If the contents of the report held true, it would affect not only the present Huskies, but the past and future of the program as well.

The allegations centered around the recruitment of Nate Miles (a player who enrolled at the school in the fall of 2009, but never played a game in a Huskies uniform) and his association with a former UConn team manager turned NBA agent Josh Nochimson. As an agent, Nochimson was allowed under NCAA rules to talk to high school players (assuming they don't provide extra benefits), but as a former team manager he was considered by the NCAA a representative of UConn, and could not speak with any UConn was recruiting.

Not that it mattered once Yahoo reporters Dan Wetzel and Adrian Wojnarowski discovered that over the course of Miles' recruitment, Nochimson had supplied money, lodging and transportation for the recruit, all of which are blatant NCAA rules violations, and all of which happened while the UConn coaching staff was in contact with him. After six months of investigation, Wetzel and Wojnarowski found a laundry list of phone calls and text messages between the player and his guardians, the agent and the school, and witnesses linking them all together. It was as serious as allegations come.

Like many in the sometimes shady world of amateur basketball, by the spring of 2009, Miles had become a bit of a cautionary tale. Born in Toledo, Ohio, Miles spent his teen years bouncing from school to school, looking for the next spot to lace up his sneakers and find a basketball home. Unfortunately it almost always seemed to end with him a burning a bridge and leaving the school under questionable or uncertain circumstances. In total Miles was linked with seven high schools in five years and attended five, but even after graduating from the Patterson School in North Carolina in January 2008, it would still be another five months of NCAA investigation into his transcript before he'd be cleared to play college basketball. Regardless, the elite basketball skill was there as at times Rivals.com had him listed amongst their top 25 players in the country in his age group. Jim Calhoun even went on the record after Miles committed and said that he had "as much basketball ability" as anyone he'd ever recruited.[1]

In what turned out to be both a gift and a curse, UConn fans never saw that talent on display. After being committed to the school for close to two years, Miles was finally cleared to play in June of 2008 and made his way up Storrs at the end of that summer. There he'd room with another highly recruited freshman named Kemba Walker.

However, his time at the school was short. On September 25, 2008, a mere couple weeks into his first full semester at UConn, Miles was arrested for violating a restraining order. Earlier that week a woman alleged physical abuse against Miles, and when the restraining order was issued, he was not allowed to have contact with her. Within minutes of being served, Miles placed a phone call to the woman, leading to his arrest. The already thin ice Miles was on at UConn was about to break.

With news of his arrest, UConn moved quickly. After his troubled recruitment and questionable high school past, the school had a zero tolerance policy with Miles and expelled him the first week of October. For a guy that UConn spent nearly two years working with and vouching for, Miles would barely last two full months on campus. He would never play a game in a UConn uniform, eventually transfer to the College of Southern Idaho, and go unselected in the 2009 NBA Draft.

But back to that recruitment because ultimately it wasn't anything Miles did while on campus that got him and the school in trouble with the NCAA. It all happened beforehand and came to light with the reporting of Wetzel and Wojnarowski.

And it all started by accident.

"I barely cover the college beat, and only knew Nate Miles vaguely as a UConn recruit," Wojnarowski, who covers the NBA almost exclusively, said of how the whole thing began.

However, the name that Wojnarowski was familiar with was Nochimson's, who in 2008 had been decertified as an NBA agent, after getting caught scamming former UConn star Richard Hamilton out of over one million dollars. With Nochimson out of a job and without the prospect of getting one, that's where Wojnarowski got his first lead and began digging, straight through to when the report surfaced in March of 2009.

"I asked someone, 'Where did all Nochimson's' money go,' and they told me to follow up on that," he said. "Not unlike a lot of other stories, all I had to do was follow the money."

According to Wojarnowski and Wetzel's reporting, a UConn assistant coach at the time named Tom Moore saw Nochimson- a friend of Moore's from his days as a student-manager at the school- at a high school event in Chicago. Moore was there to watch Miles and Nochimson was in town because at the time he was the agent of Chicago Bull Luol Deng. From there Moore mentioned that UConn had been recruiting Miles, and pointed out a man named Jerry Easter, who was a guardian of Miles. By the end of the day, Nochimson- with knowledge of UConn's recruitment of Miles- had introduced himself to Easter and Miles. Two weeks later, Miles would visit UConn and give the school a verbal commitment.

From there Yahoo uncovered a Pandora's box of illegal benefits provided by Nochimson during Miles's recruitment, including a place to sleep, food, and travel money. Even worse, throughout that time Nochimson was in constant contact with the UConn coaching staff, a clear violation of NCAA rules since—as a former student manager and alumnus—he was considered to be acting as a representative of the school (a fancy term for "booster"). A Freedom of Information Act request by Yahoo uncovered over 1,500 calls and texts between the agent and the staff, with at one point, an average of close to three contacts a day between the two parties, and over 1,100 between Nochimson and Director of Basketball Operations Beau Archibald alone. In addition, there were sixteen calls between Nochimson and Head Coach Jim Calhoun. It was under that swirl which the report was released in March 2009 and would lead to a full-scale NCAA investigation into the program.

(In an interesting side note, while UConn fans were furious about Miles's expulsion in October, his removal from the school was one of the few saving graces in the whole situation.

Because of his involvement with an agent, had Miles actually stepped on the court for the Huskies, he would've eventually been ruled ineligible by the NCAA, meaning that any game in which he participated would've been redacted and become a forfeit in the record books. Had he not been expelled and actually played for UConn, Miles would've put the whole run to the 2009 Final Four in jeopardy.

Now whether that's important context to the story or not depends on one's opinion, especially as it relates to his arrest.

But as it turned out, in pure basketball terms, being expelled from school was just about the only noble thing Miles ever did for UConn.)

Either way, on the court the report did little to impact the Huskies; if anything it only brought the team closer together. UConn knocked off Purdue in the Sweet 16 and Missouri two days later to advance to the Final Four.

But off the court? Nothing could ease the anxiety going forward.

⌘   ⌘   ⌘

After UConn's 2009 season ended in Detroit, the NCAA sent their Letter of Inquiry the following January, a notice that essentially alerted the school that an investigation into the program was underway. And after spending the next four months asking questions and conducting interviews, the NCAA released the findings of their investigation on Memorial Day weekend of 2010.

Yet it was an incident that happened the day before the announcement which signified just how bad things might get. With the report set to come out the Friday before the holiday weekend, news broke late Thursday that Assistant Coach Pat Sellers and Archibald, the director of basketball operations had resigned.

The timing was less than ironic with both playing a key role in Miles's recruitment.

Sellers was the point-man for Miles after Tom Moore (who began the recruitment) left to take the head coaching position at Quinnipiac University in the spring of 2007. Meanwhile, as director of basketball operations, Archibald wasn't allowed to recruit under NCAA rules but did have a previous relationship with Nochimson dating back to the late 1990s. At the time, Nochimson was a student-manager with the program and Archibald a rarely used backup.

Regardless, the NCAA Letter of Allegations arrived a day later and found eight very serious violations. To paraphrase (otherwise we'll be here all day), they read as follows:

- Members of UConn's coaching staff exchanged 160 impermissible phone calls and 191 impermissible texts with recruits;
- Former student-manager turned agent Josh Nochimson had provided impermissible benefits to a recruit (the NCAA

blacked out the name of the recruit, but it was, of course, assumed to be Miles);

- Beau Archibald placed a twenty-nine-minute impermissible phone call (the name of the person, again, was not listed);
- Archibald provided false and misleading information to NCAA investigators;
- Patrick Sellers provided false and misleading information to NCAA investigators;
- During the 2007 and 2008 seasons, the UConn coaching staff gave twenty-six impermissible complimentary tickets to high school basketball coaches and others;
- Jim Calhoun failed to promote an atmosphere of compliance in the men's basketball program and failed to adequately monitor the program in regards to telephone calls, text messages, and benefits; and
- Between 2005 and 2009 the university failed to monitor the conduct and administration of the basketball program.[2]

The allegations were especially tough on Calhoun, a prideful New Englander, who in thirty-eight years of coaching college basketball had never been involved with major NCAA violations (in 1996 two players did accept plane tickets and UConn had to forfeit NCAA wins involving them however).

With lawyer Rick Evrard and Athletics Director Jeff Hathaway by his side, Calhoun told reporters that day, "It's certainly not the high point in my career, as a matter of fact, it's certainly one of the lowest points, at any time that you are accused of doing something."[2]

But with the allegations now out in the open, UConn's athletics department became proactive. Along with Evrard, they hired the lawyers of Bond, Schoeneck & King and prepared their response to the NCAA, which were presented in September.

In the pre-hearing that September, the school agreed with the allegation that the coaching staff had made impermissible phone calls and texts messages to recruits and that Nochimson (as a representative of the university) had illegal contact with a recruit (assumed to be Miles) and Archibald. They did however argue that

Calhoun had failed to "promote an atmosphere of compliance," and both the school and NCAA agreed that the "failure to monitor" charge should only be invoked from 2007–2009, not from 2005 as the original Notice of Allegations read.

In addition, the school also recommended a handful of other measurements they were willing to self-impose on the program. The university recommended probation for the program for two years, a scholarship reduction for the 2011 and 2012 seasons, and agreed to limit certain contact to recruits by certain members of the staff. The school went in front of the NCAA's Committee on Infractions in October to plead their case, hoping that because they were hands on and proactive in the investigation, the NCAA would be lenient with their punishment.

And to a degree, they were.

After nearly two full years of investigation, the Letter of Inquiry in January, Notice of Allegations in May, and hearing in the fall, the NCAA finally came down with their verdict on February 23, 2011.

What the NCAA found was that Jim Calhoun did in fact fail to promote an atmosphere of compliance and did in fact fail to monitor his assistants as well as he should have. In NCAA legal speak, those are two pretty heavy hits. The school was placed on three years' probation and lost a scholarship for not only 2011 and 2012, but 2013 as well and faced additional limitations on contact with recruits.

In addition, the findings ended in different results for the two assistant coaches who'd been forced to resign nearly a year earlier.

The NCAA stuck by their claim that former Director of Basketball Operations Beau Archibald had misled investigators and hit him with a two-year "show cause" penalty. Essentially this meant that if any school had interest in hiring him for the following two years, they would need to go in front of the NCAA, plead their case, and "show cause" for the hire.

But on the opposite end of the spectrum, Sellers (who had left the United States to take a coaching job in China) had been cleared of the "false and misleading" charge after the NCAA couldn't validate that he lied to them during the initial investigation. Sellers was again free to coach college basketball and accepted an assistant coaching position at Hofstra University in June 2011. Tom Moore, the assistant who had started the recruitment of Miles back in November 2006 was also cleared of any wrongdoing, and is now in his fifth year as head coach at Quinnipiac.

Ultimately though, the onus at least publicly fell on Calhoun. Due to his failure to promote an atmosphere of compliance and failure to monitor the program, he was hit with a three-game suspension in Big East play. But in an interesting twist, he wouldn't be asked to serve it until the following season, in the case of an appeal.

Still, Calhoun was remorseful and released a statement through his attorney Scott Tompsett on February 25, just a few days after the sanctions were announced. It read:

> First of all I'd like to thank everyone who has offered support over this past week both for our program and for my family during what has been a difficult time. Regarding the NCAA's findings and penalties, I'd like to state the following:
>
> As the leader of the Connecticut basketball program and an ambassador of the University, the buck stops with me. No qualifications. No exceptions. Without going into the details of the case or addressing each of the findings and subsequent penalties, I fully acknowledge that we, as a staff, made mistakes and would like to apologize to the University and all associated with UConn on behalf of myself and the men's basketball program.
>
> Throughout my 39-year career, my intentions have been, and will continue to be, on doing things the right way, in full compliance with the rules of my profession, and more importantly, with a moral and ethical standard that has been at the center of who I strive to be as a person. I remain committed to doing my job with integrity. Clearly, through our actions, there are lessons to be learned for the University, for our basketball family, and for me personally.
>
> Unfortunately, our mistakes have caused unrelated attention to be placed on the young men in our program today who continue to write their own story this basketball season. I will not allow those distractions to continue.

*My love for my players, the game of basketball, and this University will remain my number one professional priority. As the leader of this program, I am moving forward. I owe this to our players and our staff. I have apologized to them privately for the distractions. My personal feelings about this situation and the NCAA's findings will remain private and I will not have any further public comment on this matter.*

*I am energized and excited about the remainder of the regular season and what the post-season may hold, and our program remains committed to making UConn and all associated with it proud of what we do both on and off the floor.*

The significance of Calhoun's statement was clear: The long nightmare was over. After almost two years, the school no longer had to wait and wonder what was in store for them. They had their punishment, and whether those inside the program and in the media believed it was fair, everything was final.

The program could move on and avoided the punishment that fans feared the most. There would be no postseason ban. UConn would be allowed to play in the NCAA Tournament.

No one knew it at the time, but the program would take full advantage.

# Chapter 12

## Getting to Know Everyone Else

Beyond the players already profiled, there were a handful of others who were key parts to the 2011 UConn Huskies. Just like any other basketball team, for every star like Kemba Walker, there are always others that play smaller roles, all of which are just as important to a team's success.

One of those players was Roscoe Smith.

Smith was an interesting story in that, unlike so many of his future UConn teammates, he didn't have to scrap and claw for the attention of college coaches. Instead he spent most of his high school career trying to keep them at bay.

Entering high school as a six-foot-six fifteen-year-old, Smith was an immediate star at Baltimore's Walbrook High School, leading them to a 13–7 record as a freshman and averaging a very respectable twelve points, eight rebounds, and four assists. Again, he did that as a freshman. On varsity. Not too shabby, huh? And by the time Smith's second year at Walbrook ended in the Maryland state quarterfinals, he was considered to be one of the top high school sophomores anywhere in the country. Unlike future UConn teammates Shabazz Napier and Jeremy Lamb who were barely even being recruited at that point in their careers, every college coach in America knew Smith's name before he was even old enough to drive a car.

Interestingly that talent and prestige allowed Smith to make a unique decision following his sophomore year at Walbrook. That summer he skipped the AAU circuit almost entirely.

Now understand that in the cutthroat world of high-stakes and high-level hoops, it is AAU ball—and not high school—where almost all teenage basketball stars make their name. Playing against much better across-the-board competition than at the high school level, AAU basketball has become the meat market of basketball with college coaches crisscrossing the country all summer long in search of their next star player. And with scholarship offers gained and lost with a single good or bad performance (see: Lamb, Jeremy), skipping a summer on the AAU scene is not only frowned upon, it's unheard of. For many it's quite possibly putting your entire future in jeopardy since there is always someone else ready to step in your spot as "the next big thing."

But to the credit of Smith and his father Brian Thompson, the honor-roll student spent most of that summer at home getting ready to take the college boards the following year. Instead of worrying about scoring points at the Peach Jam or Boo Williams, Smith was more concerned with points on his SAT.

When Smith did hit the scene though, there was little rust on his now six-foot-eight frame.

He was selected as one of the Top 80 high school players in the country and invited to participate at the LeBron James Skills Academy, spending four days that July practicing and scrimmaging against the nation's best. Once there, Smith was named one of the nation's twenty best, and chosen for one of two "select" teams picked to play against the world's best youth in the Nike Global Challenge. Smith scored twenty-two points in that tournament's championship game as his US 2 team beat US 1, a club which featured a number of future college stars. It included a bulky forward from Massachusetts named Alex Oriahki.

Back at Walbrook for his junior year, Smith was simply a man among boys as he averaged twenty-two points and eleven rebounds and led Walbrook to the state semifinals. A known commodity in the region for years at that point, he was also named to his second straight *Baltimore Sun* All-Metro selection.

Of equal importance, Walbrook also became a home-away-from-home for many of college basketball's top coaches that fall with a handful (including an ever-present Roy Williams of North Carolina) stopping by quite regularly to see one of the country's top juniors. By the end of that year, Smith had scholarship offers from virtually every major program in the country, and on the first day that college coaches were legally allowed to call junior recruits under NCAA rules, he heard from plenty. Bill Self from Kansas, Georgetown's John Thompson III, Gary Williams of Maryland, and Florida's Billy Donovan all made their pitch to Smith that afternoon.

However, before Smith could make a college decision, he would first have to make an equally important one for senior year of high school. With Walbrook closing its doors after his junior year, Smith transferred to the prestigious Oak Hill Academy in Virginia where he'd play on a literal high school All-Star team. Over the past twenty or so years, Oak Hill had hosted a number of future college and NBA stars including Carmelo Anthony, Rajon Rondo, Brandon Jennings, and Jerry Stackhouse. And when Smith enrolled at the school in the fall of 2009, the roster was again stacked. He was joined by Doron Lamb (who'd later attend Kentucky), Pe'Shon Howard (Maryland) and future Big East rival Baye Moussa Keita (Syracuse) on a team which would start the year ranked No. 3 in the country.

At Oak Hill, Smith got to test his skills against the best high school teams and players in the country. Whatever competition he'd missed on the AAU circuit two summers before, he made up for in Virginia. Oak Hill played a national schedule that winter going toe-to-toe with schools like St. Patrick's of New Jersey (featuring future No. 1 overall draft pick Kyrie Irving) and Northland in Ohio, which had the nation's No. 1 big man, Jared Sullinger. After traveling coast-to-coast from November to March, Oak Hill's season finally ended in a loss to Mountain State Academy of West Virginia in the ESPN Rise High School Showcase.

Of course while Smith was at Oak Hill, his recruiting only picked up steam. In the end, Smith eliminated all but three schools in the recruiting process, finalizing things, and taking official visits to UConn, Duke, and Georgetown in the fall of 2009. Interestingly, during most of the process, UConn seemed to be Smith's last choice, with local favorite Georgetown seeming to have the upper hand. Duke also made a strong push, especially after they lost out on the nation's No. 1 wing player, Harrison Barnes, to North Carolina. Within minutes of Barnes declaring for Chapel Hill, the Duke coaching staff dialed up Smith, giving him a desperate pitch to come to the school. In the end though, with Jim Calhoun at UConn and a system known for putting wing players in the NBA, Smith chose to be a Husky in January of his senior year of high school.

Unfortunately for UConn fans, his recruitment didn't stop there.

With his commitment coming in January, Smith was caught in a limbo. Because of the timing, he had already missed the early signing period, a one-week window in November in which recruits can officially sign their letter of intent. Understand that until the letter of intent is signed, the player is not technically bound to the school beyond their verbal word. Instead Smith would have to wait until April to officially become a Husky, giving every interested head coach three more months to chase after Smith. Some even took the liberty of using the additional fuel of UConn's disappointing season and questionable health of Jim Calhoun against the Huskies.

As CBS Sports recruiting analyst Jeff Borzello remembers it, while Smith never publicly discussed an interest in attending a different school, it didn't stop people from gossiping.

"Everywhere he went, people were talking about it," Borzello said. "I can't say I ever felt like he was truly interested in de-committing from UConn, but people were absolutely still discussing it."

Finally in April 2010 UConn fans finally were able to breathe a sigh of relief.

The most highly-regarded recruit, in one of the most important recruiting classes in program history, put pen to paper.

Roscoe Smith would be a UConn Husky.

⌘　⌘　⌘

When Smith arrived to campus in the fall of 2010, he would be competing with two other freshmen for playing time in the front court. Niels Giffey was set to split some minutes with Smith on the wing, while Tyler Olander would do the same at the power forward spot.

Speaking of the pair, despite sharing a room in Hilltop Dormitory, the duo shared next to nothing in common in how they got to UConn.

Olander was quite literally the "hometown" boy on the 2011 UConn Huskies squad. Growing up just minutes away from the campus, Olander attended UConn basketball games as a kid and played pickup games in Gampel Pavilion as an up-and-coming star at E.O. Smith High School.

After three successful years at the school and with scholarship offers starting to come in, Olander took the not-unusual step of heading to prep school and, like future teammate Shabazz Napier, reclassified to the class of 2011. Unlike Napier though, Olander didn't do it because of bad grades but instead to get physically more mature to play college basketball.

Unfortunately, for all the success that Napier found at the prep school level, Olander had no such luck. Within weeks of arriving at Worcester Academy in Massachusetts, Olander injured his thumb and never actually played for the school. By the time basketball season rolled around, the six-foot-nine forward had already gone home to Storrs and transferred back to E. O. Smith, and ended up finishing his last year at the school averaging twenty-one points and ten rebounds. With scholarship offers from Florida, Providence, UConn, and others, he chose to stay in the class of 2010, skip the optional year in prep school, and enroll at UConn the following fall. In the process he may have set the unofficial record for "fastest move onto campus" for a freshman in UConn basketball history.

But while Olander had to only move a mere few miles to begin his UConn career, the person he would be sharing a dorm room with had come halfway across the world to play college basketball: Niels Giffey from Germany.

Giffey grew up Berlin and from a young age had been identified as one of the top players in his age group in the country. He starred as a local club player for a youth program named Marzahn Basket

Baeren before moving on Alba Berlin, the junior team of one of the top clubs in all of Europe.

Once there, Giffey flashed a lot of the skills that he would later show at UConn.

"He did everything," said Christophe Ney who runs the popular European basketball website EuropeanProspects.com and is considered one of the foremost experts on European youth basketball. "He was never a big scorer, but he was so dominant everywhere else. In passing. On defense. He was the best player on the court." Alba would go on to win two age group titles during Giffey's time with the team.

For three summers, Giffey played for the German National Team as well. He participated with the Under-16 team in 2006 and 2007 and played with the Under-18 team at the 2008 European Championships.

And it was after the 2008 championships, Giffey had a decision to make. Alba was interested in signing him to a pro contract and was ready to move him up to their senior team. But with his parents more interested in his education, Giffey—with the help of his coach and former North Carolina Tar Heel Henrik Rödl—decided to come to the United States to play college ball. Schools like UConn, Louisville, and Gonzaga showed interest, with Giffey ultimately choosing the Huskies in June of 2010. He would join Olander and Smith as freshmen in the frontcourt, all battling for playing time.

But despite being the least known commodity of the three entering his freshman year, Giffey made the biggest early splash.

Starting from the opening game in at the small forward spot that was assumed to be Smith's, Giffey thrived, showing the smart, sound, and fundamental game that many Europeans are known for. Giffey did nothing flashy but did all the little things needed to stay on the court early in the season: he played solid defense, didn't commit dumb fouls, and occasionally was an effective offensive player, just like he had been in his time playing for Alba. In particular, his fourteen points against Kentucky in Maui stood out in the early season. Understand that while the Maui Invitational will always be remembered as "Kemba Walker's coming out party," the All-American guard couldn't do everything by himself. And against

Kentucky, Giffey was as responsible as anyone for providing an unexpected spark.

Alongside Giffey in the frontcourt, Olander earned starters minutes early in the season at power forward. But unlike his roommate, Olander's impact was much less tangible.

Early on, Olander played like most freshmen who are going against bigger, stronger, and older players for the first time. He wasn't great and wasn't terrible, but on most nights he at least provided a key big body on a roster that was somewhat short on them. Olander started a handful of games but played his most important role on nights when Charles Okwandu or, more importantly, Alex Oriahki got into foul trouble. He also provided quality minutes when Oriahki simply needed a quick breather.

And then of course there was Roscoe Smith. The highest rated of the three recruits, Smith was often the first player off UConn's bench and in total played the most minutes of the three as the season wore on.

While Smith didn't necessarily show the consistent dominance from his high school days, his versatility allowed him to become one of the most important pieces of the puzzle for Jim Calhoun. Simply put, Smith allowed his coach to tailor the Huskies' lineup to the strengths and weaknesses of that night's given opponent. When UConn wanted to put out a really big lineup in the frontcourt, they could play Smith at small forward alongside Oriahki at power forward and Okwandu at center. When they wanted to go small, Calhoun removed Okwandu and put Smith at the power forward position and shifted Oriahki to center. Over the course of the 2010– 2011 season, only Kemba Walker, Oriahki, and Jeremy Lamb played more minutes than the forward from Baltimore.

On the stat sheet, Smith's versatility showed too.

At times he could be a low-post banger, someone who had no problem grabbing ten or more boards playing up front. He did it three times his freshman year. At others he showed the soft touch of a wing player, hitting key three-pointers in big spots.

In all, none of those threes (and few shots the entire season) was more important than one Smith hit against Wichita State. It was a buzzer-beater before halftime in the Maui Invitational opener and gave UConn a 33–32 lead and the momentum heading into the break. UConn, of course, ended up winning that game and winning the tournament, in the process giving a young team a wave of confidence they'd eventually ride to a National Championship five months later. While it's impossible to say what would've happened if Smith had missed that shot, it isn't unfeasible to think the Huskies could've lost that game, altering their entire season in the process.

However, as important as that three-point bucket was, it was actually a missed three-pointer later in the season that would make Roscoe Smith famous throughout the college basketball world. Actually, the better word than "famous," would probably be "infamous."

It happened in early January, when UConn traveled down to Austin, Texas, for a crucial game between the Huskies and the Texas Longhorns. For UConn, they'd just lost their second straight Big East game to open conference play and needed a big victory to get them headed in the right direction. For the Longhorns, it was seen as one more chance to notch an impressive win in the out-of-conference slate. In the previous two weeks, they'd beaten North Carolina in Greensboro and Michigan State on their own campus in the Breslin Center.

The game was a hotly contested battle from the start with the Longhorns taking a five-point halftime lead and UConn coming all the way back to take that lead in the second half. In the final seconds, with the game tied at seventy-three apiece, Kemba Walker missed a layup which bounced into the hands of Texas guard Dogus Balbay. Balbay drove the length of the court and hit forward Gary Johnson with a chest pass, but when Johnson went up with the ball, it was blocked by Alex Oriahki, keeping the score tied.

And that is where things got interesting.

The blocked shot was tipped right into the waiting hands of Smith with a little over ten seconds left. The young freshman (still only a dozen or so games into his college career) quickly glanced at the clock, took one dribble, and heaved the ball the length of the court. He missed the basket entirely, and the ball rolled out harmlessly out of bounds with four seconds still showing on the clock.

What could Smith have possibly been thinking to take such an ill-advised shot? Well mistakenly, when Smith let go of his shot, he thought the clock read "one second" not ten.

Texas got the ball back, but much to the relief of UConn fans (and their cardiologists), the Longhorns wouldn't score on their gift final possession. The Huskies held on to win in overtime.

Still, that didn't stop everyone from having fun at Roscoe's expense. Later that week, *Sportscenter* labeled it the No. 1 play on their "Not Top Ten" list before mercifully deciding to "retire" the video from ever being broadcast again because of its sheer absurdity.

Yet in the end, the worst ribbing of all came from the relentless joking of Smith's own teammates.

"My team—man, they got on me in the locker room," Smith told the Hartford Courant's Mike Anthony after the game. "I glanced at [the clock] and threw it up there. I just saw the clock going real fast."[1]

Even Smith's grizzled head coach had some fun with him.

"I've seen a lot of things in my life," Calhoun, the college coach of forty-plus years, said. "I've never seen that. I never have, really."[1]

⌘　⌘　⌘

In addition to the three freshmen in the frontcourt, there were also two seniors who made significant contributions to the success of the 2011 UConn basketball team as well. They were Charles Okwandu and Donnell Beverly.

Beginning with Okwandu, his story starts off not unlike most kids born in his native Nigeria, where as a child, he much preferred the soccer pitch to the basketball court. And it was only after growing to over seven feet tall that Okwandu gave up his first passion and gravitated toward basketball as a sixteen-year-old in 2002.

From there no one in college basketball had a more interesting backstory than Okwandu.

With size that would make most NBA stars green with envy and a general coordination and skill acquired from a lifetime of playing soccer, Okwandu caught the eyes of local basketball scouts who set him up with the Basketball Without Borders program. Started in 2001 in conjunction with the NBA, Basketball Without Borders holds camps in Africa, Asia, Europe, and Latin America, bringing access to the sport of basketball to parts of the world where it is otherwise not played. Since its inception, Basketball Without Borders has sent a number of players from Africa to American high schools and colleges, including Baye Moussa Keita, who played with Roscoe Smith at Oak Hill Academy, and Luc Richard Mbah a Moute who went on to UCLA before getting drafted to the NBA.

But when Basketball Without Borders first came to Africa in 2003, one of the first stars was Charles Okwandu. With his strong play at the camp and under the watchful eye of plenty of scouts, Okwandu's name trickled back to the United States where a young University of Arizona assistant named Josh Pastner (now the head coach at University of Memphis) showed immediate interest. After sharing tape with then head coach Lute Olson, Okwandu was offered a scholarship, and a short time later, he gave a verbal commitment to the school.

"We were hearing these reports from people that were at the camp, people we trusted, so we went ahead and offered him a scholarship sight unseen," Pastner said when asked about Okwandu years later. "But from the beginning, it seemed like our back was against the wall to ever actually get him on campus. After a while it became obvious that it just wasn't going to happen."

It never did. For Okwandu, issues in getting a visa from the notoriously tough (and some would say corrupt) Nigerian embassy, as well as struggles on the TOEFL test (Test of English as a Foreign Language), precluded him from arriving in the United States at all. Expected to enroll in the fall of 2004, the once promising prospect was without a basketball home.

From there it would be another year or so before Okwandu re-emerged, again at a camp, this one called the Africa 50. (In the crazy world that is high-level basketball, the camp was organized by a young Nigerian-born NBA scout named Masai Ujiri. Ujiri would eventually become the first African-born person to ever hold the title of "General Manager" for a professional sports team when he accepted that role with the Denver Nuggets in the fall of 2010.) There Okwandu was again a star, and impressed scouts with his size and athleticism. But with Nigeria timid in handing out visas for fear that their citizens might never return, it'd be over a year before Okwandu was released out of the country.

Finally, at the end of 2006 and at the age of twenty (when most of his peers would be starting their junior or senior years of college), Okwandu made it over to the United States. He briefly attended the College of Southern Idaho (where Nate Miles would suit up for a few games two years later), before landing at tiny Harcum College in Pennsylvania. Harcum had formerly been a women's only school and didn't start a men's basketball program until 2006. When he arrived in the summer of 2007, Okwandu was literally and figuratively the biggest recruit in school history.

"The year before we had another Nigerian kid, and we were able to get him to Seton Hall," Harcum head coach Drew Kelly said. "People knew we'd had success, so someone gave me a call, and Charles was on his way. Next thing you knew, there's this 7'1 kid ducking through my door."

But despite that massive frame and a solid skill set honed by years of working out for scouts in basketball camps, when Okwandu was put into an actual game action, he was still woefully under prepared. Kelly found that out the hard way, the first time he worked with his new seven-foot-one project.

"When Charles first got here, we put him through a workout, and I mean, man this kid had it all," Kelly said. "He had great hands, was athletic, excellent footwork. Then we put him in a game and—this is a true story—Charles gets two or three offensive goaltending calls against him in a row. He comes back to the bench and says to me, 'Coach, what's going on?' The poor kid had never played in a game with referees before."

To his credit though, Okwandu more than held his own that winter despite playing in his first organized games. He was averaging a respectable 6.7 points a game but was eventually ruled ineligible because of confusion with his transcript. His career at Harcum was effectively done.

Yet despite all the holdups and limited time on the court, it didn't stop Okwandu from garnering interest from college teams. Within hours of arriving at Harcum, word leaked that a new seven-footer was in town, with coaches lining up outside Kelly's door the next morning to see him. Eventually Okwandu visited UConn following the 2008 season and committed that weekend. While on campus he was immediately drawn to another seven-foot African who'd overcome a ton of obstacles to get to UConn, Tanzanian center Hasheem Thabeet. Thabeet had decided to return to campus for his junior year just days before, and now Okwandu followed suit.

Once on campus though, Okwandu's struggles only continued.

Because he started college after the age of twenty-one, Okwandu was already behind the eight ball and under NCAA rules only had three years to play at UConn. And to be blunt, he wasted one of those years of eligibility in his first season as a Husky. Listed as a sophomore during the 2009 season and stuck behind veterans Thabeet, Jeff Adrien, and Gavin Edwards in the frontcourt, Okwandu rarely saw action. Not that it mattered much anyway, since at the end of his first semester Okwandu was ruled academically ineligible. After coming so far just to get to college basketball, he would have to sit out the rest of the season and watch UConn's run to the Final Four in street clothes.

Back eligible the next fall, things barely got any better.

With Edwards now a senior, Oriahki a new freshman, and Ater Majok eligible for the first time in December, Okwandu was again the odd man out in the rotation. In UConn's last twenty-two games, Okwandu would only play ten or more minutes in nine of them.

And when he did take the court, you could practically hear the groan come from the crowd.

Despite his advanced age, Okwandu was still highly immature in a basketball sense and couldn't seem to get out of his own way in game action. Passes that hit him in the hands bounced out of bounds. On defense, he got lost like a first-time visitor to Times Square. And the fouls, well, they never stopped coming. During that season, Okwandu had more games in which he fouled out (three) than games with more than five rebounds (two) or double digits points scored (one).

Incredibly, he once even fouled out in just six minutes of play, a feat which will surely mystify basketball historians for years to come. By the end of the 2010 season, Okwandu's season mirrored his team's. He wasn't just disappointing. He was a disaster.

Maybe most concerning though was that as he entered his senior year in 2011, the immature twenty-four-year-old had much less margin for error. With Edwards and Stanley Robinson graduating and Majok leaving under mysterious circumstances, UConn's frontcourt depth featured Alex Oriahki and—well, that was really the only certainty, with everyone unsure of exactly what to expect from the three freshmen. Simply put, UConn was a big man short in the paint, meaning that not only would Charles Okwandu play, he'd be asked to play quite a bit.

Against the lighter competition of the out-of-conference schedule, Okwandu was eased into the action, only playing a handful of minutes in that portion of the season.

But entering Big East play, that all began to change, although not immediately. He played twenty-plus minutes for just the second time all season in the conference opener against Pitt, thanks in large part to Oriahki's foul trouble. Unfortunately, going against a bulky Panthers frontline, Okwandu's foul problems from the previous season resurfaced. He played a respectable twenty-five minutes with four points and four rebounds but ended the game on the pine after getting his fifth foul with just under six minutes to go. As much as things change, they stay the same, huh?

Not necessarily. Because as time went on, a funny thing started to happen: Charles Okwandu actually began to play pretty well.

Granted, because of his late start to the sport of basketball, the instinct and natural "feel" of the game never totally came to him at any point during his UConn career. But again, to see Okwandu by the end of his senior season was to realize just far he'd come. Especially when you remembered that he'd never picked up a basketball until he was sixteen, and never got any consistent coaching until he arrived at Harcum nearly five years later.

But there was little doubt that he was in fact improving. Okwandu had ten rebounds in a victory over Marquette in January and eleven more boards with four blocks when UConn beat Providence at home a few weeks later. Most importantly, when he was on the court, Okwandu wasn't the foul machine he'd been the year before. In most games (depending on the matchup) Okwandu played between twelve and twenty-five minutes and went nearly two calendar months without fouling out. For some that might not be great. But for Okwandu it was no doubt an improvement.

And by the time Senior Night rolled around, the biggest player on the UConn roster, who'd come the longest way to get to that point, had softened just about everyone around the program. That included his head coach Jim Calhoun, who jokingly told reporters, "I think he's 36 [years old]. I'm not sure about that. He's come a long way."[2]

Okwandu himself said, "It's been a long road...I enjoyed being here. I had some ups and downs, but it was fun." He then added, "I would love to come back, but I'm getting too old."[2]

He might not have been thirty-six, but after first catching the eyes of college scouts way back in 2003, it was time for Okwandu to move on. And when Harcum coach Drew Kelly caught up with him during Okwandu's final NCAA Tournament games, the amount of progress his rough-around-the-edges pupil had made wasn't lost.

"To see how far Charles had come in just a few short years was incredible," Kelly said. "Like any college kid, he'd grown as a person and obviously, he'd grown as a basketball player too. Here's this kid that had been playing with just a few rows of bleachers on one side of the gym, and now he's playing at Reliant Stadium? The UConn staff did an incredible job with him."

One could only hope that the next eight years for Okwandu are as action-packed and adventurous as the previous eight.

⌘　⌘　⌘

Along with Okwandu and Kemba Walker (who was set to graduate in three years), there was one more senior to honor at the last home game of the regular season. He was the only scholarship player who'd been in the program for four years and, quite frankly, probably had ten years' worth of stories from his time on the UConn basketball team. That player was Donnell Beverly.

Beverly had seen it all during his time at UConn after arriving as an unheralded recruit in the class of 2007. He only signed with the school late in the recruiting process when a last-minute scholarship opened up.

From the beginning, Beverly was put into a seemingly no-win situation. With sophomores Doug Wiggins and Jerome Dyson and juniors A. J. Price and Craig Austrie already on the roster when he arrived, the six-foot-four Beverly quickly became the fifth guard in a four-guard rotation. There was only so much playing to be had, and the freshman got next to none of it.

That would remain a theme throughout his time in Storrs, but for one day during his freshman year, Beverly did shine.

With the Huskies playing reasonably well that winter (they'd won two games in a row), UConn went on the road in January of Beverly's first year to face the No. 8 ranked team in the country, the Indiana Hoosiers. The game came just a few weeks before the bottom would fall out for Head Coach Kelvin Sampson in Indiana, but at the time the Hoosiers were hot and amongst the nation's best teams.

Anyway, with the UConn program having a little momentum behind it for the first time in two years (they'd missed the NCAA Tournament the previous spring), news broke the morning of the game that Wiggins and Dyson were suspended and wouldn't be traveling with the team. The Huskies—which were an underdog entering that game to begin with—were in huge trouble unless someone unexpected could step up.

That player would be Donnell Beverly.

Getting his first real playing time of the season, the freshman responded. He scored just two points but played harassing defense on future NBA lottery pick Eric Gordon, limiting him to just five of sixteen shooting on the afternoon as the Huskies shocked the college basketball world with a stunning 68–63 victory in front of a national TV audience. The win would propel the Huskies for the rest of the season; they went on to win seven straight games following the victory in Bloomington.

Unfortunately for Beverly, that afternoon also marked the last big minutes he'd play his entire freshman year. Eventually Dyson and Wiggins would come back from suspension, and Beverly never saw more than nine minutes of action in any game the rest of the year. With the arrival of Kemba Walker the following season (but the departure of Wiggins), Beverly once again spent most of the season on the bench, playing the role of the proverbial "odd man out," and for a time considered transferring. Meanwhile, on the practice court, it seemed like no matter what he did, Beverly was constantly raising the ire of Jim Calhoun.

But after another mundane season as a junior, Beverly's fortunes began to change heading into his senior year. While he still wasn't projected to see a ton of minutes on the court, he was named captain of the team along with Walker and would set the tone early with so many new freshmen on campus. Under Beverly's watch, things that were tolerated in the past no longer would be.

Also, like Okwandu, while Beverly's numbers didn't totally reflect his impact, it was there, with the senior becoming the Huskies' ultimate glue-guy, both on and off the court. When Kemba Walker needed a breather, Calhoun turned to Donnell Beverly. When Shabazz Napier needed someone to vent to at the end of the bench, there he was too. All the little things that don't show up in the box score, Beverly provided. Simply put, he was the leader that the previous year's team so sorely lacked.

And while he may have spent four years under the constant critique of Calhoun, by the time his last game rolled around in Storrs, everyone, even his coach, had nothing but praise for the senior who'd been through so much.

"Donnell has been a coach's dream in a sense that when you need someone to yell at, you can yell at him," Calhoun joked before the game. "He's a tough, prideful kid, who has been really good for our basketball team."[3]

The player himself added, "I take pride in what I did here…Even if it didn't go well, or if it did, I still have the same mindset. I can just say I'm proud to be a Husky."[3]

Little did Beverly know that as he approached the end to his rocky career there'd been plenty more for him and his teammates to be proud of.

Next stop?

The Big East Tournament. And a date with history.

UConn's Two Seniors (And Kemba Walker) Hold The Big
East Championship Trophy

**Credit: Ed Ryan/The Daily Campus**

Shabazz Napier Did All The Little Things To Help UConn
On Their Title Run

**Ashley Pospisil/The Daily Campus**

Alex Oriahki Was UConn's Rock Down Low All Season

**Credit: Ed Ryan/Daily Campus**

Kemba Walker And Roscoe Smith Catch Their Breathe
At A Wild Big East Tournament

**Credit: Ed Ryan/The Daily Campus**

Jeremy Lamb Became A Much Needed Second Scorer For UConn Over The Course Of The Season

**Photo Credit: Ashley Pospisil/The Daily Campus**

The Team Celebrates The Title In Houston

**Credit: James Anderson/The Daily Campus**

Senior Donnell Beverly Provided A Little Bit Of
Everything For The Huskies

**Credit: Ed Ryan/The Daily Campus**

The Man, The Myth, The Legend: Kemba Walker

**Credit: Ed Ryan/The Daily Campus**

Reliant Stadium: Home Of The 2011 Final Four

**Credit: Aaron Torres**

Kemba Walker Can't Hold Back Tears When He Is Introduced Into UConn's
Ring Of Honor During The Championship Celebration

**Photo Credit: Ashley Pospisil/The Daily Campus**

# Chapter 13

## A Fresh Start in the Garden

With the NCAA sanctions out, a large cloud lifted from above the UConn program. But for those who thought it'd end their late season skid, well, they were wrong. Very wrong.

The day after the NCAA's announcement, the Huskies returned to the court in a seemingly winnable home game against Marquette. Just like when they came to Hartford the previous year, the Golden Eagles' season was on the brink of spinning out of control, losing five of eight entering their matchup with UConn. Included in that streak was an eight-point loss to the Huskies in Milwaukee when Jeremy Lamb went off for twenty-four points.

This time it'd be Marquette with the upper hand, thanks in large part to another frustrating effort by the Huskies. In particular, UConn's star player was to blame.

After falling down big early, UConn clawed their way back into the game, thanks in large part to Marquette missing their first eleven shots of the second half. But up 59–57 with less than two minutes to go, Kemba Walker—of all people—basically gave away the game for the Huskies.

On UConn's last four possessions, Walker missed two shots and had two key turnovers, the second of which led to a Darius Johnson-Odom layup to tie the game with just five seconds to go. UConn (which was without Jim Calhoun because of a death in the family), would go on to lose in overtime in one of their sloppiest efforts of the year. The Huskies committed seventeen turnovers and shot just 36 percent from the field, losing despite a plus-seventeen rebounding margin, including twenty-six offensive boards. But it was Walker, who was maybe most disappointing. The guard shot just ten of twenty-seven from the field and forced shots and the action all night in another poor effort.

With the loss and just three remaining games on their schedule, time was running out for UConn to turn things around. But to their credit, the Huskies did bounce back the following Sunday with a win over Cincinnati. UConn led for all but twenty-nine seconds of the game and shot exactly 50 percent from the field in the victory. The win wasn't exactly reason to celebrate, but after struggling so much in the proceeding weeks, any victory was a needed ego boost for the young team.

Unfortunately that victory proved to be more of an aberration than an upward trend.

Next was the final road game of the regular season where UConn faced the always tough West Virginia Mountaineers. West Virginia wasn't quite as talented as the previous year -when the program had gone to the second Final Four in school history- but there was no question that plenty of heart and toughness remained.

Those two traits showed through when the two teams tipped off. West Virginia controlled the boards (out-rebounding UConn 30–23) and played defense late in the game that the Huskies simply weren't prepared to handle. With a 47–46 score and ten minutes to go, UConn shot a brutal two of seventeen as a team to close out the game, resulting in another loss seemingly worse than the last. Final score: 65–56.

Beyond just another check in the loss column, of more concern was UConn quickly digging themselves a hole in the conference standings they might not be able to get out of.

After the defeat at West Virginia, for the first time all season, the Huskies faced the real possibility of finishing outside the top eight of the conference standings, which would mean no first-round bye in the Big East Tournament. That was a death knell for any conference school, meaning that they'd have to play the opening day of the tournament on Tuesday, and face a five-games-in-five-days gauntlet to get to the championship. And while it wouldn't impact the team's ability to make the NCAA Tournament, it did likely end any hope that the Huskies could pick up a few confidence-building wins before the Big Dance.

Unfortunately the reality of a Tuesday Big East Tournament opener happened when the Huskies lost their finale to Notre Dame on Senior Day.

Before the game, all signs seemed to point toward a storybook ending for the Huskies' veteran players. As is tradition, all the seniors were honored before tip-off, walking hand-in-hand with their parents to center court, to the cheers of the home crowd prior to the final home game of their careers.

But this Senior Day there was a catch. Beyond Donnell Beverly, Charles Okwandu, and manager Jordan Rich, there was another, unexpected, honoree: Kemba Walker. Although he was listed as a junior on the roster, Walker had taken the necessary coursework over the previous summer to graduate from the school after three years and, if he chose, it opened up a path toward entering the NBA Draft a year early. And as a likely high pick, that was exactly what was expected to happen, meaning that the Notre Dame game was very likely the last time Walker would wear a Huskies uniform at home.

The ceremony was elegant and emotional, and, for a while, it seemed like the ending that everyone wanted. It appeared that for one final time, Kemba would be the conquering hero.

Trailing late in the second half, UConn got a huge break when Notre Dame guard (and eventual Big East Player of the Year) Ben Hansbrough fouled out with over eight minutes to go. The fact that he was even in the game with that much time left was a surprising move, but it was the little break the Huskies needed. At the time Notre Dame was ahead 60–52, but without their floor leader, no one expected them to retain the lead.

And they didn't.

Behind a raucous crowd at Gampel Pavilion, the Huskies made an epic run thanks almost exclusively to their superstar. With Hansbrough looking on with a towel draped over his head, UConn scored thirteen straight points (with eleven from Walker) to storm back and go ahead. Within minutes that 60–52 deficit had turned into a 65–60 lead, and the Huskies seemed to be headed toward a win.

But the good times wouldn't last.

Much like they had against West Virginia, UConn lost their composure at the worst possible time. The Huskies shot just one for ten from the field in the final four minutes of the game and saw a five-point lead swing back to a four-point deficit before a Jamal Coombs-McDaniel bucket eventually stopped the hemorrhaging. Notre Dame still led 69–67, and after a free throw made it a three-point game, the Huskies had one last chance.

With just seconds left, the ball was inbounded to Walker who sensed a swarming defense and quickly threw an errant pass to Beverly. Beverly never got clean possession of the ball, and a final shot never went up. The Huskies had again lost, 70–67, and given the circumstances, this seemed like it might've been the worst loss of all.

"I remember going into the locker room after the game, and it was like a morgue," former Fox Sports and current CBS Sports writer Jeff Goodman said about the post-game atmosphere. "It was pretty clear by that point that Kemba wasn't coming back, this was supposed to be his big going out party, and it just didn't go as planned. Seeing those guys after that game, you thought their season was done right there."

And really, looking at the context of the situation, there was plenty of reason to think that the season was over. The dreams of Maui, Texas and even the early portion of the Big East schedule were gone and replaced with the reality that this UConn team just wasn't that good. They'd lost four of five to close the regular season and, worst of all, had regressed and transformed into everything they'd been expected to be in the preseason. In the Notre Dame loss, Walker scored thirty-four points. The rest of his teammates had combined for thirty-three. UConn was—as had been projected in the fall—a one-man team. Even worse, there seemed to be no time to figure things out.

With the loss, as feared, UConn now had to open the Big East Tournament on Tuesday. It was a proverbial death sentence for a team looking for any kind of positive momentum.

Simply put, time was running out on the 2011 UConn Huskies. They'd need a prayer and a miracle to make it out of New York alive.

And the NCAA Tournament? It was the last thing on anyone's mind.

⌘　⌘　⌘

When it comes to a must-see event on the bucket list of any college basketball fan, the Big East Tournament might very well be No. 1 (and with the future of the Big East Conference more uncertain by the day, it's this author's recommendation to get to it while you can). While the quality of a Final Four depends on the teams participating and venue which is hosting, the Big East Tournament always delivers. Every year the conference hosts five days of wall-to-wall basketball, featuring some of the nation's best teams in the "World's Most Famous Arena," Madison Square Garden. The 2011 tournament was certainly no exception, hosting a record eleven teams which would eventually qualify for the NCAA Tournament.

And really, just looking back on past Big East Tournaments provides a who's who of some of the great moments in college basketball history. There was the epic "Allen versus Allen" game in 1996 when Ray Allen and the UConn Huskies got the better of Allen Iverson and Georgetown. A decade later Gerry McNamara led Syracuse to a then-record four wins in four days, making himself a folk hero in the process and securing the Orange an NCAA Tournament berth which hadn't been guaranteed just a few days before. And then there was 2009 when UConn and Syracuse played one of the most memorable games in college basketball history. It took seventy minutes and six overtimes before the Orange prevailed 127–117 in a game that will likely be talked about for decades to come.

Interestingly, 2009 was also the first in which a rule came into play which would greatly alter the tournament going forward. For the first time since the conference expanded to sixteen teams prior to the 2006 season, all sixteen would be invited to Madison Square Garden to compete for the tournament championship. Prior to 2009, only the top twelve finishers qualified, with the bottom four stuck at home as spectators.

But with sixteen teams playing for the title, it also gave the Big East Tournament a structure unlike any in the sport of college basketball. The tournament now started on Tuesday with the top eight teams receiving a bye until Wednesday and the top four getting a double bye into Thursday's quarterfinals. While it was beneficial for the top of the conference, it made for a next-to-impossible task for the bottom eight. To win the Big East Tournament, they'd have to win five games in five days. And to at least one of college basketball's top analysts, to do that was tougher than actually winning the NCAA Tournament.

"Oh I absolutely believe it is," ESPN analyst Jay Bilas said when asked to compare the two. "To win an NCAA Championship, you've got to win six games in three weeks. You've got time to prepare, time to adjust, and of course time to rest. But five games in five days, especially against the competition you traditionally see in the Big East? Come on."

And it was that next-to-impossible task which UConn had in front of them when they opened the 2011 Big East Tournament. The loss to Notre Dame dropped the Huskies to ninth in the regular season standings, meaning they were forced to play lowly DePaul on a quiet Tuesday afternoon in the tournament opener. At that point, the topic of winning five games in five days wasn't broached; UConn just wanted a victory in that Tuesday game. For all the talk about four losses in their last five games of the regular season, it was easy to forget that no player on the Huskies' roster had ever won a Big East Tournament game. As a program, they hadn't won one since a 2005 quarterfinal opener against Georgetown. Most of the players on the 2011 roster were in middle school at the time of that game.

But for at least one day, the Huskies looked like the UConn of old. Sure they were playing DePaul, a team which went just 1–17 in Big East play during the regular season. The Huskies left nothing to chance though, and after jumping out to a 45–28 halftime lead, cruised to a 97–71 win. Five players scored in double figures for the Huskies, and while the victory wasn't exactly a reason to celebrate, it was still important for the struggling team.

"We had a nice bounce back game," Jim Calhoun told reporters following the victory. "We're happy to get a win. It's been awhile."[1]

The next day brought another noon tip-off and another struggling team in Georgetown. After UConn ended the Hoyas' eight-game win streak a few weeks before, Georgetown hadn't really been right since. With star point guard Chris Wright out with an injury, they'd lost three straight games to end the season.

And it was because of the injury to Wright that optimism was still tempered when the Huskies beat Georgetown to advance to Thursday's quarterfinals. Without their starting point guard, the Hoyas' offense never really got going, and UConn cruised to another win. Kemba Walker had another strong game with twenty-eight points on an efficient ten of eighteen shooting from the floor. Add in twelve points from Jamal Coombs-McDaniel and eleven from Jeremy Lamb, and the game was never really in doubt. Final score: UConn 79, Georgetown 62. Most importantly, the Huskies seemed to be getting some confidence back.

"You could definitely see that the swagger was back a bit after the Georgetown win," Goodman, who was at Madison Square Garden all week long, said of the victory. "Whether it was contrived, or they really believed it, I don't know. But it seemed like they were starting to revert back to the team that we'd seen earlier in the year."

But even with the two victories in the opening two days, the real work had just started. Next up was the team which had embarrassed the young Huskies early in the season, the Pittsburgh Panthers.

Pitt was one of the beneficiaries of the double-bye format, and UConn was already two games in by the time Pitt opened up their Big East Tournament against the Huskies. With plenty of rest, the Panthers came into the game as huge favorites, not only because of their dominant early season win, but also thanks to their 15–3 conference record and Big East regular season title. They came to New York as the No. 1 seed in the tournament.

And early on in their quarterfinal matchup with UConn, they showed why, jumping out to a twelve-point lead seven minutes in and maintaining the same margin with under six minutes to go in the first half. But to the Huskies' credit, they battled back, and by the time the horn sounded for intermission, UConn trailed by just one, 41–40.

From there, the second half went back and forth with Pittsburgh building a lead and UConn clawing their way back. Pitt went up 54–47, and UConn made a run. The Panthers went up 60–54, and the Huskies came back before eventually it was UConn who had the lead. And when the Panthers' Ashton Gibbs hit a three to even things up at 74, the game would go into the final seconds all tied up.

Following a Pittsburgh time-out, the Huskies got the ball back. But before Kemba Walker could provide any magic, he would need some help from a teammate.

That teammate was Jamal Coombs-McDaniel, and as easy as it is to forget now, he made a crucial play to set up the Huskies' game winner. With just over twenty seconds left, Walker went up for what would've been the game winner and missed it before it was quickly tracked down by an alert Coombs-McDaniel who quickly called a time-out. That play, lost in the lore of UConn's run, was one of the great unsung moments of the entire season.

But back to the action.

Out of the time-out, the ball not surprisingly went to Walker who had the option to take the final shot himself or, if he sensed trouble, dish it off to Coombs-McDaniel for a corner jumper. With fear of the jump-shooter, Pitt elected not to double team Walker, and after a defensive switch left Walker with a mismatch against six-ten Panthers center Gary McGhee, the decision had been made. It would be Kemba Walker's shot.

Giving away a foot in height, but with an overwhelming advantage with his quickness, Walker dribbled down the clock, waiting and waiting until just seconds remained. Then he made his move. Walker gave McGhee a quick jab-step and even quicker pull-back which crossed the center's legs up and sent him sprawling to the floor. Unguarded, Walker went up for an uncontested jumper.

The ball hung in the air before finally falling through the net as the buzzer sounded.

UConn 76, Pittsburgh 74. Madison Square Garden became complete pandemonium.

Within seconds of the ball going through the net, Shabazz Napier quickly ran over to Walker and lifted him off the ground before the two were swarmed by their teammates. March had officially gone mad, and so too had everyone in the arena. Everyone that is, except Kemba Walker.

"Everybody was excited," a smiling Walker told the media after the victory. "We came into this game as underdogs, everybody saying we were going to lose, but everybody stayed with each other, and we stayed together, and we came out with this victory."[2]

With the win, the Huskies' improbable run toward a Big East title continued with their next game against a familiar foe. On Friday night, UConn would play Syracuse, and once again the two teams would need extra time to decide things.

Like the Pitt game, UConn held the edge late against the Orange, but this time there'd be no Husky heroics at the end of regulation; instead Syracuse's Scoop Jardine provided the excitement. Trailing 68–62 in the final minute, Jardine hit a three to cut the lead to three, and after Napier missed a free throw, Jardine again came through with a long-range bomb. Thanks to Jardine's personal 6-0 run, the game was tied at 68, and the two teams were again headed to overtime. A mere twenty-four months after they'd played six in the same building.

This time though, Kemba Walker- who along with Beverly was one of the two Huskies who'd played in the six overtime thriller two years before- wouldn't let the game carry late into the night.

"I didn't want to go into another six overtimes," Walker would later say about his mindset at the end of regulation. "I was mad when it went into the first overtime, and I thought at the six overtime game, and I wanted to get the win in that first OT."[3]

And that's exactly what Kemba and Company did. The Huskies played lockdown defense from the start, and Walker and Lamb outscored the entire Orange team 8–3 in the extra period, holding on for a five-point victory. Incredibly, the team that couldn't buy a win late in the season pulled off four in four days, including three against college basketball's Top 25 teams. Now they readied for a final with Louisville, the team they'd been unable to figure out and lost to twice in 2011.

Beyond just the championship game and a Big East title, history too was on the line. No team in college basketball history had won five games in five days, in any event, anywhere, ever.

Did the Huskies have enough left in the tank for one more victory?

# Chapter 14

## UConn's Big East Championship: How Sweet It Is (Published March 13, 2011)

It's not often you'll see me get up to write on a holiday. But this past Thanksgiving was a very special exception.

What was the exception? Well, my UConn Huskies had just taken home the Maui Invitational title,[1] an unprecedented and surprising run, which saw them rip of three epic wins in three days over three really good teams. UConn entered the tournament as national nobodies and left as a Top 10 team in the country, a stunning turn of events that I had trouble putting into words the following day. Regardless, it was—and likely always will be—one of my favorite moments ever as a sports fan.

Of course the story within the story at Maui was Kemba Walker. The junior guard wasn't just good that week, or even great, but almost transcendent in leading the Huskies to the crown. He scored ninety points in three games, carrying an overmatched cast of young guys to the unexpected title. Walker was so dominant in Maui that upon winning the tournament, his teammates actually gave him a standing ovation when he got on the team bus heading to the airport. As Jim

Calhoun tells it, it was the only time in his forty years coaching he'd ever seen that happen.

Anyway, fast forward four months to the here and now, and I'm once again up and writing at some very strange hour after another unprecedented UConn run. This one was on the mainland, in the Big East Tournament, and 40 percent better: five wins, in five days, a feat which has never happened in college basketball history.

And much like Maui, Walker was the focal point.

By now you know the Walker narrative from the last five days. He slashed and dashed, scored and dished, set up his teammates, and set up himself for game winners. The highlights are too many to count, but just for fun, let's rattle off a few. The most famous of course was Thursday's game winner against Pitt where Walker crossed poor Gary McGhee, sending him sprawling to the floor and eliciting my friend Mark to text me right after, "We gotta chip in to get Gary McGhee some crutches." Then there were the thirty-three big points Walker put up against Syracuse, including the Huskies' last two in an overtime win. But my favorite play of the week was in the final minute Saturday night when Walker spun into the lane just slightly out of control before finding Jeremy Lamb for the final field goal in regulation. It wasn't the game winner (there were foul shots to ensue), but that one play was symbolic of Walker's entire week and, really, UConn's entire season.

It summed up Walker's entire week because to his credit, over the last five games, he somehow played the role of cold-blooded scorer who also happened to get all his points within the flow of the offense. Yes, Walker averaged twenty-seven a game over the first four nights in New York, but despite that, he never forced things. There were no out of control drives, no wild three-point attempts, no forced jumpers. Just smart, sound basketball. Which wasn't how he always played this season.

Really though, that play summed up the Huskies' season in a nutshell.

You see, when this whole wild ride started in Maui, this team was essentially Kemba Walker and twelve backup singers. I think I even once described it as similar to how the Dave Matthews Band has Dave

Matthews as the headliner and a bunch of nameless and faceless guitarists, bassists, and drummers standing behind him. Well, that was UConn in Maui. Everyone except Walker (and to a lesser degree Alex Oriahki) were nameless and faceless, just happy to be along for the ride.

But as the season wore on, a funny thing started to happen: Those nameless and faceless young guys found their wings. It didn't happen all at once, and understand that it wouldn't have happened at all if they didn't have a Kemba Walker security blanket. But it did happen. Jeremy Lamb became a solid second scorer, Jamal Coombs-McDaniel was instant offense off the bench, and Shabazz Napier became one of the perimeter defenders in the Big East. The young guys all of a sudden had their sea legs.

And the problem was that at times I did wonder how that new dynamic would affect the team. Yes, Kemba was still the front man, but those other guys were ready to take some of the spotlight too, and Walker wasn't quite ready to relinquish it. Not because he's selfish or a bad teammate, but because (justifiably) he has an innate confidence in himself to make plays at the end of games (And really who can blame him?). Still, it doesn't mean there weren't some uneasy moments at the end of games when the young guys carried the Huskies for big stretches, and Walker tried to do too much, as opposing defenses focused on him in the waning seconds. Two losses in particular, the first Louisville and second Marquette games come to mind as low points.

That's also why that play in last night's game was so special. There was Walker, the best player in college basketball, the guy who felt obligated to make every big play all season, driving…attacking…and dishing the ball to Lamb for the layup. After playing out of his mind for five straight days (and five straight months, really), and playing on legs made of Jell-O, Walker's biggest play of the game—of an All-American season—was setting up a teammate. It was completely symbolic of Kemba being "the man" while still handing off some responsibility to the younger guys.

And getting back to what I was saying about the young guys, that play was also quite symbolic of UConn's entire season. Because the truth is, while everyone was busy writing the "Kemba Takes New York" script, his teammates became—and ultimately were—the difference on Saturday night.

Yes, Walker was spectacular, but even he admitted that by those last couple minutes he had nothing left in the tank. (By the way, you know what the most amazing stat of Walker's entire week was? How about that he played 190 of a possible 205 minutes during UConn's Big East Tournament run, and would've played more if not for some early foul trouble against Louisville. Gives a new meaning to the term, "New York Marathon," huh?)

Anyway, back to what I was saying. Because as much as Saturday night (and this week really) was about Walker, it was really about everyone else too. It was about Lamb being at the right place at the right time for that lay-in against Louisville. It was about Roscoe Smith scoring in double figures for just the third time since the start of February. It was about Shabazz Napier hitting two clutch free throws at the end of the game. It was about Oriahki once again being a warrior in the paint. And it was about Tyler Olander, Jamal Coombs-McDaniel, and Charles Okwandu stepping up in key spots. Yes, Kemba Walker was the star of the show, but over the last five days, everyone else got their on-stage solo too.

(While we're here, I'd be remiss if I didn't take a second and absolutely, positively bow down to Louisville. Saturday night's game was a war on both sides, and the Cardinals left just as much on the court as UConn did. Peyton Siva in particular was outstanding, and he did it on one good ankle. It isn't hyperbole when I say that I've never been more impressed by any team the Huskies have ever played, win or lose. Louisville left everything on the court too, and at the sake of sounding like a Little League mom, they've got nothing to be ashamed of.)

So what now? I'm honestly not sure.

Everyone is quick to point out that for all the heroics of the last five days, all the fun, drama, and excitement that it brought, none of it means anything if the Huskies flame out in the NCAA Tournament. And you know what? Everyone is right. Five wins in five days in the

Big East Tournament is an incredible accomplishment. But six wins over three weeks in the NCAA's is much more significant.

Still, regardless of what happens going forward, there's something to be said for what happened this past week. As UConn stepped to the podium on Saturday evening, I couldn't help but think back to something Bobby Knight said a few weeks ago when he mentioned that in his eyes, winning the Big East Tournament was just about as tough as winning an NCAA Tournament. I didn't fully appreciate that comment at the time, but after seeing my team win five games in five days, four against ranked opponents, I do now.

Ultimately what I will take away from this win and this UConn season in particular is the following: every time someone has counted this team out, they've come on stronger and more resilient than before. It happened when they went to Maui as nobodies, it happened after early season losses to Pitt and Notre Dame (which in hindsight, don't seem so bad, huh?), and it happened when they came to New York on a losing skid.

Will it happen again in the NCAA Tournament? Maybe and maybe not. But if I've learned one thing, it's not to bet against this team.

Until then, it's just time to relax and enjoy the ride.

Reflecting on everything from Maui to Manhattan, it's important to realize that seasons like this just don't come around too often.

# Chapter 15

## Are These Guys for Real? Early NCAA Tournament Play

With the win over Louisville, the college basketball world was again buzzing about the Huskies. Sure, there were plenty of other teams had won conference tournaments: Duke avenged a late season loss to conference rival North Carolina to take home the ACC title; San Diego State finally got by BYU, the only team that had beaten them during the 2011 season; and Kentucky similarly put their enormous talents together to win the SEC. But ultimately no one had won with the style and pizzazz, not to mention fortitude, of the Huskies.

"Simply put, I didn't think five games in five days could be done," said ESPN analyst Jay Bilas who was courtside for the Huskies' win over Louisville in New York. "It's not a stretch to say that what UConn did was the greatest accomplishment ever in conference tournament history."

Still, no one remembers what happens in the Big East Tournament if you lose early in the NCAAs, a reality that the Huskies faced head-on when their draw came out the following day on "Selection Sunday." UConn was placed as the No. 3 seed in the West, matched in a region that was just about as tough as any in the 2011 tournament.

The No. 1 seed were those Duke Blue Devils, a team which entered the year at No. 1 and closed it out with their third straight ACC conference tournament title. Duke had it all, including two key seniors who helped the Blue Devils to the NCAA Tournament title just a season before. Nolan Smith and Kyle Singler were as good as any duo in college basketball (both had played with Kemba Walker on the US Select Team the summer before), and when combined with role players that added size in the paint and scoring on the perimeter, Duke was clearly one of the most complete teams in the field.

And much to the dismay of the rest of the field, the rich only got richer when the Blue Devils welcomed back point guard Kyrie Irving right before the NCAA Tournament. Irving had been sidelined since early December with a toe injury but, when he had been on the court, was the best player in college basketball. The true freshman who later went on to be the No. 1 pick in the NBA Draft was averaging a cool seventeen points and five assists prior to the injury.

But before the Huskies could even get to Duke, there were plenty of other stumbling blocks in the way.

The No. 2 seed in the region was the San Diego State Aztecs, a club which had burst onto the college basketball scene for the first real time in 2011. The laid back Southern California school hadn't ever won an NCAA Tournament game in program history prior to 2011 but still entered the tournament at 32–2 with their only two losses to conference rival BYU. Maybe even more concerning was that if the Huskies played San Diego State, it'd be in the Sweet 16 at the Honda Center in Anaheim, California. The host city of the West Regional semifinals and final was only about two hours away from the San Diego State campus, meaning that if the two schools matched up, San Diego State would have a decidedly "home court" advantage.

Filling out the rest of the bracket were plenty of other grenades and landmines.

The NCAA Tournament selection committee surprised many when they elected to put the Texas Longhorns as the No. 4 seed in the region. Yes, Texas had struggled down the stretch and lost three of their final four games of the regular season. Then again those three losses came on the heels of a 23–3 start in which the Longhorns had been ranked as the No. 1 team in the country. Most everyone expected the Longhorns to—at worst—be a No. 3 seed. Yet there they were at No. 4 in the West.

Beyond those top three, plenty more challenges remained for UConn.

The No. 5 seed were the Arizona Wildcats, a team which was coming off a thrilling conference tournament of their own with a Pac-10 Championship Game in overtime against Washington. The Wildcats also featured one of the top players in the country, explosive forward Derrick Williams, who'd been named the Pac-10 Player of the Year just a few weeks before.

Even the Huskies' second round game wouldn't be easy: if UConn beat Bucknell in their opener, they'd get the winner of a tough matchup between Missouri and Cincinnati. Missouri was a team that had been ranked in the Top 25 for most of the season, and Cincinnati was a Big East club that knew the Huskies like a pair of brothers playing pickup ball in the driveway. Sure UConn had beaten them just a few weeks before in the Queen City, but the Huskies had also lost to them twice in the 2010 season as well.

However, to some truly savvy UConn fans, placement in the West Region was actually a strange blessing in disguise. Yes, the Huskies had a tough draw and potentially faced San Diego State (and maybe Arizona) under what would be decidedly disadvantageous circumstances. At the same time, history was also on the Huskies' side. Of the three times in program history that they'd advanced to the Final Four, in all three cases UConn had come out of the West Region. It happened during the championship seasons of 1999 and 2004 and also two years prior to 2011 when the Huskies had gone to the Final Four in Detroit in Kemba Walker's freshman year.

Then again those situations were also much different than the one UConn walked into in 2011. In all three of those seasons, UConn had been the favorite in their region. They were the No. 1 seed in both 1999 and 2009 and, even as a No. 2 seed in 2004, were picked by many not only to win the region, but also win the title. That club may have been a two seed on paper, but it also had more talent than a lot of NBA rosters with All-Americans Ben Gordon and Emeka Okafor flanked by freshman studs Josh Boone and Charlie Villanueva. Frankly that team was so good that even a little used backup named Hilton Armstrong would later become a first-round NBA Draft pick.

But 2011 was different.

Sure some liked UConn to make a big run, including Bilas who selected them to go all the way to the NCAA title game. Plenty of others worried about how the Huskies' run at Madison Square Garden might impact fatigue entering the NCAA Tournament. As history showed, the two clubs who'd previously won the Big East Tournament after winning four games in four days would both later lose in the opening weekend of the NCAA Tournament. What would five games in five days mean? Especially for a UConn club which relied so heavily on freshmen and sophomores, none of which had ever played an NCAA Tournament game?

And on paper at least, the Huskies' opening opponent, the Bucknell Bison, proved to be the perfect foil for the Huskies. Bucknell entered the tournament with ten straight wins and nineteen victories in their previous twenty games dating back to the Christmas holiday, not to mention that they had played Marquette and Villanova tough early in the season before that. The Bison would not be afraid of the Huskies.

Maybe most important was that despite being a mid-major school in name, Bucknell didn't look anything like it when they walked in the gym. The Bison's best player, Mike Muscala, had averaged fourteen points and seven rebounds a game and, at six-foot-eleven, was a commodity that most small schools just don't have. Looking at the big picture, all the ingredients seemed to be in place for an upset. At the very least, many believed that if the Bison didn't win the game, they'd at least keep things close.

Which they did—for a few minutes anyway. But even before halftime hit, it was clear the game wouldn't be much of a contest.

After Bucknell cut an early UConn lead to 27–20 with under eight minutes to go, the Huskies went on a 12–2 run to open things up and close the first half ahead 39–22. And from there it only got uglier. After the two teams traded three points each to open the half, a one-sided game turned into an embarrassing rout. UConn went on to score the next fifteen points and led by as many as thirty-two in the second half before Jim Calhoun mercifully called off the dogs late. The Huskies cruised to an 81–52 win.

But really, to just look at statistics following the victory would take away from how well UConn had truly played. It was simply the best overall effort of the Huskies' season, and at times, about as efficient as a team can look on the offensive end of a basketball court. UConn shot 48 percent from the field as a team, with Walker again leading the way with eighteen points. But in continuing their success from New York, Walker didn't do it alone. With Bucknell's defense focused on slowing him down early, Walker's passing set the tone for the rest of the team. He finished with twelve assists, the most ever for a UConn player in an NCAA Tournament game. One more page of the UConn record books belonged to Kemba, much to the delight of his teammates.

"Every time he came off a pick, he had two guys on him," a smiling Alex Oriahki said in a post-game interview. "They don't know we have other guys on this team that can score as well. He made them pay."

Oriahki's coach agreed.

"Their choice was simply, 'Kemba Walker is not going to beat us,'" Jim Calhoun said after the victory, which was the 850th of his historic career. "But he did. He beat you by making other people better."[1]

Following the win over Bucknell, a familiar foe awaited the Huskies in the next round: Big East rival Cincinnati. The Bearcats cruised into the second round after a surprisingly easy win of their own over Missouri.

But before the game could even tip-off, there were plenty of fireworks surrounding the game. It involved the two coaches and one star player.

The whole situation had really started a week before at the Big East Tournament, after the Huskies beat Georgetown, when Jim Calhoun came to the post-game press conference a little miffed. The coach started the press conference in defense of Walker who hadn't been unanimously picked to the All-Big East conference team. One coach had left him off his first team ballot.

And while Calhoun didn't name any names at the time, he did imply that the coach who might have left Walker off the ballot, could've been one who still held a vendetta against Kemba for not choosing his school during the recruiting process. Whether it was a real accusation or Calhoun just stirring the pot, only the coach knows. But with the implication, all signs seemed to point toward Cincinnati coach Mick Cronin, who as you may remember, made Walker a top priority after getting the Bearcats coaching job. At the time, Walker seemed set on committing to Cincinnati until UConn swooped in with an offer.

But regardless of whether there was any actual bad blood between the two coaches or just a media-created story angle to sell newspapers, Calhoun quickly defused the rumors the day before tip-off.

"It's all cleared up," Calhoun said prior to the matchup between the two schools. "We had a good conversation."[2] Well then. I guess that settles that.

Once the two teams did actually get on the court, it was clear that bad blood or not, this was going to be no easy game for the Huskies. Cincinnati took a one point lead minutes into the second half and stayed close all the way throughout.

In the end though, the difference proved to be Walker and his ability to get to the foul line down the stretch. He finished the game with thirty-three points (and in the process became UConn's all-time single season scoring leader) and went fourteen of fourteen from the charity stripe, including six straight in the final minute to seal the win. After their recruiting battle all those years before, the difference in the 2011 NCAA Tournament between UConn and Cincinnati was that one had Kemba Walker and the other didn't. It was enough for the Huskies to advance to the Sweet 16. Afterward, a reflective Calhoun explained how his team's confidence had grown in the previous few weeks. "All of a sudden, you just pull away because you believe you're going to win," Calhoun told reporters following the victory. "When you've won five, six, seven, and played really good teams that happens."[3]

With the victory, the Huskies had advanced to the second weekend of the NCAA Tournament for an astounding thirteenth time in Calhoun's tenure at the school. However, when they arrived in Anaheim for the Sweet 16, a worst-case scenario had become a reality: UConn would play San Diego State, the school whose campus was mere hours from the site of the game.

Speaking of San Diego State, to understand why their fans were so willing to make the trek up to Anaheim, you first have to understand how far they had come in just a few short months.

To say that the Aztecs had "little" tradition entering the 2010–2011 season would be a gross understatement; they had next to none. Despite starting their basketball program all the way back in the early 1920s and moving to Division I level in 1970, the school still had a total of just seven NCAA Tournament appearances, four of them since Coach Steve Fisher took over prior to the 1999–2000 season. And with that little history came a sad reality: Prior to the 2011 season, the San Diego State Aztecs had never won a single NCAA Tournament game. Not one.

"Really, there wasn't a lot of reason to follow the team closely prior to 2011," said Yahoo Sports college basketball writer and California native Jeff Eisenberg. "They were an adequate program, competitive enough to occasionally make the NCAA Tournament. Not much beyond that though."

But for everything that San Diego State lacked in history, they made up for with a brilliant 2011 season.

It started just two games into the year when they went up to Spokane, Washington, and shocked the Gonzaga Bulldogs in a 79–76 road win. At the time Gonzaga was ranked No. 12 in the country, and the loss was just the fifth in their home building since it'd opened up in 2004. And following that victory, San Diego State only continued to roll. They won twenty straight to start the season and moved all the way up to No. 4 in the country before their first loss of the season at BYU.

But beyond just their 34–2 record entering the Sweet 16, a bigger concern loomed for UConn: the Aztecs were a club perfectly built to beat the Huskies. San Diego State was a veteran team that started three seniors, and against a smallish Huskies club, had a front line as big as any in the Big East. All three starters in the frontcourt stood at least six foot seven, including All-American forward Kawhi Leonard.

Thanks to elite athleticism, long arms, and hands that Eisenberg once had described to him as "bigger than toilet seat covers," Leonard played much larger than his six-foot-seven frame and very well might have been the best post player UConn faced all year up to that point. He'd led the Aztecs with fifteen points and eleven rebounds a game in the season.

Also, it wasn't just who San Diego State put on the court but how they played. The Aztecs used a slowed-down offense and a physical, in-your-face brand of defense to control tempo and wear down opponents. The fifty-nine points a game they allowed was the seventh fewest in college basketball, a concern for UConn, which liked to play up-tempo and fast break at every opportunity. And while others had tried to slow down the Huskies in the past, San Diego State not only had the players to do it, but enough talent to win as well.

Factoring all that in though, there was still one more advantage that San Diego State had that UConn just couldn't counter: their fans. After Fisher literally had to give away tickets his first few years on campus, San Diego State had developed one of the most loyal, passionate, and loud fan bases of any team in the country. They filled Viejas Arena on campus whenever the Aztecs played and made San Diego State as intimidating an arena as there was in college basketball. Just to show how strong the fan base had become, there was even a crowd of twelve thousand in the stands on New Year's Eve to see the Aztecs play Division III Occidental College.

"That game was really the most surprising thing to me. They outdrew both UCLA and USC that weekend, which is something you never heard of happening," Eisenberg said. He then added, "San Diego State basketball became the thing to do, not only on their campus, but in the entire city of San Diego."

And it was that kind of passion that would lead San Diego State fans to make the drive up to the Honda Center to support their team in droves for the Sweet 16. Despite everything UConn had been through to that point in the season, dealing with a crowd quite that loud hadn't been one of them. When the two teams played, the Honda Center would be anything but a "neutral" court.

"Even the people in the arena who weren't San Diego State fans, the Duke and Arizona fans there for the later game, were pulling for the good, 'underdog story,'" Eisenberg said.

But no matter where it was, a neutral court or otherwise, when the action tipped off between the two schools, it undoubtedly had "the feel" of a big-time, win-or-go-home college basketball game. The road warrior UConn Huskies took a nine-point lead into the locker room, but it wouldn't last as San Diego State used their size down low and skill on the perimeter to battle back after halftime. Forward Malcolm Thomas made three straight buckets, and guard D.J. Gay added five points of his own before a Billy White layup put the Aztecs up 53–49 with just under nine minutes go. At that point Jim Calhoun was forced to call a time-out as the game appeared to be slipping away from his young Huskies.

But before the two teams could make it to the bench, something happened. Something innocuous and petty and dumb. Something that would swing the game and alter the seasons of both San Diego State and UConn.

San Diego State guard Jamaal Franklin bumped into Kemba Walker.

Really, "bumped" might not even be the right word. But with Walker looking the other way as the two teams walked to their respective benches after Calhoun's time-out call, Franklin did casually put his shoulder down and bump Walker in the chest. It sent the guard sprawling to the floor, and immediately a technical foul was called. Whether it was a little acting on Walker's part or not, only Kemba knows, but the play proved to be the kick in the butt UConn needed. Walker went to the line and made two free throws, and all of a sudden, things swung back in the Huskies' favor. It also ignited Walker, and after the two teams next traded baskets, the star guard put on a show.

Out of the under eight-minute time-out, Walker got to the rim for a layup. Then he hit a jumper. And then a three-pointer, all as San Diego State went ice cold from the field, and suddenly became incapable of stopping Walker on the defensive end. And by the time that Kawhi Leonard had made a free throw to end the bleeding,

Walker had done his damage. He went on a personal 12–3 run, and a one-point deficit had become an eight-point lead at 65–57.

To the Aztecs' credit though, the veteran and experienced group refused to go away and countered back. Gay hit two quick threes. Thomas added a free throw. And the Aztecs found their legs again on defense. Within a few short possessions, that eight-point lead was cut down to one entering the final two minutes of the game. The crowd was again deafening.

But as they'd done all year, UConn proved to be tougher than their age and experience might indicate. It started when Jeremy Lamb hit a three out of the time-out to end San Diego State's run. It was a crucial play since Walker would later say after the game that he had little left in the tank by that point. And when Lamb added a bucket after that, it started to look like UConn might just hold on for a win. Two Walker free throws and a Lamb dunk in the final minute did exactly that. Incredibly, UConn continued to do defy the odds. They were one game away from the Final Four.

As usual, the coach summed things up about as well as anyone could. The win, the 2011 season really, wasn't even about basketball at that point. "This run has been sensational, and I haven't been able to put it in perspective," Calhoun told the media following another surprising victory. "I couldn't have asked for a better gift than this team, and then we get this. I don't remember anything quite like this."[4]

With the win, the improbable dream continued. Next stop: the Elite Eight.

But when the Huskies got there, they were in for a bit of a surprise. Following their emotional win over San Diego State, most assumed they'd get the No. 1 seed Duke Blue Devils who were set to play Arizona in Anaheim later in the evening. Looking through college basketball history, a matchup between UConn and Duke seemed almost predetermined by fate as UConn had to beat the Blue Devils to get to each of their championships in 1999 and 2004. The two schools had also played in the Elite Eight in 1990, when Christian Laettner ended the run of Calhoun's first great team at UConn. It only seemed fitting the two would play again for a trip to the Final Four.

It wasn't meant to be this time. Instead, a relatively close game between Duke and Arizona got blown open in the second half when the more explosive and athletic Wildcats put on a wild fifty-five-point scoring showcase after halftime, embarrassing the Blue Devils 93–77. It was Arizona who'd play UConn for a trip to Houston and the Final Four.

And while Arizona lacked some of the name cache that Duke held, they more than made up for it in raw basketball skill. Most importantly, the Wildcats had one of the few players in college basketball that could go point for point, score for score with Kemba Walker, forward Derrick Williams. Williams had scored a career-high thirty-two points in the win over Duke and would later go on to be the second overall pick in the 2011 NBA Draft.

With a trip to college basketball's Mecca on the line, UConn again had another tough test in front of them. They'd have to win again in Anaheim, and again win in an arena that would feel and sound like the toughest road venue they'd play in all season, with plenty of Wildcats fans making the trip from Tucson after the Duke win.

But like they had been all season, UConn was again up for the challenge.

# Chapter 16

## UConn's Dream Run Continues to the Final Four (Published March 27, 2011)

I've spent the last half hour trying to figure out how to start this column, and the best I can come up with is this: I cannot believe I'm still writing about UConn basketball at this point in the season. Amongst everything that I consider feasible on this planet, the idea that I'm still talking about Jim Calhoun, Kemba Walker, and the Huskies, ranks somewhere just above "The Cleveland Indians winning the World Series" and just below "Jennifer Aniston actually being attracted to David Schwimmer on the TV show *Friends*."

Then again, that last analogy isn't as far off as it might seem. Yes, *Friends* is just a TV show. It's fiction. But to continue the parallel with UConn basketball, it does kind of seem fitting. That's because while UConn fans might argue about a lot of things, there's something everyone is in agreement with: this season doesn't seem real.

And it really doesn't seem real when you think back and consider all the dark places UConn basketball has been since their last Final Four run in 2009. Because to understand where UConn is today, you've got to understand where they've been. And believe me when I say, it isn't pretty.

Starting with the obvious, by now you all know a lot of the surface level stuff that's been going on with the program. You know about the NCAA snooping around like the Hardy Boys over the last two years, looking for any dirt they could find to bring down the team. You know about the firing of assistant coaches Beau Archibald and Patrick Sellers. You know about the NCAA hitting the school with sanctions just a few months ago, limiting scholarships, and recruiting in the coming years.

What's crazy though is that there's been plenty more going on beneath the surface. It might be stuff that didn't get talked about as much. But for a while it did change the vibe around the program.

It's only fair to start with the actual 2010 season, which—as you might have heard—didn't go well. The story of that team probably didn't really hit as hard nationally as it did at home, but was one of the most crushing in recent memory.

Ultimately the 2010 UConn Huskies were the antithesis of everything that people hate about sports. Individually it was a good group of kids, but collectively it was nothing short of a grease fire. At a certain point, I really felt like Jim Calhoun might have to call in the National Guard to run interference.

If anything, the 2010 team was actually quite insufferable. On the court they were selfish, self-serving, and disinterested. They lacked leadership and heart. Their level of play yo-yoed with whomever they were playing. It was a club that beat the No. 1 team in the country (Texas) and a future Final Four participant (West Virginia) but also lost more winnable games in one season than the Washington Generals have in their entire history. In full disclosure, I will say that 2010 was the first time that I've ever openly rooted for my team's season to end. Having no UConn basketball at all was better than having to watch another second of that pathetic 2010 club.

Off the court, there was other stuff too. Calhoun missed time with an illness. He bickered with Athletic Director Jeff Hathaway over a contract extension. The school lost a handful of elite recruits, all unsure of the future of the program.

And much like the recruits, the future of the program left a lot of people in Connecticut in a funk too.

Understand that like a lot of places, UConn basketball probably means a little *too* much to a lot of people, myself included.

Yes, Connecticut is a progressive state. But really, the Huskies are one of the few things that separate us from everyone else, that we can call our own, and that we don't share with Boston or New York, the Northeast, or the tri-state area. UConn basketball has the same meaning to us that Boise State football does to the people of Boise, the Spurs have to San Antonio, and Kentucky hoops does to the commonwealth. It's what sets us apart from everyone else.

And it's because of that, that the last eighteen months or so were really pretty tough. In a lot of people's eyes, our program, our coach, and our team were self-imploding, or at the very least losing traction as one of the nation's elite. With NCAA sanctions, lost recruiting battles, and defeats on the court, it left a lot of people wondering, "Is this it? Is this the end of our run on top?"

Which, bringing it full circle, is why this season has become about so much more than basketball for UConn fans.

Look, I could sit here and tell you all about the merits of Calhoun, Kemba, and Alex Oriahki, but you watch the games just like I do. You know the stories of Maui, of the midseason struggles, and of the epic Big East Tournament run. I could babble on about those things all day (and believe me, I'd love to), but why bother? We've already been there. That's old news.

So instead, let's talk about all the little stuff I've already mentioned, and let me explain *why* it's so important. Because understand this: Not only did no one in Connecticut see this Final Four run coming, ultimately I don't know if anyone really wanted it. All we did want was a little bit of our pride and self-respect back and for people to start talking about the games on the court, rather than the crap off of it.

Not that anyone's complaining.

Because if last year's club was every reason to hate sports, well, this one is every reason to love them. This is a group that's team-first, selfless, and cares about W's more than any other stat. This is a group that's seen players shuffled in and out of the lineup all year, has seen roles change, seen stats change, but has never, ever seen anyone's attitude change.

Remember, Niels Giffey began the year playing big minutes and now gets next to none. We haven't heard a single complaint from him. Tyler Olander plays in short spurts and usually is done on the court by the midway point of the first half. We haven't heard a complaint from him. Donnell Beverly is a scholarship senior, likely playing the last meaningful basketball of his life. We haven't heard a single complaint from him. Alex Oriahki has basically had to fend for himself in the paint all year. No complaints. Roscoe Smith, Jeremy Lamb, and Shabazz Napier have seen their roles fluctuate back and forth, good and bad. No complaints from them.

And while we're here, what about Kemba Walker?

Yes, he's everyone's All-American, and yes, he's put up more than thirty points twice in the tournament. And you know what else? His role has changed over the course of the season too. Yes, he still gets his points, but he also gets everyone else way more involved than he did, even a month ago. Understand that this team wouldn't have won in Maui or had their incredible regular season run without "Kemba being Kemba." They also wouldn't be on a nine-game postseason win streak if he hadn't altered what he was doing along the way too.

Finally, you know who I've been most surprised by? Jim Calhoun.

Understand that I've been watching UConn basketball about as long as I can remember. I'm not joking when I say that outside my immediate family, Jim Calhoun probably had about as much an impact on my childhood as anyone else (what that says about *me*, is another story).

And I can never remember Calhoun acting the way he has this year. Maybe he's been mellowed by the unrelenting media, the health problems, whatever. But whatever it is, I never remember him *this* relaxed. On the sideline. In interviews. In everything. Maybe it's armchair analysis, I don't know. But I've got to be honest, I think he's enjoying the ride as much as anyone.

One more thing. I know I haven't talked about basketball much at this point, and honestly I'm not going to. You know why? Because as I mentioned before, this isn't just about basketball.

This UConn basketball season is about why grandfathers bring their sons to games, and why those sons do the same with their kids twenty years later. It's why you grow up a Dodgers fan, or a Cubs fan, an Alabama football fan, or UConn hoops fan. It's why you keep following teams through thick and thin, coaching changes, scandal, whatever. It's because sometimes a team takes you on such an unexpected and wild ride that it makes all the bad worth it. We've all heard the stories of the 2004 Boston Red Sox, Kentucky's "Unforgettables," and the Super III New York Jets, about how win or lose, following those teams was about more than sports. It was an experience.

And that's how I feel about this UConn team.

Eight days from now the college basketball season will end and a new NCAA Champion will be crowned. Maybe it'll be UConn or maybe it won't, but either way I'm going to be pretty upset.

Not because my team won or lost. But just because this season has been so fun I don't want it to end.

# Chapter 17

## Final Four Preview: Picking Winners for Saturday's Games (Published April 1, 2011)

One of the most underrated parts of having a wildly unpredictable Final Four is how tough it makes it on us writers. Wait, I'm supposed to have an opinion on Saturday's games? Geez! Doesn't anyone ever think of us anymore?

Honestly I've never been more torn heading into a Final Four weekend, in large part because I would've never guessed in a million years that any of these four teams would be here. I watched UConn all season and gave up on them as actual contenders sometime in mid-February. As I explained in my column Monday,[1] I just never saw "it" with Kentucky, at least not until super-late in the season. In regards to Butler, well, I would've been less surprised seeing the UConn women's team playing in Houston Saturday night than these guys. And VCU… forget about it. I couldn't even spell VCU three weeks ago. Although in my defense, the spelling is tougher than it looks.

Yet incredibly, here we are with one of these four teams just seventy-two-ish hours away from taking home a national title. Only in America. Only in March.

Here's who I think will be playing for the title Monday.**VCU vs. Butler: Saturday, 6:09 p.m.**

To any Butler or VCU fan who may have stumbled across this site, I want to start with an apology. The breadth and depth of this preview won't come close to what I'm about to spit out on UConn-Kentucky later. So, I'm sorry. Although really, I probably shouldn't be writing about this game at all. Quite frankly, I'm about as qualified to talk about these two teams as I am to discuss fifteenth-century Renaissance art or the keys to a successful relationship. In other words, I actually have no qualification at all.

What I will say though, is that this game will ultimately come down to tempo. Whoever dictates it will win.

Starting with VCU, it'll be interesting to see how they handle Butler's slow and methodical pace. Looking back at this tournament for the Rams, when teams have wanted to run with them, VCU has blown them out of the building, Georgetown and Kansas in particular. As for everyone else, well, once Purdue fell down early, they had no choice but to run with VCU, and while USC was successful at slowing things down, they didn't have nearly enough offensive firepower to keep things interesting. Really, Florida State was the only team able to slow down VCU and, not coincidentally, the Seminoles played them tougher than anyone in the tournament. Well, on Saturday, not only does Butler want to keep this game in the 60s, they will keep this game in the 60s.

And actually, that's where I don't think Brad Stevens gets enough credit as a coach. Sure we fawn over him for many things, whether it's for his tournament poise, big game chops, or the fact that he looks like the sixteen-year-old who works at your local movie theater. But we never give him credit for how well his players execute the game plan and force the other team to play their style.

To prove my point, I'll take something that I wrote about last year's Butler run and use it this year, because I think it's important. What's most impressive about Butler getting to a second straight Final Four is that they've had to beat every kind of team to get there. They've beaten ones who play fast (Florida) and slow (Wisconsin). Ones who are physical in the paint (Old Dominion) and physical on the perimeter

(Pitt). Teams which rely on athleticism (Florida) and more on smarts (Wisconsin). Some that live by the three (Wisconsin) and others which barely shoot any (Pitt). And much like their coach, nothing has rattled them along the way. All they do is win, win, win.

And I think they'll do it again Saturday.

One more thing as well. The biggest concern for VCU entering this game has to be that they've gotten crushed on the boards all tournament long. Looking at the numbers, it's really staggering. VCU has been out-rebounded by an incredible 180 to 144 margin over their five games in the tournament, which comes out to minus 36 overall and by an average of 8.8 a game. If you take out their "First Four" win over USC (where they actually out-rebounded the Trojans by six), the Rams rebounding margin is minus 42 overall, and they're getting out-rebounded by over 10 boards per game. The fact that they're still standing isn't just staggering, it's inconceivable.

Of course the reason that VCU has been able to keep winning is because of their three-point shooting. They're 43 percent in the tournament and 45 percent overall if you take out that first, hideous USC game.

Well, Butler allows opponents to shoot just 32.5 percent from three, and with Matt Howard, Andrew Smith, and Khyle Marshall down low, I firmly believe they'll be able to crush VCU on the boards as well.

Simply put, if VCU gets out-rebounded by ten to Butler, they will lose. Which is exactly what I expect to happen.

Incredibly, Butler will be playing for their second straight title Monday night.

## Kentucky vs. UConn: Saturday, 8:49 p.m.

Let's start from the beginning, and completely debunk the most important myth this week: There is nothing to take out of the game that these two played in Maui in November. Each team couldn't be any more different today than they were five months ago, and while it's a fun talking point, it's ultimately irrelevant.

Starting with UConn, you all know their narrative by now. In November it was Kemba Walker's team, Kemba Walker's island,

and Kemba Walker's week. Now obviously guys like Jeremy Lamb, Shabazz Napier, and Niels Giffey had some role in Maui. But I'm not so sure Jim Calhoun couldn't have picked up a couple stoned surfers off the beach, plopped them into the lineup, and got the same results. Kemba was just that good. For the most part, everyone else (except maybe Alex Oriahki) was simply a nameless, faceless, interchangeable extra on the Kemba Walker Show, happy to come along for the ride.

But as I've mentioned multiple times since, it was because of Walker's heroics early that allowed the rest of the team to get their sea legs sometime around the middle of January. Again, UConn doesn't win the title in Maui without Lamb, Napier, Roscoe Smith, and whoever else contributing some. But that doesn't mean they're the same players they are now. Not even close.

Same with Kentucky. Looking at that box score for the Wildcats is a lot like looking at your old high school yearbook picture—you just want to laugh. Things couldn't be any more different.

Starting with Brandon Knight, whatever he was that day, he isn't now. Knight is cool, confident, and a stone-cold killer, especially in this tournament. While the numbers don't tell the complete story on him, he's a million times better than he was in November, just like UConn's Jeremy Lamb and Shabazz Napier are too. Still, the most important reason for Kentucky's success recently isn't Knight's scoring; it's how he's taking care of the ball. Knight had eighteen turnovers over the three games in Maui (including five against UConn) but only fourteen in four NCAA Tournament games this March. Believe me, that's no small deal.

As for the rest of the team, well, Terrence Jones was Kentucky's high scorer that night with twenty-four points, and now he's, to a large degree, an afterthought for the Wildcats (he hasn't scored twenty-plus since February 12). Then again, that's not necessarily a bad thing as Josh Harrellson, DeAndre Liggins, and Darius Miller are all more involved. As a matter of fact, if there's one word to describe the evolution of both teams this year, I think it'd be "balanced."

Speaking of Harrellson, I've got to ask, why aren't more people talking about this kid's story? The guy scored a total of twenty-two points in all of the 2010 season, yet scored seventeen in the Elite Eight alone. Maybe it's because of his goofy nickname (Jorts) or because of his dad's camouflage hat, I don't know, but Harrellson isn't getting nearly the publicity he deserves. As one Kentucky fan told me earlier this week, "A treadmill has never treated anyone better."

And really, I think he could be a key to this game. If Kentucky establishes him early, I just don't think UConn has anyone who can handle him one-on-one. Alex Oriahki is prone to foul trouble, and because of that I don't think Calhoun will start him on Harrellson. And if that means Charles Okwandu gets the call defensively, Harrellson could have a double-double by halftime. I'm not kidding.

For UConn, I believe their key offensively is different than what most people expect me to say, and that is that I think someone besides Kemba Walker needs to carry the offense early. My biggest fear is that Kemba tries to do too much, forces a few bad shots, and Kentucky gets a few easy threes or dunks and gets the crowd in Reliant Stadium going early. On offense, UConn needs to execute in the half court, and much like playing on the road in an NFL playoff game, take the crowd out of it.

As for their defense, I think this is where it gets interesting. To me, the key for UConn is Shabazz Napier.

The truth is that for all the heroics Knight has had in this NCAA Tournament, he wasn't all that good against Ohio State, especially when Aaron Craft was guarding him. Yes, Knight hit the game-winner over Craft, but he also finished just three for ten from the field against the Buckeyes and one for six from three with six turnovers.

Well, I've seen both Ohio State and UConn a lot this year, and truth be told, Napier is a better defender than Craft is. I know that sounds like blasphemy to a lot of people, and I will admit that fundamentally, Craft is the better pure defender. But based on quickness and pure instinct, I'll take Napier. And remember too, if Napier can come in and take the pressure off Walker to guard Knight that will only help Kemba have fresh legs on the offensive end too.

Speaking of Kemba and the offense, I'm not as concerned as most that Kentucky's best defender DeAndre Liggins is guarding him. Now that's no disrespect to Liggins who's done a hell of a job this tournament on the defensive end, most notably on North Carolina's Harrison Barnes.

Still, I don't think Liggins's size and length will be as much of a factor as most do. For one, San Diego State tried to do the same thing, essentially rotating a bunch of bigger, longer, and more athletic guys on Walker all game long. And we all saw what happened there as Kemba ripped off thirty-six points, including fourteen in a row in the second half.

And actually, I think that unlike what people tried to do with Jimmer Fredette this year, putting bigger guys on Kemba is actually beneficial to him.

It allows Walker to use his favorite move, that quick, herky-jerky jab step where he gets into the lane, fakes his shot, and gets fouled. I've seen him do it a million times against a million different kinds of defenders. And having watched every UConn game this year, I know that the big, physical guys aren't actually the ones who give him problems. It's the small, quick guys like Peyton Siva from Louisville, or even—as crazy as this sounds—Ben Hansbrough from Notre Dame. The ones that are low to the ground and in his grill give him problems. The bigger ones he just goes right around or, in some cases, right through.

Finally, I don't think the "home-court" advantage that Kentucky will have is much of a big deal either. UConn is an incredible 12–0 on neutral courts this year, and, to a degree, I think they actually like the stage. It didn't affect them last week when they basically played two road games against San Diego State or Arizona in Anaheim, the latter of which my buddy Mark (who was at the game) called "The craziest sporting event" he's ever been to. And believe me, this guy has been to a sporting event or two in his life.

In the end there's no way the score of this game is anything like the 84–67 final in Maui five months ago, but the result is the same.

UConn and Butler will play for the title Monday.

# Chapter 18

## UConn-Kentucky: The Huskies Are Playing for a Title (Published April 3, 2011)

There's no right way to start this article. Believe me, I've tried.

I've tried to be funny and serious. Sarcastic and stupid. Light-hearted and with an edge. But there's nothing, no words in our beautiful English language which can describe how I feel right now. UConn will be playing for a National Championship Monday night, and I, Aaron Torres, am speechless. Ask anyone who knows me, and they'll tell you that doesn't happen often.

The road to get here wasn't easy. It came with a bunch of pot holes that I've already mentioned a million times and really don't need to repeat. You already know plenty about them: The midseason struggles this past winter. The NCAA sanctions which were smacked down on the school in February. The health of Jim Calhoun which has fluctuated like the weather over the last couple years. And I haven't even mentioned some team named Kentucky that the Huskies had to play on Saturday night.

Speaking of Kentucky, this article is bittersweet if only because I love that program nearly as much as I love my own. Starting with their fans, I won't let anyone say a damn bad word about them. Yes, Big Blue Nation is zany, but truthfully, they'll be the first to fess up to that zaniness and admit that yes, maybe they care about their team a little too much. If you don't believe me, I've got a bunch of e-mails in my inbox that admit to just that.

At the same time, you know what else the folks in Kentucky are? Some of the most kind and sincere people I've ever dealt with. I can't tell you how many e-mailed me this week just to wish me luck heading into Saturday's game. Some did it in twenty words and some did it in two thousand words, but that's just what makes Kentucky fans so darn fun. Nobody loves their school, and nobody loves basketball more than they do. As far as I'm concerned, we should all strive to care about our team that much.

And on the court Saturday night, they once again had something to be proud of. Understand that this Wildcats team was hardly the most talented since the school's last Final Four trip in 1998. Really, they're not even the most talented of the last two years. If the 2010 squad played the 2011 squad in shirts and skins, it'd be a massacre. Patrick Patterson, DeMarcus Cousins, and John Wall would've worked this group like a speed bag.

But what this team lacked in talent and experience, they made up for in heart and grit. The Wildcats showed it when they battled to win three straight tough games to close the regular season. They showed it when they blitzed through the SEC Tournament and avenged an early season loss to Florida. They showed it with a close win over Princeton early in this NCAA Tournament and back-to-back thrillers to beat Ohio State and North Carolina last weekend.

And there's no doubt they showed it again Saturday night when Kentucky fell down by double digits at halftime, only to scrap and claw back, eventually turning a ten-point deficit into a 35–33 lead just five minutes into the second half.

From there it was on, and the two teams went back and forth like the great heavyweight fighters they are. UConn took the lead. Then UK took it right back. Then it was tied. Eventually UConn seemed to seize control, leading by six with under two minutes to go.

But like they've been doing for the last six weeks, Kentucky refused to quit. After DeAndre Liggins made a three-pointer and then the front end of two foul shots, a six-point lead was all of a sudden just two. To say my heart was racing at this point would be factually incorrect. I'm pretty sure it stopped all together.

After getting the ball back with under a minute to go and up two, UConn left the playmaking duties (and ultimately their season) in the hands of Shabazz Napier. Now understand that wasn't totally by design, but with Liggins draped all over Kemba Walker, UConn had little choice. And unfortunately for the Huskies, for the first time in a long time, Napier looked like exactly what he is—an inexperienced freshman. With the shot clock winding down, Napier tried to split two defenders, took one misstep, and turned the ball over. Kentucky had the ball back with just a few seconds to go.

From there the drama only intensified. After a time-out, Brandon Knight got the ball and tried to work some of his March Magic. He tried to get into the lane, tried to get a good look, but with Kemba Walker defending him and Charles Okwandu (of all people) helping out, he couldn't. Knight forced the ball to Liggins, who forced an errant three that was no good. Two Napier free throws later, and that was the ball game. UConn will play Butler Monday for a championship.

But before we talk Butler, let's go back to that last play for a second, because I think it perfectly symbolized UConn's night.

Understand that this was a game where if the Huskies were going to win, it was going to have to be on the backs of their defense. Kemba Walker was gassed by the last few minutes, Jeremy Lamb's game was as quiet as his shy personality, and Napier was missing shots he normally makes. Simply put, the offense was an albatross the entire second half, and after shooting over 50 percent from the field in the first twenty minutes of the game, UConn was just seven for twenty-two from the field after the intermission (that's less than 33 percent for those of you who are as bad at math as I am).

Yet just like they have been for the last four weeks, this team just found a way to win. As a matter of fact, if you came up with one theme for this club, that's exactly what it'd be. Not matter who the opponent is, or what the stage is, someone, somehow, is going to make a play.

Against Pitt in the Big East Tournament, it came on Walker's game-winning jumper. Against Louisville in the Big East Final, it was a Walker pass to Jeremy Lamb. Against Arizona last weekend, Lamb had a couple late crucial steals. And on Saturday, it was smothering defense that forced the tournament's most clutch player—Knight—to become a bystander for the biggest shot of Kentucky's season. Looking back on UConn's season, none of their games seems to have anything in common, except that they always seem to end in a win.

So here we are, and forgive me for being repetitive, but I'm just as shocked on this (very) early Sunday morning as I have been all season. From Maui to Manhattan, and through Anaheim last weekend, this whole season has seemed one unreal dream, and one that I really don't want to wake up from.

As for Monday night, I honestly don't know if this whole tournament run will end in a win or a loss. With the way this Butler team has been playing, nothing is a certainty. Well, except that as fans, we're in for a great game.

So will UConn win Monday? I don't know. But at this point, nothing would surprise me.

# Chapter 19

## Butler-UConn: Thirteen Keys to Decide a National Championship (Published April 4, 2011)

HOUSTON—I bet you wouldn't be surprised if I told you that I didn't sleep well last night. After getting into Houston around midnight and falling asleep sometime around 2:00, I was back awake at 6:00 a.m., staring at the ceiling, thinking about Monday night's National Championship Game.

Eventually I stopped staring and started writing. Here are thirteen keys I came up with for tonight's game:

**1. Shelvin Mack:** I've been sitting here for twenty minutes thinking about Mack (weird, I know), and I keep coming back to the same thought on him: if you went into a laboratory and built a prototype of the guard which would give UConn the most trouble, it has to be the guy, right?

Think about it. Kemba Walker and Shabazz Napier can handle the super-quick guards. Jeremy Lamb can guard the bigger, more athletic ones. But who exactly on this UConn roster is going to guard a guy like Mack? Someone who's super-quick, with deep three-point range, and shoulders like Rosie O'Donnell? A guy just as comfortable pulling up from twenty-four feet or bowling over his defender to get into the lane? Someone who get his points in a million different ways?

Really, I can't find anyone on this UConn roster, and the more I think about it, the more I'm just making myself nauseous. So I'll stop. Still, looking back on UConn's season, the only opponent I can come up with who had a comparable game to Mack's was Notre Dame's Ben Hansbrough. And oh, by the way, Hansbrough had a pair of twenty-one-point games against the Huskies.

Well news flash, Mack is better than Hansbrough. That's a scary proposition for UConn.

**2. Tempo:** Reflecting on Butler's NCAA Tournament runs the last two years, the one thing that has remained eerily consistent is the following: no team in the country is better at making you play *their* game than Butler is.

And if there was ever a case where that was most evident, it was Saturday night against VCU. After the Bulldogs jumped out to a 5-0 lead, VCU smartly lulled Butler into playing *their* game, sped up the tempo, and before you could blink, the Rams had hit four straight threes and led 15–7.

Smartly, Brad Stevens called a time-out, and all of a sudden, it seemed like Butler was a different team. Rather than going up and down and forcing bad shots, the Bulldogs would get the ball past half-court, pull it out, set up their offense, and run time off the clock. And that's ultimately what the game came down to. For the first five minutes, VCU played their game. For the next thirty-five, VCU played *Butler's*. Not surprisingly, after that 15–7 run to open the game, Butler outscored VCU 63–47 to close things. And they won going away.

As for UConn, well, I'm curious to see how they handle things Monday night. Looking back on their tournament run, pretty much everyone has allowed them to get out and run, dating back to the Cincinnati game in the second (third) round. Arizona let UConn run. Kentucky let UConn run. Even cerebral (and some would say boring) San Diego State let UConn run. Well, Butler won't.

Which leads to the following question: We know UConn can win playing their game. But can they win playing Butler's?

**3. Alex Oriahki:** Look, we all know that Kemba Walker is far and away the best player on this UConn team. I don't think I'm breaking any news there. But ask any UConn fan and they'll tell you that it's actually Oriahki who might be the team's most *important* player.

Of course the problem was that at times this season it seemed like Oriahki kind of forgot that. The sophomore showed his age often, getting into foul trouble and disappearing for long stretches. In a related story, when that happened, UConn tended to lose.

Well, to Oriahki's credit, he has been much better during this NCAA Tournament. While his scoring numbers are down (thanks in large part to a hideous hook shot that sometimes works and sometimes looks like it's going to break the backboard), the important numbers are up. Oriahki has averaged almost ten boards per game and hasn't fouled out of a single tournament game.

If he can continue those trends, I like UConn's chances Monday night.

**4. Zach Hahn:** Apparently I'm getting old, because I could've sworn I remembered seeing Hahn hit like five huge threes in Butler's win over VCU on Saturday night. Looking at the box score, it was actually two. But, damn, did it feel like five. Again, apparently my mind isn't as sharp as it once was.

Still, UConn needs to watch out for this guy. Points are going to be at a premium Monday night, and the last thing the Huskies need is some unassuming guy coming off Butler's bench and swinging the game with a big three. Or five. Whatever it may be.

**5. Roscoe Smith vs. Khyle Marshall:** Two true freshmen. Two goofy names. Two of the secret keys to this game.

For Marshall, he's pretty much the only big off Butler's bench and, athletically, pretty much the only guy who can match up with UConn in the post (Sorry, Matt Howard and Andrew Smith. It's true). And to his credit, Marshall has been killing it all tournament long, especially in the last three games. Since the start of the Sweet 16, he's averaged over eight boards a game, a number that is even more impressive since he's barely playing twenty minutes a night. (By the way, I'm not much into the stat PER, or any advanced metrics in basketball for that matter. But if I was, I feel like Marshall's numbers would make my head explode)

As for Roscoe, his six points and five rebounds per game don't jump out at you, but like Marshall, he's prone to random outbursts in big games. He had twelve points in the Big East Tournament final against Louisville and has grabbed at least seven rebounds in three of UConn's five NCAA Tournament games. Plus, nobody pounds their chest harder after meaningless plays than Roscoe does. It really is his trademark at this point in the year.

Of these two guys, whichever has the bigger game gives his team a huge advantage. And each team needs every advantage they can get Monday.

**6. The Coaching Factor:** Don't worry, I'm not about to pull out the "Naive young guy versus wily veteran" story angle like every other writer in America. Honestly, I'm better than that. (Actually I'm not. But still.)

What I will say though, is that if Calhoun has the edge here, it isn't because of his "basketball experience" as much as his "real life" experience too. For Calhoun the end of the tunnel is near, and he's smart enough to know that opportunities like these just don't come around very often. And I've got to believe that more than ever, Calhoun will leave everything on the sideline Monday night. (And this is where you can make the joke, "He won't take a dime back" with him to the locker room. Good one. I totally wasn't expecting that.)

Understand that's not to take anything away from Stevens. But at thirty-four, I just don't think he can or will have the same desperation (for lack of a better term) Monday night. Calhoun knows this might be his last shot. Stevens can't possibly think the same thing.

Advantage: UConn.

Speaking of advantage UConn…

**7. Niels Giffey:** Easily my favorite German-born Husky ever. Sure he might not play at all Monday night, but whatever. This is my preview. And Niels is getting his shout out.

**8. Matt Howard:** …(Oh man…

Approach this slowly Aaron…

Remember what your mom always told you, if you don't have anything nice to say...)

Aww, screw it. I hate Howard!

Well, OK, I don't hate Matt Howard, at least not on a personal level. In a basketball sense though, he's about as likeable as the Asian bird flu or Carrot Top's stand-up act. And don't even get me started on Howard's hair. Pleeeeease don't get me started on that hair.

Still, I can't deny that Howard is an incredible player and has been one of the most impactful of this tournament. Quite frankly, I can't think of one "smarter" big man in college basketball this year. Howard always seems to be in the right position, always seems to make the right play, and always seems to do five to six little things that don't show up in the box score that impact the game. The guy is just a winner, straight up. He's also easily the scariest, un-athletic, pale, six-foot-eight white guy UConn has played all year.

Don't let the look fool you. The guy is terrifying.

**9. Shabazz Napier:** Who, when you think about it, is kind of like Matt Howard. Well, minus the size, game, hair, and pretty much everything else actually.

The one thing you can't deny though is that like Howard, Napier does all the little things to help UConn win. On defense he takes the other team's best guard (Hello, six for twenty-three shooting from Brandon Knight), and on the other end of the court, he takes control of the offense and lets Kemba Walker play off the ball. I cannot tell you how important that's been to UConn's success this year.

On a deeper level, Napier doesn't care about shots, but when he gets them, makes the most of them. He's hit big buckets in the Big East Tournament, the Elite Eight win over Arizona, and against Kentucky Saturday night.

You can win without a lot of things in college basketball. But you can't win without a guy who does all the little things like Napier.

**10. Jeremy Lamb:** I've got some good news and bad news on Lamb if you're a UConn fan.

The bad news is that Lamb seemed totally disengaged and maybe even a little taken aback by the moment on Saturday night.

Yes, he finished five of eight from the field, but he didn't play with that assertive swagger he's been carrying the last month or so.

The good news? UConn won anyway.

And the better news is that Lamb will be much better Monday night. I can promise you that.

**11. The Crowd:** Let's be honest. If you're not a UConn fan, from Connecticut, or one of Stanley Robinson's illegitimate children, you probably won't be rooting for UConn on Monday night. You can admit it. We're all friends here.

And really, it's OK, because for whatever reason, this UConn team has enjoyed playing the role of underdog all year. It wasn't a factor in Maui, in the Big East Tournament, or when they played San Diego State and Arizona in what amounted to back-to-back road games in Anaheim. And it certainly wasn't a factor Saturday night when there seemed to be more Kentucky fans in Reliant Stadium than there were left back home in the state's borders.

That knack for playing well on neutral courts is always why I think any talk of "experience" is moot at this point. Yes, Butler is older, and yes, they played in this game last year. Still, it seems like every UConn game over the last five weeks has come down to the last possession, and UConn keeps coming out on top.

Butler may have more experience overall. But nobody has more experience in tight, pressure situations than UConn.

**12. Defense:** If I asked you, "Off the top of your head, which of these teams do you think is better defensively?" instinctively you'd say Butler, right? Well, in actuality, they're pretty darn even. Butler allowed fewer points per game this year, although many would say that's more because of their style of play than anything else. As for defensive field goal percentage (a better gauge of how a team really plays), UConn actually had the edge. They held opponents to 39.8 percent while Butler held theirs to just 42.

And to me, that's one of the things that I don't think Jim Calhoun and his staff have gotten nearly enough credit for this season. It's always easy to get a young team to play hard on offense, but on defense, that's a whole other story. Hell, last year's UConn team started three seniors and they had about as much interest in playing defense as I have in European art. That is to say, basically none at all.

Well, this UConn team takes pride in their defense, and it showed Saturday night. UConn was phenomenal all game but especially in the first twenty minutes against Kentucky. They held the Wildcats to 28 percent shooting in the first half and 33 for the game, and it was their defense more than their offense which was the difference in getting the win.

Finally, let's be honest. We could sit here and break down a million different stats, matchups, and keys, but there's one thing that can't be factored in. That's the play of…

**13. Kemba Walker:** And I can't help but think it'll be the difference in Monday night's game. (Shocking revelation, I know.)

Watching Kemba play this year has been as much of an "experience" as anything else. As a fan, I've never trusted a guy to make the big play down the stretch like I do this guy. He did it in Maui. He did it in the regular season and the Big East Tournament. And he's been doing it all NCAA Tournament-long too. Understand that Walker might not make every play all game long, but at the college level, I can't remember anyone ever making more plays when his team absolutely needed them.

And really, I can't see UConn getting all the way to this point, all the way to the National Championship Game, and Kemba letting them lose it. When two teams are even like these two are, more often than not, it comes down to which side has the best player on the court. And that's Kemba.

In the end, I expect a back-and-forth game, but he'll be the difference.

UConn 66, Butler 62.

UConn will be your National Champions.

# Chapter 20

## The Perfect Ending to an Unforgettable Season: The UConn Huskies Are National Champions (Published April 6, 2011)

**H**OUSTON—When UConn won Saturday night's Final Four semifinal, I just *knew* I'd be in Reliant Stadium for Monday night's National Championship Game. I didn't know how I'd get to Houston. Or where I'd find the tickets. Just that I'd be there. It was a surreal feeling and reminded me of one of those wedding shows on TLC that you stumble across and see some bright-eyed girl in her late twenties say, "The second I just met Jason, I just *knew* he was the one." That was me Saturday night. I just *knew*.

Now understand that the whole trip was about more than basketball to me. Yes, I'm a UConn fan. Yes, I went to the school. And yes, I'm wildly spoiled by everything the program has done over the past two decades. But it wasn't about that. Being in Houston Monday night was about this team in specific.

As I've mentioned many times before (and I'm sorry, but it needs to be repeated), this is the type of team that as a fan you hope to root for just once or twice in your life. They were the ultimate blue-collar, hard-hat, "sum is greater than the parts" group. Nobody cared about stats and minutes, not any more than wins and losses anyway. Being a fan of this specific team and getting to watch the team all year was like being a computer nerd who wakes up one day and finds himself dating a supermodel. You know eventually things probably won't work out as you hope. But you still want to enjoy the ride while it lasts.

Beyond that, maybe the coolest part of the whole 2011 UConn Huskies season was how outsiders began to view this team. The rivals that used to hate UConn, hate Jim Calhoun's outbursts, and hate the swagger the program walked around with, all of a sudden came full circle. I can't tell you how cool it was to hear Louisville, Syracuse, and Kentucky fans tell me all March, "Once my team got knocked out, I've been rooting for you guys. I don't know what it is, but there's just something about them that I just love." It hasn't been often that UConn is the scrappy underdog that's somehow relatable, yet that's exactly what they were this year.

So now hopefully you can understand why I decided to go to Houston. It wasn't just about a basketball team, because really, basketball teams come and go. It was about *this* team in specific. It was because I realized that if fifteen guys could sacrifice so much over the course of six months, the least I could do was sacrifice three days and a whole bunch of money I didn't have for them. In a weird way, I feel like they'd do the same for me (corny, I know).

Now let's get to the game Monday night. By now you've had a chance to swallow it and digest it, and truthfully, we can all be honest here: it was ugly. You know that. I know that. My ninety-four-year-old grandma who thinks basketball is a game with nine innings and three outs per inning knows it too.

Still, the result on the court doesn't take away from the experience of just being there.

It doesn't take away from the experience of seeing Reliant Stadium on TV a million times, then walking up a ramp in downtown Houston, turning a corner, and being overwhelmed by it in person. It doesn't take away from spending thirty-six hours wondering how you'll get a ticket to the game, finally getting one, holding it in your hand, and just thinking to yourself, "Wow am I blessed." And it certainly doesn't replace walking into an empty football stadium, a building that looks like you could land a fleet of 747s in it, and thinking, "I'm seriously about to watch my team play for a title."

Speaking of which, the experience before the game was one I can't fully describe.

Understand that I've been going to big-time college basketball games for a long time. I've seen fist fights break out over next to nothing. Which is why I wasn't totally prepared for the lead up to Monday night's game, an atmosphere I'd call "respectfully tame." There was no yelling or shirt popping, just a bunch of UConn and Butler fans walking around the concourse in Reliant Stadium, nodding, acknowledging each other and smiling. Nobody was boastful or arrogant, as much as just surprised their team was playing Monday night. It was the most easygoing "Prelude to a Championship" I could ever imagine.

Come to think of it, walking around as the teams warmed up, I've got to admit it was pretty surreal. Maybe it's because I'd only gotten into Houston the night before and could barely get my bearings before heading to the stadium Monday evening. I don't know. Yet as my friend and I first took our seats, it almost seemed like we were there to watch a basketball game in a huge stadium, not a basketball game to determine a National Champion. I almost had to pinch myself and say, "Dude, you're sitting in the arena minutes before the National Championship game. *Get excited!!!!!!!!!*"

Luckily that feeling started to change right before tip-off. The stadium inexplicably filled up to darn near capacity, like some secret side door had all of a sudden been opened and let sixty thousand people in at once. Looking down from the second deck, all you could see was a sea of Kentucky blue and VCU yellow, and a whole lot of UConn and Butler royal blue with little blotches of every other color of the rainbow filling in the rest. It really felt like a big-time event a few minutes later when a giant American flag draped the court and Leann Rimes belted out the most perfect version of the National Anthem I've ever heard. I'm not much of a crier, but the combination of my team, the moment, the flag, and the song nearly brought me to tears.

Once the game tipped, well you know what happened from there. It was slow, and when both teams started missing shots early, it took the air out of an otherwise excellent and supportive crowd.

A few things on the pace and play of the game. Obviously it was ugly. I'll give you that. I do think it was a little overblown though.

Understand that as a team, UConn spent most of the first half in foul trouble purgatory with Kemba Walker, Jeremy Lamb, and Alex Oriahki each ending the half on the bench with two fouls each. Yes, it was ugly, but as I said to my friend at the time, "I'd be willing to bet money that these five guys haven't been on the court together all year, at least not in any meaningful situation." And then they were being asked to keep their team in contention in the biggest game of their lives? No wonder they didn't look so hot. I don't think it's much of a surprise that the offense was much more fluid in the second half.

As for Butler, well, what can you say? Things eventually got so ugly that I actually started feeling bad for them. Now obviously I wanted my team to win, but at the same time I've still got nothing but respect for the Bulldogs program. More importantly, I've seen them enough to know that if the National Championship Game were played one hundred times, in ninety-nine of them Butler would've looked better than they did Monday. It just wasn't their night, which happened to be on the worst night possible for that to happen. Everyone affiliated with the program deserved better than what happened against UConn.

(One quick side note: To all the NBA fans who choose to watch one college basketball game a year and then spend the next forty-eight hours making sweeping judgments and bad jokes about the sport as a whole, please, just go away. This was the highest-rated NCAA Tournament ever and the most attended Final Four ever. College basketball doesn't need you.

And by the way, when you get a chance, take that stick out of your you-know-what and get some facts straight. UConn shot 34.5 percent in victory, a number which, yes, was kinda, sorta ugly. At the same time, guess what? The Lakers won Game 7 of last year's NBA Final shooting 32.5 percent.

Thought I'd throw that out there. )

Anyway, back to the game.

As the second half wore on and UConn started making shots and Butler kept missing theirs, it became pretty clear the Huskies were going to win. I went from anxious and uneasy in an upper deck filled with Butler fans, to strangely at ease, and finally at the under four-minute time-out, my friend and I got out of our seats and made our way down to the lower level. It took two escalators, some sprinting through the concourse, and a little cajoling of the ushers, but eventually we ended up about twenty rows off the court for the final few minutes of the game.

From there, it really is just a blur.

Understand that it's one thing to see your team win a title, and it's another to be in the building when it happens. But when they win the title, you're in the building, *and* the final few minutes aren't in doubt? It's pure nirvana. To be able to just clap and yell and hug and high-five without a care in the world? It doesn't get any better. To hear the final horn sound, to see the guys on the bench run onto the court to hug their teammates, watch the confetti fall, and to realize, "Good God... we are National Champions?" What can top that?

Not much, especially when it's followed by a million other little things you can't experience watching the game on TV. Like watching the stadium crew quickly set up a makeshift podium at center court. Or seeing Jim Nantz hand your head coach the trophy only to follow it up with a dumb question that makes you think, "If I saw him walking down the street, would I punch him? Yeah, actually, I think I would." Or being there as every player climbs up on a ladder and cuts down the nets. Or having the chance to watch "One Shining Moment" on a scoreboard five hundred feet in the air rather than on a TV five feet off your living room floor? Wow.

And to me the best and toughest part of the night was sitting in Reliant Stadium after all that and simply not wanting any of it to end. Long after the game was over, and even after the team had already retreated to the locker room, I was still in the stadium, sitting in a folding chair, drained, and trying to take in every last moment. The empty seats. The loose confetti. Everything. I'm not joking when I say that if the cleaning crew hadn't kicked me out, I might still be there.

Eventually we did get kicked out though, and after a long walk, short cab ride, and a bunch of yelling at no one in particular, we made it back to our hotel.

Once there, we didn't get too wild and just enjoyed some cheap beer with a few other UConn fans we'd met along the way. We celebrated and smiled, watched replays on *Sportscenter*, and passed the time talking about everything that'd happened from November through the end of Monday night. It was the perfect end to the perfect day which capped a completely perfect season, with no one concerned about anything but that exact moment.

It reminded me a lot of our basketball team actually.

# Chapter 21

## A Goodbye to Kemba Walker
## (Published April 13, 2011)

*C*hances are pretty good that Kemba Walker doesn't read this Website. My guess is it'd be more likely that Jim Calhoun, John Calipari, and Rick Pitino got together for a picnic in Central Park this weekend than that Kemba's eyes ever cross this article.

*But on the off chance they do, I just wanted to thank him for the incredible ride he took the fans on this season. With the announcement yesterday that he is leaving UConn for the NBA Draft, here is my thanks to him in letter form.*

Dear Kemba,

So, word on the street is that you're leaving UConn, huh?

Can't say that I totally blame you. Actually, I take that back. I can't think of one good reason you should come back to UConn. Well, unless you enjoy the sorority parties and fifteen-degree January nights that much. Really, looking at this thing objectively, I can't remember a college basketball player with *less* reason to come back to school for another year of college ball.

First of all, you just won a National Championship (Did I thank you for that, by the way?), and really, what's cooler than going out on top?

Come to think of it, Brett Favre really could've learned a thing or two from your example.

Also, you should be commended for earning your degree in three years. As someone who needed a full four years and still barely got my piece of paper, you really ought to be just as proud of yourself. At some point your basketball skills will be gone, but that degree with be with you forever.

Plus, with all this fear about an NBA lockout and a whole bunch of your pals deciding to come back to school for another year, it seems like you just keep climbing up everyone's NBA Draft board. Every time I hear that a Perry Jones or Jared Sullinger or John Henson is coming back to school, all I can think is, "There's some more money (deservedly) in Kemba's pocket." On a different note: can a friend get a loan? Kidding, buddy. You earned every penny you're about to get. Spend it carefully.

But whatever happens at the next level is kind of unimportant right now. Because, at least for today, we need to celebrate everything you did at UConn.

For starters, everyone knows about the raw stats. Your 23.5 points per game was fourth in the country this year and second in the Big East to only Providence's Marshon Brooks. Not too shabby, huh?

Of course for those of us who had the privilege of watching you every night, your scoring prowess was just a small part of the Kemba Walker Experience this past season.

It's easy to forget now, but you were also second on UConn in rebounding, a number that's all the more impressive considering that you weigh about as much as one of Alex Oriahki's thighs. You also finished with almost a two to one assist-to-turnover ratio and averaged almost two steals per game, proving that the game of basketball is about much more than just putting the ball in the basket.

While we're here, I should probably also mention how you took the UConn record book and lit it on fire. (It's Ok. According to a source within the athletic department, all records were backed up onto floppy disk, so need to worry about said fire.) Did you know that only two players in the history of the UConn program have ever scored more than 800 points in a season prior to this year? That's right, Donyell Marshall scored 855 in 1994, and Ray Allen followed up with 818 two years later.

Well, not only did you join those two in the 800-point club, you also became a charter member of the 900-point club, crushing Marshall's record with 965 points this year. Incredibly, not only did Marshall and Allen never come close to scoring 900 points in a season (let alone 965), but neither did Ben Gordon, Rip Hamilton, Rudy Gay, or Caron Butler. And all those guys turned basketball into a pretty nice livelihood, no?

But Kemba, you're a smart guy (again, congrats on that diploma you'll be getting this May), so you know that stats only tell part of the story. After all, stats told voters to give Jimmer Fredette the National Player of the Year award this year. And not to take anything away from Jimmer, but do you think he'd trade spots with you right now? My guess is no. Not only do you have a National Championship, but... you can drink alcohol whenever you please! Kidding, Jimmer! Besides, that's not entirely true anyway since you don't turn twenty-one for another few weeks.

Really though, the fact that you're still twenty is the perfect segue to the next part of this letter. Because despite being a boy in the eyes of the law, you played like a man all year.

As I mentioned before, looking at your stats won't do your season its full justice.

Looking at the stats won't tell someone just how much of a burden you had to carry early on. Sure the stats may say that you averaged thirty points a night over three games in Maui back in November, but how can any numbers signify the leadership you had to show over that same stretch? How can they explain that despite defenses being focused on you night after night at Lahaina Civic Center you got the ball in key spot after key spot and came through just about every time? How can looking at a box score explain how much sun and sleep Gregg Marshall, Tom Izzo, and John Calipari (three pretty darn good coaches) lost worrying about you? And how no matter what they tried, you refused to be stopped? Stats can't do that. Like I mentioned before, they're wildly misleading.

The stats also can't tell the story of how your teammates looked up to you in those early weeks like the surrogate big brother you'd become.

Now obviously UConn won the Maui title because of contributions other than your own. Alex, Jeremy, and Shabazz were all phenomenal. Then again, it needs to be mentioned that those guys rose to the occasion in large part because of the confidence *you'd* instilled in them. They had what I called at the time, "The Kemba Walker Security Blanket." In other words, they didn't worry about making mistakes because they knew that no matter what happened, you'd come in, clean things up, and make everything better. Like any good big brother would.

Stats also don't tell the story of how much your game morphed over the year. Believe me, I watched every one of your games (What's that? Yes, I know I'm lame.), and whether you fully realize it or not, your game did in fact change.

At the beginning of the year (in Hawaii and in early league play), you carried the boys, a lot like how Charlie Sheen carried Jon Cryer and that chubby kid over the first few seasons of *Two and a Half Men*. Those guys relied on you for an unhealthy amount of support. Unlike the television show though, over time the guys began to spread their wings and began to hold their own. Jeremy became the second scoring threat the team needed, Shabazz became one of the best perimeter defenders in the country, and Roscoe, well, he sure is a goofball, huh? And as I already mentioned, your game changed over that time as well. It wasn't obvious to those who weren't watching closely, but it did happen nonetheless.

After some mid-season struggles when everyone—including yourself—was still figuring out their role on this team (Which seems like a lifetime ago, doesn't it?), your game continued to evolve, and you became a perfectly unstoppable superstar for this team. I'm not quite sure when everything clicked, but by the end of the year your play was even more valuable than anything you did in November. You toed the line perfectly between phenomenal teammate who got everyone into the game early before taking over and becoming a straight-up assassin late. Jason Bourne would've been proud.

The first signs were obviously at the Big East Tournament, to start this whole wild March ride. You heard about that whole "Five wins in five days" thing, right? The play that will always stand out to most was the crossover game-winner you had on Gary McGhee, the one which made you a March star, and made him a permanent poster boy for "ankle breakage." That was Kemba being Kemba, the superstar returning from a bit of a midseason lull.

You know what I'll remember though?

I'll remember two nights later against Louisville in the Big East Championship game. In the closing minute, when everyone in the arena knew you were getting the ball, when you penetrated into the lane, when you...passed to Jeremy Lamb for the game winner. That's when I knew you'd arrived as a complete player, Kemba. Not only could you do it on your own—we all knew that—but the fact that you had confidence in your teammates took this team to a new level. And that's when everyone started to realize that things were getting interesting.

And it only continued into the NCAA Tournament where your game continued to evolve. At times you were deferential, like when you took just eleven shots in the opening-round win against Bucknell. But at times you went back to being assertive and dominant, like when you dropped thirty-four points on San Diego State, including, what was it, twelve UConn points in a row in one stretch?

Maybe I'm naive (or really, "stupid" is the right word), but after that game was when I started to think you guys might just take home the title after all. And the credit all goes back to you. November's Kemba Walker was dynamic, exciting, and the best player in college basketball, but UConn wasn't winning a title with him. The Kemba Walker of March, though? That dude was dynamic, exciting, and the best player in college basketball...who also had an unrelenting faith in the other four guys on the floor and made everyone around him better. Just understand that in November Kemba Walker *was* the UConn team. In March he was just the biggest part of it. There's a big difference. And an important one too.

Speaking of the title, it automatically vaulted you into the discussion of the greatest players in UConn history. Now honestly,

Kemba, I'm not really good at putting these things into a historical perspective, so you'll have to forgive me. But if Ray Allen, Caron Butler, and Donyell Marshall didn't even play in a Final Four, how could they rank ahead of you? And as great as Rip Hamilton, Emeka Okafor, and Ben Gordon were, you can claim something they never could: you were a contributor on two Final Four teams, the only person in school history that can really say that. (Tell your boy Donnell Beverly I'm sorry, but it's true.) Because for all your March heroics this time around, it's easy to forget now that UConn probably wouldn't have gotten to Detroit in 2009 without your twenty-three points in the Elite Eight against Missouri. Don't worry, I didn't forget.

Ultimately though, Kemba, what I will remember about your time at the school beyond the wins and titles is just how fun it was to watch you play.

Starting with your physical "prowess," I hate to bust your chops (OK, who am I kidding, I love to!), but you're not much taller than me and certainly not any heavier. (I know, I know. I've got a few pounds to lose) So the fact that you took all those hits and fouls this season and kept bouncing up, going to the free throw line, and hitting clutch shots was incredible to watch. It was Iverson-ian, really.

Beyond that though was the mental toughness you brought to the court every night. It seemed like no matter the situation, the time left on the clock, or the amount your team trailed by, you never doubted your own ability to get things done. Not early, not late, and not when you were tired. You were like the Energizer Bunny mixed with Superman. And because of it, I've never had more faith in a guy to get things done in crunch time. Again, I just can't describe how fun it was to watch you. Hopefully someday you'll be able to sit back and appreciate everything the fans got to this year.

Alright, Kemba, this letter has gone on long enough. By now you've probably stopped reading and gone to shoot jump shots somewhere. If you haven't, well, you're an even better guy than all those reporters say you are. Because if you can deal with my babbling, you truly are a saint.

So let me conclude by saying thank you.

Thank you for an unforgettable season. Thank you for making this UConn team maybe the most fun to follow ever. Thank you for the most unlikely of championships in any sport I can ever remember.

But most of all, just thanks for being you. I speak for a lot of people when I say it was our pleasure watching these past six months and these past three years.

Good luck going forward, but honestly, you don't need it.

See you down the road.

—Aaron Torres

# Epilogue

They lined the streets eight and nine deep. Young and old. Rich and poor. Black and white. From Avon and Andover, Wilton and Waterbury, and everywhere in between. They came on April 17, 2011, forty thousand strong to the state capitol of Hartford. They came to see the UConn Huskies. Kemba and Company. College basketball's National Champions.

As players and coaches rode on double-decker buses through the city streets to the cheers of a state and region that adored them, so much had changed since returning from Houston just a few weeks earlier.

It started at the celebration immediately following the return from the Final Four. One hundred or so fans met the Huskies at the airport at Windsor Locks, and many thousands more at Gampel Pavilion after their bus had made its way down I-84 to Storrs.

Upon getting into the arena, the Huskies emerged one by one, each to the deafening roars of the crowd. First the assistant coaches. Then the players, bleary-eyed and in sweat pants, still wearing the hats they'd been handed on the podium in Houston the previous night. Next was Jim Calhoun, looking as fresh and energetic as any sixty-eight-year-old possibly could. And of course finally, holding the

National Championship trophy, Kemba Walker received the loudest ovation of all.

By that point of course, Walker was as beloved as any player in UConn history. Parents that couldn't afford tickets to actually see the Huskies play brought their children to Gampel Pavilion that day to catch the state's newest hero in the flesh. Walker's male peers painted their chests with the letters of his name. Young women asked for his hand in marriage, either with written signs held over their heads, or simply by yelling over each other, one louder than the last. This was Kemba's time. It was Kemba's kingdom.

But as Kemba and his teammates took the podium that day, the school which Kemba had given so much to, reciprocated and had done something for him. At the celebration in Storrs, Kemba's jersey was set to be raised to the rafters and placed into UConn's "Ring of Honor" alongside the program's greatest players. It was an honor that no active player had ever received, the brainchild of a conversation between Sports Information Director Kyle Muncy and Administrator Tim Tolokan just days before. Jim Calhoun later approved (assuming the team won the championship of course), and when Kemba stepped on stage, only those three knew what was coming next.

When the curtain did drop and his jersey revealed to the thousands in the arena, emotion overcame Kemba as he fell weakly into the arms of his coaches and teammates. Finally, through tears he told the crowd, "Sorry, I'm a bit emotional right now. I never thought I'd see this day, with my name up there,"[1] wiping away the wet spots surrounding his eyes as he spoke. Kemba Walker had officially arrived amongst the greats of the UConn basketball program, just as he was getting ready to leave Storrs. Within a few days, he'd declare for the NBA Draft.

Right around the same time, things proved to be equally busy for Head Coach Jim Calhoun. The off-season is always crazy for any coach. It's that much more so for a coach with a new ring on his finger.

The Jim Calhoun summer whirlwind started almost immediately upon his return to Storrs. He rang the opening bell on the New York Stock Exchange a few days after coming in from Houston. A couple days later, the lifelong Red Sox fan threw out the first pitch at Fenway

Park (Walker would do the same just at a Yankees game later in the week). He spoke at events across the state of Connecticut. And organized and participated in the fifth annual Jim Calhoun Cancer Challenge Ride and Walk with proceeds going to cancer research. Calhoun was even expected be a speaker at Dedham High School, one of the first coaching stops of his career way back in the early 1970s. Unfortunately rain cancelled that event.

But neither rain, nor sleet, nor snow could stop Calhoun and his team from heading down to Washington, DC, in mid-May. There they would spend the early part of the morning on May 16 conducting a clinic with some elementary school kids in the area. Of course like every college and pro team that wins a title, they were also there to meet the President of the United States. Calhoun and his team had met Bill Clinton following the Huskies' first title in 1999 and George W. Bush five years later. Now it was time to meet Barack Obama.

"I have to be honest—this is a bittersweet day for me," the President said when addressing the UConn players and coaching staff. "On the one hand, I get to congratulate a great team and a great coach and a National Champion. But on the other hand, I am reminded once again that my bracket was a bust."[2] The comment brought laughs and smiles to all in the room. After all, that's what you do when the President of the United States makes a joke in your presence.

Unfortunately, at the same time, the off-season wasn't all fun and games for college basketball's reigning kings of the court. No championship team can be kept entirely intact, and with Donnell Beverly and Charles Okwandu completing their eligibility and Walker headed to the pros, the Huskies were no exception. The attrition continued just days after the team returned from Houston when Assistant Coach Andre LaFleur left to become the associate head coach at Providence College.

After playing for Calhoun at Northeastern, LaFleur had spent ten years at UConn, both as the director of basketball operations and later as an assistant. He was the man who tracked down Kemba Walker through Moe Hicks and Book Richardson early in the guard's recruiting process and the same who once famously took a twenty-four-hour flight to Australia to scout Ater Majok only to stay for a few hours and fly right back. But with George Blaney entrenched as Calhoun's associate head coach, LaFleur jumped at the opportunity for a promotion at Providence where he'd be new Head Coach Ed Cooley's right-hand man. With his departure, Glen Miller was elevated from director of basketball administration to LaFleur's spot as an assistant. And eventually former UConn assistant and recently fired George Washington head coach Karl Hobbs would return to Storrs to take over the spot vacated by Miller.

The staff wasn't the only spot where changes took place.

With three departed players, the likely assumption would naturally be that UConn had three scholarships to give away to the next group of Huskies. Instead, they were in a curious limbo entering the off-season.

UConn gave one of those scholarships to incoming recruit Ryan Boatright, a guard expected to replace some of Kemba Walker's production with Shabazz Napier moving into the starting lineup. The Huskies also lost one scholarship because of the sanctions handed down by the NCAA in February. In addition, the school lost an extra two scholarships because they were unable to meet the NCAA's minimum Academic Progress Rate (APR) requirements. The APR is a system put in place to monitor how a program's players have progressed academically in years past, losing points for any player who leaves the school (either by their own choice or because their eligibility is up) with unfinished coursework. And even though the mark released in the summer of 2011 didn't reflect the previous year's team (only from 2006–2007 to 2009–2010 clubs), UConn's score of 893 was well below the NCAA's requirement of 925 points (out of a possible 1,000). In addition to losing a scholarship for the sanctions, they'd lose an additional two because of the APR. It also cost Calhoun a hefty contract bonus of over $87,000. He'd also have to make a $100,000 donation to the school's general scholarship fund for falling below the APR minimum as well.

Despite that, another scholarship did open up when Jamal Coombs-McDaniel left the school in May.

Coombs-McDaniel had a tumultuous career at UConn, dating all the way back to his arrival at the school with childhood friend Alex

Oriahki in the summer of 2006. But on the court, Coombs-McDaniel never could seem to stay in the good graces of Jim Calhoun and more than once ran afoul of his coach. He even considered transferring in January of 2011, before sticking it out and becoming a contributor later on in the season.

In the end, Coombs-McDaniel's best game would go down as his twenty-five-point explosion against Providence College, but his most important undoubtedly was in the Big East Tournament against Pittsburgh. While everyone will always remember Kemba Walker's heroic shot to win the game, what's easier to forget is that Kemba had missed a jumper just seconds before that Coombs-McDaniel rebounded before quickly calling a time-out. Out of a time-out, Walker hit the shot that beat Pittsburgh and in some ways propelled UConn to a title. Coombs-McDaniel's AAU coach Leo Papile said of his former pupil that he constantly made "winning plays," the kind that don't necessarily show up in the box score but are impactful in the final outcome of the game. Well, that play was exactly that. Had UConn not beaten Pitt in the Big East Tournament, it's impossible to say if they'd have gained the confidence needed to make a run at the National Championship.

Even with all that, it seemed time for Coombs-McDaniel to leave the school and find a place where he'd have the opportunity to play more. An off-season, non-basketball related incident helped expedite that process. It happened in late April when he and two friends (no one on the basketball team) were arrested with marijuana and a grinder, and charged with possession of a controlled substance and possession of drug paraphernalia. Eventually Coombs-McDaniel would enter a Diversion program as a first-time offender, and should he complete it, will have his record cleared.

Still, the arrest didn't push Coombs-McDaniel out the door as much as his desire for more playing time. With Jeremy Lamb returning at shooting guard and Roscoe Smith at small forward, there was no guarantee that he would start or even what his role would be. On May 5, Calhoun released a statement which said in part: "Jamal and I met recently and, although he loves the program, he would like more playing time. He and I both agree that he may have more opportunity for that playing time in another program."[3]

After weighing his options, Coombs-McDaniel eventually decided to transfer to Hofstra University where he'd be joined by former UConn assistant coach Patrick Sellers. As you may remember, Sellers resigned from UConn just prior to the NCAA's Notice of Allegations in May 2010, but upon the release of sanctions in February, Sellers had been cleared of an original charge of "Providing False and Misleading Information" to investigators. With that clearance, he was allowed to coach in college basketball again. Sellers—who'd spent the 2011 season coaching in China—returned to the United States just in time to see the Huskies take home the title, and signed on at Hofstra in late April. His former UConn recruit followed suit a few weeks later.

Beyond Coombs-McDaniel's brush with the law and transfer, there was other negative press around the program following the championship. Even Kemba Walker, the player who'd done next to nothing wrong all season, couldn't escape the media scrutiny.

A seemingly harmless quote by Walker to a *Sports Illustrated* reporter after the championship win over Butler became a national headline when the magazine hit newsstands a few days after the team returned from Houston. The reporter had seen the book *Forty Million Dollar Slaves* in Walker's duffel bag in Houston, and when he asked the star guard about it, Kemba replied, "It's the first book I've ever read [cover to cover]."[4] Eventually Walker cleared up the quote (he meant a book outside of required academic reading), and given that he was graduating from one of the top public schools in the country in three years, most understood that it was taken out of context. Still, it gave the national media plenty of fodder in the following days.

Really though, that snafu was minor compared to a public firestorm in late July when new University President Susan Herbst hired an outside consulting firm to audit the Athletics Department and Athletics Director Jeff Hathaway in particular. The timing seemed a bit surprising given that it a banner year for the department (the football team, baseball team, and men's and women's basketball teams had all won the Big East Conference) and that Hathaway had been named the chairman of the NCAA Tournament Committee for the 2012 season. It's one of the highest honors an athletics director can receive.

But read between the lines, and many saw it as a power play by the school's head basketball coach to get a man he'd openly bickered with for years out of office. Coming off a third National Championship, Calhoun's power—perceived or real—had never been higher, and he spent most of the summer making non-committal remarks about his future, leaving many to wonder if it had anything to do with Hathaway. In Calhoun's defense, when news leaked of the situation, Herbst publicly acknowledged that as a new president, she was doing audits of all the university's departments, and athletics just happened to be next. To cynics though, the timing was nothing if not ironic.

Eventually everything came to a head on August 20. On that date, under conditions known only to him and a handful of others, Hathaway announced his retirement from the school effective immediately. As part of the agreement, neither side was allowed to speak of the other publicly, unless under the oath of an NCAA investigation. It brought an end to Hathaway's eight-year run as the man in charge of UConn's Athletics Department and close to twenty overall that he'd spent at the school.

Back on the basketball court, the returning UConn Huskies got to work.

UConn welcomed two new recruits to the mix for the 2011 championship defense: Boatright, the guard from Chicago, and the highly regarded DeAndre Daniels. Daniels received Coombs-McDaniel's scholarship and the last roster spot on the 2011–2012 squad.

Or so everyone thought.

That's because on August 28, one of the biggest surprises in the history of college basketball landed on UConn's doorstep, gift-wrapped for Jim Calhoun. That was the No. 1 high school senior in the country, Andre Drummond, who decided that he wanted to enroll at UConn—effective immediately—to play in the 2011–2012 season.

If you're confused by that last sentence, don't be. It requires plenty of explaining and nearly four years' worth of background information.

Drummond was a fascinating story in the sense that he was the rare superstar who grew up wanting to play for the Huskies that was actually from Connecticut. For all the success that Calhoun had over the years in recruiting players like Walker from New York, Oriahki and Napier from Boston, and others from all corners of the country and globe, there was rarely ever a player from within the state's own borders good enough to suit up for the school. Even when someone with Connecticut roots did play for the Huskies, most never took on more than a contributing role with the team. As you can imagine, a state with a population of barely over three million people just doesn't produce a ton of elite basketball talent.

Well, Drummond was certainly elite as the six-foot-eleven center who grew up in Middletown, Connecticut, was considered to be far and away the No. 1 player in the high school class of 2012. He had all the intangibles any coach could ever want in a center: the size of a near seven-footer, with the skills of a wing player, and athleticism that could match anyone on the court. Some recruiting analysts believed that he was the best high school center prospect since Dwight Howard seven years before him.

Add in that combination of size and skill with his love of the home state team, and it was assumed that Drummond was a lock to end up at UConn.

If he ever decided to play college ball, that is. You see, there was a catch with Drummond.

Early on in his high school career, Drummond had repeated a year of school, meaning that by the time the 2011–2012 season rolled around, he was nineteen-years-old and set to start his fifth year of high school. The catch was that given Drummond's age, and the fact that his original high school class graduated in the spring of 2011, it meant that according to current NBA rules, Drummond could enter the professional ranks without ever having to step on a college campus. It seemed like the ultimate Catch-22: The best player the state had ever produced, the one that generations of fans had waited to watch and embrace their entire lives, would likely never have any obligation to attend college.

And it was expected to stay that way. At least until late August.

That's because on a cool, crisp Friday night, just days before classes were set to begin, Drummond called Calhoun and told him that he wanted to play for UConn—that year. Because Drummond had already been in high school for four years, he had all the needed coursework and SAT scores done to enroll in college for the fall of 2011 if he chose. And in late August, Drummond had a change of heart, elected to skip his last year of high school, and do exactly that. He announced his decision via Twitter to the shock of the entire college basketball world. No player of Drummond's caliber had ever showed up on a college campus that late in the process. UConn was set to start classes for the fall semester just days later.

Of course like most of the things that had happened in UConn's off-season, Drummond's decision didn't come without some criticism. Since UConn was at its scholarship limit, a player that was currently under scholarship would be forced to either give theirs up or leave the school entirely. Even if Drummond chose to pay his own way he couldn't; NCAA rules still stipulated that because he was a recruited player, someone else had to be taken off scholarship.

That player was Michael Bradley, a raw six-foot-ten center prospect in his own right, who had redshirted during the 2010–2011 season. With his background (Bradley spent seven years of his childhood in the Tennessee Baptist Children's Home), Bradley was reportedly able to secure a significant financial-aid package, meaning that even in giving up his scholarship, he would incur very few out-of-pocket expenses.

Still, even with Bradley's blessing and even considering that just about any other college would've made the same decision, UConn received national criticism nonetheless. Many were incensed that Bradley gave up his scholarship when he had done nothing wrong to have it removed. Even more so, many saw the Drummond situation as UConn's way of skirting their NCAA punishment after they'd lost a scholarship because of sanctions. Simply put, had they not committed NCAA violations and if they'd had the necessary APR scores, UConn wouldn't be missing any scholarships to begin with.

Regardless, Drummond arrived just in time to start college classes in late August, along with Boatright and Daniels, who'd been on campus since the spring, along with many of the returning key pieces of the 2011 title team. During the off-season, Oriahki and Napier were named captains for the 2012 season, with Jeremy Lamb expected to take on a starring role after a breakout freshman campaign. Over the summer Lamb continued his ascent into the discussion of college basketball's best players. He was selected for the United States Under-19 National Team, leading them in scoring on their way to a fifth-place finish at the World Championships in June. It seemed like a far cry from where Lamb had been just two summers earlier when he was an unknown high school junior on the AAU circuit.

Then again, the entire UConn Huskies basketball program is a far cry from who they were prior to the 2011 championship season. With four starters returning off the title team and the addition of Drummond, UConn is expected to be firmly in the National Championship hunt from the beginning of the season, looking to become just the second team in twenty years to win back-to-back National Championships. It certainly is a much different scenario the Huskies saw themselves one calendar year before, when they didn't receive a single vote in the preseason polls. The next six months proved to be a wild ride that no one could've foreseen coming, and in the process, changed the perception of a coach, his program, and of course, one superstar player.

"When I look back on this UConn team, I think they'll be remembered for taking on the character of their coach and best player," CBS Sports college basketball writer Jeff Goodman said. "They took on the heart of Kemba Walker, and the stubbornness of Jim Calhoun."

Starting with Calhoun, one of the greatest coaches in the history of college basketball didn't need a third National Championship to prove himself to anyone. But by winning that third one, he did put himself in the rarest of rare company. He is now one of only five coaches in the history of the sport to win three or more National Championships, joining John Wooden (ten), Adolph Rupp (four), Mike Krzyzewski (four) and Bobby Knight (three) in that category.

"Coach always talked about not wanting to catch lightning in a bottle," his former assistant Tom Moore said. "Any coach can get one good recruiting class, and be good for two or three years. But coach always talked about building a great program, not just a great team.

"And to me, that's the greatest testament to him. If you go back through all his years at UConn, and take any five years, basically four of them would be highly successful; Sweet 16's, Elite Eight's, Big East titles. That's a great *program*. I know how much he loves UConn basketball, and after everything he went through the previous year, I know how much that hurt. I couldn't be happier for him."

Beyond just the enormity of the title itself though, was how UConn won it. In an era where the best high school players are usually celebrities by their pre-teen years, and too often come to college entitled and disengaged, there was something charming about the old-school approach to the way the 2011 UConn Huskies played basketball. Not just in their ability to overcome the odds, but to do it in a tough, gritty way. In that regard, the 2011 UConn Huskies had Calhoun's fingerprints all over it.

"Through the years Jimmy's best teams would out-work you, out-tough you, out-compete you," Leo Papile, Calhoun's friend, dating back 30 years to their days in Boston said. "That's exactly what that team was all about. It was his perfect team. This was Jimmy's masterpiece."

And then of course there was Kemba Walker, who had quite a busy spring and summer in his own right. It started when he was inducted into the Ring of Honor and included many other stops from there. He threw out the first pitch at Yankee Stadium in mid-April, sat courtside with New York City Mayor Mike Bloomberg at a New York Knicks playoff game, and made a handful of other public appearances across the Northeast.

More important than any public appearance or basketball game though, Kemba fulfilled a promise he'd made over a year before. On May 8, 2011, he gave his mother Andrea Walker the ultimate Mother's Day gift, graduating from the University of Connecticut a year ahead of schedule with a degree in sociology. In a truly Shakespearean twist, the same day that Kemba Walker entered the world as a man, he also became one in the eyes of the law. May 8, 2011, was also Kemba Walker's twenty-first birthday.

Following the ceremony, Walker's sole focus became the NBA Draft. He declared right after the championship celebration in April, and by the time June came around, was believed by most everyone to be a Top 10 pick.

Still, that didn't stop pundits, experts, and average fans from picking his game apart and wondering how he would transition to the pros. Mainly the questions on Kemba focused on two things: Was he big enough for the pros? And was he a true point guard or just a pure scorer?

Of course by that point in his career, those were questions pretty familiar to Kemba Walker. By the time the NBA Draft rolled around, he'd faced them at any number of points in his career: when everyone told him he'd never play at Rice High School in New York; prior to the Arizona Cactus Classic; and as he entered his junior year at UConn. At every step of the way, Kemba answered those questions, and, thankfully, he'll get the chance to do them one more time. On June 23, 2011, the Charlotte Bobcats made him the ninth overall pick of the NBA Draft.

But whether Walker goes on to be a multiple time NBA All-Star or just another average player in the league, it will do little to take away his legacy at the University of Connecticut. Simply put, he was one of the greatest players at one of the best programs in college basketball history, someone who not only left everything he had on the court but proved to be everything a student-athlete should and can be off of it too.

And for one glorious winter, Kemba was *the* story as he took college basketball fans on a wild ride and in the process took a group of nobodies and turned them into somebody. He turned them into a team greater than anyone in college basketball circles could've ever imagined.

Ultimately the 2011 UConn Huskies will be remembered for a lot of things, both within Connecticut's borders and beyond. They'll be remembered for their wild run in Maui, their epic five wins in five days at Madison Square Garden, and their continued success in the NCAA Tournament. They'll be remembered as a team whose sum was greater than its parts and one that proved superior chemistry could overcome talent alone. Mostly though, they'll be remembered as "Kemba's team" and for Kemba Walker himself.

We'll remember Kemba going from town to town, arena to arena, and ripping the heart out of the chests of opponents. We'll remember him for doing it with skill and flair and heart that couldn't be quantified. And mostly, we'll remember that smile. The one that made Syracuse and Pitt, Louisville and Kentucky fans agree, "I may not like UConn. But I do respect Kemba Walker."

In the end, ESPN college basketball analyst Jay Bilas summed up the 2011 UConn Huskies in one sentence about as well as this entire book could. "I don't know if they'll go down as one of the greatest teams in college basketball history," Bilas said of the Huskies.

He then added, "But they will definitely go down as one of the best stories ever."

Couldn't have said it better myself.

# Acknowledgments

I'll spare everyone the sappy, overindulgent fluff that you normally find in these Acknowledgments sections, and just say that like every book, this one wouldn't have been possible without the influence and support of an incredible group of people.

Thank you to the folks at CreateSpace for giving a young author an avenue to get this book published, when no one else in the industry would. And thank you for making me feel like my book was always your No. 1 priority, even as you worked on countless others at the same time.

Thank you to my agent Neil Salkind. If you hadn't believed in, and vouched for me from the beginning, I'm not sure I would've seen this book through to the end. I'm sorry things didn't work out quite as planned, and can only say that I look forward to working with you again in the future.

Thank you to Matt Norlander for writing the foreword to this book. When I pitched the idea to you, this book was much more a vision in my head then a piece of work put to paper. But you never questioned me, never asked for more details, and only wanted to know what you could do to help me along. Seriously, Matt, you're the man.

Thank you to the countless people who took time (often on short notice), and agreed to interviews with me for this book, despite not knowing who I was, or what my intentions were. Your words made this book a million times than my own did, and I can honestly say that there wasn't one person I interviewed who wasn't fully gracious with their time, and helped me out however they could. Not to mention that getting to know people I'd heard of- but never gotten to connect with- was maybe my favorite part of this experience. I'll never forget tracking down Book Richardson and talking to him well after midnight on the East Coast, speaking with Rolando Lamb for over an hour about everything *but basketball*, or being in awe when a journalist the caliber of Adrian Wojnarowski took my call. And really, I've got a story like that with just about who spoke to me throughout this process, and I only wish I had more space here to share those stories. In addition, I can only hope that everyone I interviewed for this book enjoyed talking to me as much as I did them.

Beyond that, an indelible amount of gratitude goes out my friends and family for their unbelievable support, encouragement and belief in me through the years. Thank you to all my buddies from UConn and home, for giving me someone to drink beers with and vent to, when the writing process became overwhelming. Thank you to my uncle for legal advice that hopefully won't get me sued. Thank you to Kristin for your patience, and Gloria for laughing at all my terrible jokes, and to everyone else I can't squeeze into this spot. You know who you are, but what you probably don't know is how much your support means to me.

Of course thank you to my parents. I said it at the beginning of this book, and it's true: I can't think of two people who have any less in common than you two do. Seriously, how the hell did you end up together? But I'd also like to add that one of the few things you do share is your love and support for me. You've never questioned my decisions, or the path that's led me to where I am today. All you've ever told me was to work hard, believe in myself, and find something to do with my life that'll make me enjoy getting up out of bed every day and going to work. I believe I've found that. I only hope that in the process, I've made you proud.

And finally, thank you to the 2011 UConn Huskies.

One of my favorite quotes in this entire book was when Jim Calhoun's long-time friend Leo Papile called the 2011 season Calhoun's "masterpiece." I love, love, love that quote.

And in a lot of ways, I feel like this book is *my* masterpiece.

I am hopeful that over the course of my life I get an opportunity to write another book or two, but I doubt that I will have more fun getting to learn the ins and outs of a particular program, school and team as much as I did this one. If that makes me a homer, I don't care (plus it's already a bit late for such a confession, huh?). The 2011 UConn Huskies will always have a special place in my heart, a sentiment that I'm sure I share with a lot of people around the state.

In conclusion, to anyone associated with the 2011 team, I'll tell you what I've told anyone who has tried to congratulate me on writing this book: The congratulations doesn't go me, it goes to you guys. The 2011 UConn Huskies were incredible without me. All they needed was for someone to put their story into words.

I'm blessed to be that person.

# Citations and References

**Prologue:**
**References:**

Lawlor, Christopher. "N.Y.'s Rice Topples Simeon 53-51, Despite Rose's 22," USA Today, January 15, 2007. http://www.usatoday.com/sports/preps/basketball/2007-01-15-weekend-roundup_x.htm
Arizona Cactus Classic. http://www.jimstoreyproductions.com/arizonacactusclassic/2007.html
Arizona Cactus Classic Championship Game. http://www.jimstoreyproductions.com/arizonacactusclassic/gamestats07/b0001000079.html

**Chapter 1:**
**Citations:**
[1] Associated Press. "Five Huskies Hit Double Figures In Victory Over Colgate," ESPN.com, November 16, 2009. http://espn.go.com/ncb/recap?gameId=293200041
[2] Anthony, Mike. "UConn Men Beat LSU 81-55," Courant.com, November 26, 2009. http://articles.courant.com/2009-11-26/sports/hc-ucmen1126.artnov26_1_time-i-saw-connecticut-blowout-of-unranked-lsu-work-ethic-meter

[3] Associated Press. "Duke Stays Unbeaten, Hands UConn First Loss," ESPN.com, November 27, 2009. http://espn.go.com/ncb/recap?gameId=293310150

[4] Torres, Aaron. "UConn-Kentucky: A Final Four In December," AaronTorres-Sports.com, December 10, 2009. http://www.aarontorres-sports.com/articles/college-basketball/kentucky-uconn-a-final-four-in-december.html

[5] "No. 13 UConn Falls To No. 12 Georgetown, 72-69," UConnHuskies.com, January 9, 2010. http://www.uconnhuskies.com/sports/m-baskbl/recaps/010910aaa.html

[6] Associated Press. "Calhoun Taking Medical Leave," ESPN.com, January 20, 2010. http://sports.espn.go.com/ncb/news/story?id=4839919

[7] Associated Press. "Dyson Drops 32 As No. 21 UConn Demolishes No. 1 Texas In The Second Half," ESPN.com, January 23, 2010. http://espn.go.com/ncb/recap?gameId=300230041

## References:

Associated Press. "Duke Stays Unbeaten, Hands UConn First Loss," ESPN.com, November 27, 2009. http://espn.go.com/ncb/recap?gameId=293310150

Associated Press. "Dyson Scores 15 Straight In The Final 7:11 To Secure UConn's Victory," ESPN.com, November 17, 2009. http://espn.go.com/ncb/recap?gameId=293210041

Associated Press. "UConn Assistant Blaney Leads UConn Past St. John's," ESPN.com, January 20, 2010. http://espn.go.com/ncb/recap?gameId=300210041

"Harangody, Villanova Coaches' Picks In The Big East," NCAA.com, October 29, 2009. http://www.ncaa.com/news/basketball-men/2009-10-20/harangody-villanova-coaches-picks-big-east

O'Neil, Dana. "Robinson Picks Himself Up Off The Scrap Heap For UConn." ESPN.com, December 15, 2008. http://sports.espn.go.com/ncb/columns/story?columnist=oneil_dana&id=3769359

## Chapter 3:
## Citations:

[1] Wetzel, Dan and Wojarnowski, Adrian. "Probe: UConn Violated NCAA Rules," Yahoo Sports, March 25, 2009. http://rivals.yahoo.com/ncaa/basketball/news?slug=ys-uconnphone032509

[2] Anthony, Mike. "UConn Addresses NCAA Violations," Hartford Courant, May 29, 2010. http://articles.courant.com/2010-05-29/sports/hc-uconn-ncaa-inquiry-0529-20100528_1_josh-nochimson-basketball-operations-beau-archibald-assistant-coach-patrick-sellers

[3] Davis, Ken. "Jim Calhoun Defends Himself At Big East Media Day," AOL.com, October 20, 2010. http://www.aolnews.com/2010/10/20/jim-calhoun-defends-himself-at-big-east-media-day/

## References:

Anthony, Mike. "Calhoun Signed Through 2013-14," Hartford Courant, May, 7, 2010. http://articles.courant.com/2010-05-07/sports/hc-calhoun-contract-0507-20100506_1_calhoun-and-hathaway-jeff-hathaway-jim-calhoun

Anthony, Mike. "Glen Miller On Being Hired By UConn," Hartford Courant, July 2, 2010. http://blogs.courant.com/uconn_mens_basketball/2010/07/glen-miller-on-being-hired-by.html

Anthony, Mike. "Kemba Walker Comfortable As A Leader," Hartford Courant, October 21, 2010. http://blogs.courant.com/uconn_mens_basketball/2010/10/kemba-walker-comfortable-as-le.html

Anthony, Mike. "Kemba Walker Dominating UConn Practices," Hartford Courant, October 28, 2010. http://blogs.courant.com/uconn_mens_basketball/2010/10/kemba-walker-dominating-uconn.html

Anthony, Mike. "Sellers And Archibald Resign," Hartford Courant, May 28, 2010. http://articles.courant.com/2010-05-28/sports/hc-uconn-ncaa-inquiry-coaches-0529-20100528_1_beau-archibald-patrick-sellers-resignations

Borges, Dave. "Majok Leaves UConn To Pursue Professional Career," New Haven Register, September 2, 2010. http://www.nhregister.com/articles/2010/09/02/sports/mmajok090210090210.txt

Katz, Andy. "Ollie Says He's Joining UConn's Staff," ESPN.com, July 2, 2010. http://sports.espn.go.com/ncb/news/story?id=5348090

"Pittsburgh Chosen As Big East Hoops Favorites," BigEast.Org, October 20, 2010. http://www.bigeast.org/News/tabid/435/Article/214542/Pittsburgh-Chosen-As-BIG-EAST-Hoops-Favorite.aspx

## Chapter 4:
## Citations:

[1] Anthony, Mike. "A.J. Price And Kemba Walker," Hartford Courant, October 18, 2008. http://blogs.courant.com/uconn_mens_basketball/2008/10/aj-price-and-kemba-walker.html

[2] Associated Press. "Walker's 23 Points Leads UConn To A Final Four Berth," ESPN.com, March 28, 2009. http://espn.go.com/ncb/recap?gameId=294000015

[3] Torres, Aaron. "40 Most Valuable College Basketball Players: Part I," AaronTorres-Sports.com. February 25, 2010. http://www.aarontorres-sports.com/articles/college-basketball/40-most-valuable-players-in-college-basketball-part-i.html

[4] Pedulla, Tom, "Walker, UConn Brimming With Confidence For NCAA Tourney," USA Today, March 15, 2011.

## References:

Associated Press. "Dyson Has Knee Surgery," ESPN.com, February 16, 2009. http://sports.espn.go.com/ncb/news/story?id=3911596

Associated Press. "Walker's 23 Points Leads UConn To A Final Four Berth," ESPN.com, March 28, 2009. http://espn.go.com/ncb/recap?gameId=294000015

"The 2008 FIBA U-18 Championships," FIBA.com, July, 18, 2008. http://www.fiba.com/pages/eng/fa/event/p/sid/4009/tid/379/_/2008_FIBA_Americas_U18_Championship_for_Men/index.html

Huff, Doug and Tennis, Mark. "Rivals.com's Fab 50 Countdown: No.'s 11-30," Rivals.com, October 31, 2007. http://basketballrecruiting.rivals.com/content.asp?SID=1132&CID=733318

"The Rivals 150 Prospect Ranking," Rivals.com, August 19, 2008. http://rivals.yahoo.com/basketballrecruiting/basketball/recruiting/rankings/rank-rivals150/2008

Rabinowitz, Theo, "Rice Gets Blaised By Holy Cross," NYCHoops. net, March 6, 2008. http://basketballrecruiting.rivals.com/content. asp?CID=782669

"Rice Beats St. Ray's," New York Daily News. February 2, 2008. http:// articles.nydailynews.com/2008-02-02/sports/17892218_1_rice-omari-lawrence-clock

Rivals.com Recruiting Staff. "McDonald's All-American Game Rosters," Rivals.com, February 19, 2008. http://basketballrecruiting.rivals.com/ content.asp?CID=776431

## Chapter 5:
## Citations:

[1] Torres, Aaron. "Kentucky-UConn: A Final Four In December," AaronTorres-Sports.com, December 10, 2009. http://www. aarontorres-sports.com/articles/college-basketball/kentucky-uconn-a-final-four-in-december.html

[2] Torres, Aaron. "College Basketball 2011: A Dozen Things I Think I Know So Far," AaronTorres-Sports.com, November, 17, 2010. http://aarontorres-sports.com/articles/college-basketball/college-basketball-2010-a-dozen-things-i-think-i-know-so-far.html

## Chapter 6:
## References:

"2008 Nike Global Challenge." NYC Hoops.net, July 22, 2008. http:// basketballrecruiting.rivals.com/content.asp?CID=829370

"Boston Athletic Amateur Club: Team Awards." http://www.thebabc. com/BABC/Team_Awards.html

Goodman, Jeff. "UConn Nabs Two Mass Studs Early," Boston Herald, August 12, 2006.

Kasiecki, Phil. "BABC Wins Boo Williams Tournament," New England Recruiting Report, April 9, 2007. http://www. newenglandrecruitingreport.com/news/article/18/BABC-Wins-Boo-Williams-Tournament.php

Longo, Hector. "Brooks Phenom Transferring to Winchendon." Eagle Tribune, July 8, 2006. http://www.eagletribune.com/sports/ x1876238951/Brooks-phenom-transferring-to-Winchendon

"National Championship Belongs To Tilton," New England Recruiting Report, March 11, 2009. http://www.newenglandrecruitingreport. com/news/article/728/National-Championship-Belongs-to-Tilton. php

"NEPSAC Finals-Event Recap," New England Recruiting Report, March 9, 2009. http://www.newenglandrecruitingreport.com/news/ article/725/NEPSAC-Finals-Event-Recap.php

"Signing Day Is Here," New England Recruiting Report, November 12, 2008. http://www.newenglandrecruitingreport.com/news/ article/604/Signing-Day-is-Here.php

"Stars Shine At NEPSAC Finals," New England Recruiting Report, March 3, 2008. http://www.newenglandrecruitingreport.com/news/ article/334/Stars-Shine-at-NEPSAC-Finals.php

"UConn Elite Camp- Event Recap," New England Recruiting Report, August 11, 2007. http://www.newenglandrecruitingreport.com/ news/article/146/UConn-Elite-Camp-Event-Recap.php

Young, Justin. "King James-Sunday," Rivals.com, April 27, 2008. http:// rivalshoops.rivals.com/content.asp?CID=801994

## Chapter 7:
## Citations:

[1] Anthony, Mike. "UConn Men Rejoined Elite In Hawaii," Hartford Courant, November 25, 2010. http://articles.courant.com/2010-11-25/sports/hc-uconn-basketball-men-maui-1126-20101125_1_ shabazz-napier-niels-giffey-roscoe-smith

[2] "UConn vs. UNH Post Game Quotes," UConnHuskies.com, November 30, 2010. http://www.uconnhuskies.com/sports/m-baskbl/ recaps/113010aad.html

[3] "No. 6 Pitt Tops No. 4 UConn In Big East Opener, 78-63," PittsburghPanthers.com, December 27, 2010. http://www. pittsburghpanthers.com/sports/m-baskbl/recaps/122710aab.html

[4] "UConn vs. Texas Post Game Quotes," UConnHuskies.com, January 8, 2011. http://www.uconnhuskies.com/sports/m-baskbl/ recaps/010811aad.html

[5] Associated Press. "Kemba Walker, Huskies Hand Blue Demons 18th Straight Big East Loss," ESPN.com. January 15, 2011. http://espn.go.com/ncb/recap?gameId=310150305

[6] "UConn 61, Villanova 59," UConnHuskies.com, January 17, 2011. http://www.uconnhuskies.com/sports/m-baskbl/recaps/011711aab.html

[7] "UConn vs. Tennessee Post Game Quotes," UConnHuskies.com, January 20, 2010. http://www.uconnhuskies.com/sports/m-baskbl/recaps/012211aac.html

**References:**

Associated Press. "Kemba Walker Tallies First Career Triple-Double As UConn Cruises," ESPN.com, December 3, 2010. http://espn.go.com/ncb/recap?gameId=303370041

Associated Press. "SEC Suspends Bruce Pearl 8 Games," ESPN.com, November 20, 2010. "SEC Suspends Bruce Pearl 8 Games," ESPN.com. http://sports.espn.go.com/ncb/news/story?id=5824966

"AP Poll: Duke Unanimous No. 1; UConn Joins Top 25," NCAA.com, November 29, 2010. http://www.ncaa.com/news/basketball-men/2010-11-29/ap-poll-duke-unanimous-no-1-uconn-joins-top-25

"Jamie Dixon," PittsburghPanthers.com. http://www.pittsburghpanthers.com/sports/m-baskbl/mtt/dixon_jamie00.html

"UConn 61, Villanova 59," UConnHuskies.com, January 17, 2011. http://www.uconnhuskies.com/sports/m-baskbl/recaps/011711aab.html

**Chapter 8:**
**Citations:**

[1] Bishop, Gregory. "Freshman Eases The Pain His Father Caused Calhoun," New York Times, March 25, 2011.

**References:**

"Georgia High School Basketball: All-Metro Boys Teams," Atlanta Journal-Constitution, March 27, 2010. http://www.ajc.com/sports/high-school/all-state-boys-teams-410225.html

Bishop, Gregory. "Freshman Eases The Pain His Father Caused Calhoun," New York Times, March 25, 2011.

"Career Win/Loss Record For Connecticut Coach Jim Calhoun," StatSheet.com. http://statsheet.com/mcb/coaches/jim-calhoun/career_record

Chirinos, Christie Cabrera, "Brandon Knight Named National Gatorade Player Of The Year," South Florida Sun-Sentinel, March 23, 2010. http://articles.sun-sentinel.com/2010-03-23/sports/sfl-brandon-knight-gatorade-player-of-year-10_1_brandon-knight-male-high-school-athlete-gatorade

Holcomb, Todd. "All-State Boys Teams," Atlanta Journal-Constitution, March 27, 2010. http://www.ajc.com/sports/high-school/all-state-boys-teams-410225.html

"Norcross High School Varsity Boys Basketball Records," NorcrossBasketball.com http://www.norcrossbasketball.com/varsity_boy_s_records

Ostrout, Neill, "Shooting Guard Lamb Says He'll Play At UConn," Stamford Advocate, September 15, 2009.

"Reggie Lewis Career Stats," Sports-Reference.com. http://www.sports-reference.com/cbb/players/l/lewisre01.html

## Chapter 9:
## Citations:

[1] "UConn vs. Louisville Coach Calhoun Quotes," UConnHuskies.com, January 29, 2011. http://www.uconnhuskies.com/sports/m-baskbl/recaps/012911aab.html

[2] Anthony, Mike. "Jim Calhoun Asks, Huskies Answer," Hartford Courant, February 6, 2011. http://blogs.courant.com/uconn_mens_basketball/2011/02/post-1.html

[3] Torres, Aaron. "College Basketball Power Rankings Part II: The Contenders," AaronTorres-Sports.com, February 11, 2011. http://www.aarontorres-sports.com/articles/college-basketball/college-basketball-power-rankings-part-ii-the-contenders.html

[4] Associated Press. "Jamal Coombs-McDaniel Scores 12 More Than Previous Career High As UConn Cruises," ESPN.com, February 13, 2011. http://espn.go.com/ncb/recap?gameId=310440041

**References:**
Anthony, Mike. "A Good Night For Jamal Coombs-McDaniel," Hartford Courant, December 31, 2010. http://blogs.courant.com/uconn_mens_basketball/2010/12/a-good-night-for-jamal-coombsm.html
Anthony, Mike. "From Blowing Up To Breaking Out," Hartford Courant, November 27, 2010. http://blogs.courant.com/uconn_mens_basketball/2010/12/a-good-night-for-jamal-coombsm.html
Associated Press. "Jared Swopshire To Have Groin Surgery," ESPN.com, January 12, 2011. http://sports.espn.go.com/ncb/news/story?id=6015766
"Karen Sypher Sentenced To Seven Years In Prison In Rick Pitino Extortion Case," AOL.com, February 18, 2011. http://www.aolnews.com/2011/02/18/karen-sypher-sentenced-to-more-than-seven-years-in-prison/

**Chapter 10:**
**Citations:**
[1] Anthony, Mike. "Shabazz Napier Learning From Kemba Walker," Hartford Courant, July 15, 2010. http://blogs.courant.com/uconn_mens_basketball/2010/07/shabazz-napier-learning-from-k.html
[2] Anthony, Mike. "Shabazz Napier's Showmanship," Hartford Courant, December 9, 2010. http://blogs.courant.com/uconn_mens_basketball/2010/12/shabazz-napiers-showmanship.html

**References:**
"2009-2010 NEPS Boys Basketball Players Of The Year," NewEnglandPrepStars.com, April 6, 2010. http://newenglandprepstars.com/news-events/2009-2010-neps-basketball-players-of-the-year
"2009 St. Mark's Boys' NEPSAC Class C Champions," NEPSAC.com, http://www.nepsac.org/page/2884/nocat_page/page1/91

Anthony, Mike. "Selby Doesn't Make Visit; Shabazz Napier Does," Hartford Courant, February 28, 2010. http://blogs.courant.com/uconn_mens_basketball/2010/02/selby-doest-make-visit-shabazz.html

Anthony, Mike. "Shabazz Napier's Showmanship," Hartford Courant, December 9, 2010. http://blogs.courant.com/uconn_mens_basketball/2010/12/shabazz-napiers-showmanship.html

"AAU National Comes To An End," New England Recruiting Report, August 1, 2009. http://www.newenglandrecruitingreport.com/news/article/936/AAU-Nationals-Comes-to-an-End.php

Chirinos, Christy Cabrera, "Brandon Knight Named National Player Of The Year," South Florida Sun-Sentinel, March 23, 2010. http://sports.espn.go.com/ncaa/recruiting/basketball/mens/news/story?id=5087281

"Dorchester Crime Rate Index," CLN.com, http://www.clrsearch.com/Dorchester_Demographics/MA/Crime-Rate

"ESPN And Rivals Release Rankings," New England Recruiting Report, August 29, 2009. http://www.newenglandrecruitingreport.com/news/article/936/AAU-Nationals-Comes-to-an-End.php

Estrada, Chris. "Eastie Stymies Charlestown," Boston Globe, February 24, 2010. http://www.boston.com/sports/schools/basketball/articles/2008/02/24/eastie_stymies_charlestown/

Forsberg, Chris. "Hoops: Marsden Magic: The Sequel," Boston Globe, March 4, 2008. http://www.boston.com/sports/schools/extras/schools_blog/2008/03/hoops_marsden_m.html

Lawlor, Christopher. "Heralded Recruit Knight Bound For UK," ESPN.com, April 14, 2010. http://sports.espn.go.com/ncaa/recruiting/basketball/mens/news/story?id=5087281

"Lawrence Academy Wins 2010 Class C Boys Title," NEPSAC.com, March 11, 2010. http://www.nepsac.org/page/2884/nocat_page/page1/86

"Locals Held Their Own At Reebok All-American Camp," New England Recruiting Report, July 11, 2009. http://www.newenglandrecruitingreport.com/news/article/898/Locals-Held-Their-Own-at-Reebok-AllAmerican-Camp.php

Murphy, Brendan. "Selby Picks Kansas, Lamb To Kentucky," ESPN.com, April 17, 2010. http://sports.espn.go.com/ncaa/recruiting/basketball/mens/news/story?id=5106954

"Orlando Update," New England Recruiting Report," August 1, 2008. http://www.newenglandrecruitingreport.com/news/article/502/Orlando-Update.php

"Scout.com Announces New National Rankings," September 7, 2009. http://www.newenglandrecruitingreport.com/news/article/1003/Scoutcom-Announces-New-National-Rankings.php

## Chapter 11:
## Citations:

[1] "Nate Miles Timeline," Hartford Courant, March 26, 2009. http://articles.courant.com/2009-03-26/news/timeline0326.art_1_cornerstone-christian-enrolled-jim-calhoun

[2] Associated Press. "UConn, Calhoun Cited For 8 Violations," ESPN.com, May 28, 2010. http://sports.espn.go.com/ncb/news/story?id=5228593

## References:

"A UConn Men's Basketball NCAA Timeline," Hartford Courant, February 23, 2011. http://www.courant.com/sports/uconn-men/hc-uconn-ncaa-timeline,0,2641453.story

Altimari, Dave. "UConn Athletic Department Paying Large Legal Bills To Defend NCAA Basketball Team In NCAA Investigation," Hartford Courant, May 10, 2010. http://articles.courant.com/2010-05-11/news/hc-hc-uconn-legal-fees0511.artmay11_1_legal-bills-legal-fees-ncaa-investigation

Anthony, Mike. "Patrick Sellers, Beau Archibald Resign From UConn Positions," Hartford Courant, May 27, 2010. http://blogs.courant.com/uconn_mens_basketball/2010/05/patrick-sellers-beau-archibald.html

Anthony, Mike. "Positive For Sellers, Not For Archibald," Hartford Courant, February 22, 2011. http://articles.courant.com/2011-02-22/sports/hc-ncaa-archibald-sellers-0223-20110222_1_ncaa-fate-beau-archibald-patrick-sellers

Associated Press. "Jim Calhoun To Be Suspended In 2011-12," ESPN. com, February 23, 2011. http://sports.espn.go.com/ncb/news/ story?id=6146656

Associated Press. "UConn At Hearing Over NCAA Infractions," Greenwich Time, October 15, 2010. http://www.greenwichtime.com/ default/article/UConn-at-hearing-over-NCAA-infractions-708849.php

Ellsbury, Chris. "UConn Admits Violations, Imposes Sanctions On Men's Basketball Program," Connecticut Post, October 8, 2010. http:// www.ctpost.com/local/article/UConn-admits-violations-imposes-sanctions-on-693574.php

Smith, Jeff. "Jim Calhoun Issues Statement On NCAA Ruling, Apologizes For Mistakes," Hartford Courant, February 25, 2011. http:// blogs.courant.com/uconn_mens_basketball/2011/02/jim-calhoun-issues-state-on-nc.html

Wetzel, Dan and Wojarnowski, Adrian. "Probe: UConn Violated NCAA Rules," Yahoo Sports, March 25, 2009. http://rivals.yahoo.com/ncaa/ basketball/news?slug=ys-uconnphone032509

## Chapter 12:
### Citations:

[1] Anthony, Mike. "Roscoe Smith…The Shot…Or Whatever It Was," Hartford Courant, January 9, 2011. http://blogs.courant.com/uconn_mens_basketball/2011/01/roscoe-smith-the-shot.html

[2] Anthony, Mike. "Senior Day For Charles Okwandu," Hartford Courant, March 4, 2011. http://blogs.courant.com/uconn_mens_basketball/2011/03/senior-day-for-charles-okwandu.html

[3] Anthony, Mike, "Senior Day For Donnell Beverly," Hartford Courant, March 4, 2011. http://blogs.courant.com/uconn_mens_basketball/2011/03/senior-day-for-donnell-beverly.html

### References:

Anthony, Mike. "E.O. Smith Coach Ron Pires On Tyler Olander," Hartford Courant, March 25, 2010. http://blogs.courant.com/uconn_mens_basketball/2010/03/eo-smith-coach-ron-pires-on-ty.html

Anthony, Mike. "Mailbag Question, 2/4: Donnell Beverly," Hartford Courant, February 4, 2011. http://blogs.courant.com/uconn_mens_basketball/2011/02/mailbag-question-24-donnell-be.html
Atkins, Eric. "All-Metro Boys Basketball: First Team," Baltimore Sun, March 26, 2009. http://www.baltimoresun.com/sports/high-school/bal-va.bhoops26mar26,0,1260423.story
"Basketball Without Borders," NBA.com http://www.nba.com/bwb/facts_2004.html
Bishop, Greg. "Long Path To The Final Four For UConn's Okwandu," New York Times, April 2, 2011. http://www.nytimes.com/2011/04/03/sports/ncaabasketball/03okwandu.html
Borges, Dave. "Nothing Iffy About Giffey," New Haven Register, June 18, 2010. http://borgesblognhr.blogspot.com/2010/06/nothing-iffy-about-giffey.html
Chardis, Phil. "UConn Men: Is UConn Looking At The Next Thabeet?" Manchester Journal-Inquirer, March 31, 2008. http://www.journalinquirer.com/articles/2008/04/01/sports/uconn/doc47f11042667cf007455660.txt
Hansen, Ben. "SP Special: Josh Pastner On Charles Okwandu," GoAZCats.com, May 25, 2004. http://arizona.rivals.com/content.asp?CID=299722
Jordan, Jason. "Roscoe Smith Still Considering Three," HighSchoolHoop.com, November 20, 2009. http://highschoolhoop.com/recruiting-news/2009/11/roscoe-smith-still-considering-three/
Meyer, Jerry. "Four-Star Smith Off The Board," Rivals.com, January 8, 2010. http://basketballrecruiting.rivals.com/content.asp?CID=1037516
Meyer, Jerry. "Smith Emerging As An Elite Prospect," Rivals.com, May 7, 2008. http://basketballrecruiting.rivals.com/content.asp?CID=805518
Meyer, Jerry. "Top Underclassmen From LeBron Academy," Rivals.com, July 12, 2008. http://basketballrecruiting.rivals.com/content.asp?CID=826217
"Nike Global Challenge: Championship," HighSchoolHoop.com, August 11, 2008. http://highschoolhoop.com/recruiting-news/2008/08/nike-global-challenge-championship/

O'Donnell, Pete. "Olander Talks Transfer, Season, Future," New England Recruiting Report, January 9, 2010. http://www. newenglandrecruitingreport.com/news/article/1192/Olander-Talks-Transfer-Season-Future.php

Quinn, Jason. "In The Gym With 2010 Star Roscoe Smith," MDHigh. com, August 27, 2010. http://basketballrecruiting.rivals.com/barrier_noentry.asp?ReturnTo=&sid=&script=content.asp&cid=706889&fid=&tid=&mid=&rid=

Rhoden, William. "Journey To NBA, Via England And Nigeria," New York Times, March 12, 2011. http://www.nytimes.com/2011/03/13/sports/basketball/13rhoden.html

Telep, Dave. "SF Roscoe Smith: Four Head Coaches Call," Scout.com, June 16, 2008. http://scouthoops.scout.com/a.z?s=75&p=9&c=2&cid=762588&nid=3226332&fhn=1&pg=4

## Chapter 13:
## Citations:

[1] Associated Press. "Kemba Walker Leads No. 19 UConn Past DePaul," ESPN.com, March 8, 2011. http://espn.go.com/ncb/recap?gameId=310670041

[2] "Post-Game Quotes: Connecticut vs. Pittsburgh," BigEast.Org, March 11, 2011. http://www.bigeast.org/News/tabid/435/Article/222208/post-game-quotes-connecticut-vs-pittsburgh.aspx

[3] Post-Game Quotes: Connecticut vs. Syracuse," BigEast.Org, March 12, 2011. http://bigeast.org/News/tabid/435/Article/222321/post-game-quotes-connecticut-vs-syracuse.aspx

## Chapter 15:
## Citations:

[1] Associated Press. "Kemba Walker Powers Huskies' Rout Of Bison," ESPN.com, March 17, 2011. http://espn.go.com/ncb/recap?id=310760041

[2] Anthony, Mike. "Calhoun, Cronin…Buddies," Hartford Courant, March 18, 2011. http://espn.go.com/blog/collegebasketballnation/post/_/id/25417/calhoun-snipes-at-cronin-cronin-fires-back

3 Associated Press. "Kemba Walker's 33 Points Powers UConn Past Big East Rival Into The Sweet 16," March 19, 2011. http://espn.go.com/ncb/recap?gameId=310780041

4 Associated Press. "Kemba Walker, Jeremy Lamb, Lead UConn Past San Diego State," ESPN.com, March 24, 2011. http://espn.go.com/ncb/recap?gameId=310830021

**References:**
Anderson, Kelli. "Madness Of Mesa," Sports Illustrated, February 28, 2011.

Associated Press. "Billy White Has 'Best Game' As Aztecs Top Gonzaga 79-76," ESPN.com, November 16, 2010. http://espn.go.com/ncb/recap?gameId=303202250

Associated Press. "Kemba Walker, Jeremy Lamb, Lead UConn Past San Diego State," ESPN.com, March 24, 2011. http://espn.go.com/ncb/recap?gameId=310830021

Brennan, Eamonn. "Calhoun Snipes At Cronin, Cronin Fires Back," ESPN.com, March 10, 2011. http://espn.go.com/blog/collegebasketballnation/post/_/id/25417/calhoun-snipes-at-cronin-cronin-fires-back

Gonzalez, Agustin. "SDSU Makes History With First Ever Tournament Win," The Daily Aztec, March 17, 2011. http://www.thedailyaztec.com/2011/03/sdsu-makes-history-with-first-ever-ncaa-tournament-win/

"NCAA Basketball Tournament History: San Diego State Aztecs," ESPN.com. http://espn.go.com/mens-college-basketball/tournament/history/_/team1/7272

**Chapter 17:**
Torres, Aaron. "It's Kentucky's Turn To Celebrate," AaronTorres-Sports.com, March 28, 2011. http://www.aarontorres-sports.com/articles/college-basketball/its-kentuckys-turn-to-celebrate.html

**Chapter 21:**

Ostrout, Neill. "Kemba To Make NBA Plans Official On Tuesday," Connecticut Post, April 12, 2011. http://www.ctpost.com/news/article/Kemba-to-make-NBA-plans-official-on-Tuesday-1332187.php

**Epilogue:**
**Citations:**

[1] Anthony, Mike. "Kemba Walker Added To UConn's Ring of Honor," Hartford Courant, April 5, 2011. http://articles.courant.com/2011-04-05/sports/hc-uconn-men-kemba-walker-huskies-of-honor-blog-0405_1_uconn-huskies-gampel-pavilion-history-of-uconn-basketball

[2] Lewis, Charles J. "Calhoun To Obama In Ceremony: 'Yes We Did,'" Connecticut Post, May 17, 2011. http://www.ctpost.com/uconn/article/Calhoun-to-Obama-in-White-House-ceremony-Yes-1380987.php

[3] "Jamal Coombs-McDaniel To Transfer," UConnHuskies.com, May 5, 2011. http://www.uconnhuskies.com/sports/m-baskbl/spec-rel/050511aab.html

[4] Layden, Tim. "UConn's Drive To Survive," Sports Illustrated, April 11, 2011.

**References:**

Abraham, Peter. "Calhoun Goes The Distance," Boston Globe, April 10, 2010. http://articles.boston.com/2011-04-10/sports/29404016_1_coach-fires-fenway-park-red-sox-fan

Anthony, Mike. "Jim Calhoun Guest At Dedham (Mass.) High Graduation," Hartford Courant, June 2, 2011. http://blogs.courant.com/uconn_mens_basketball/2011/06/jim-calhoun-guest-at-dedham-ma.html

Anthony, Mike. "UConn Men's Basketball To Lose Two Scholarships," Hartford Courant, May 20, 2011. http://articles.courant.com/2011-05-20/sports/hc-uconn-apr-0521-20110520_1_ryan-boatright-eligibility-and-retention-jamal-coombs-mcdaniel

Associated Press. "Jamal Coombs-McDaniel Sorry For Arrest," ESPN.com, May 19, 2011. http://sports.espn.go.com/ncb/news/story?id=6566373

Associated Press. "UConn AD Jeff Hathaway Retiring," ESPN.com, August 20, 2011. http://espn.go.com/college-sports/story/_/id/6878820/connecticut-athletic-director-jeff-hathaway-announces-retirement

Associated Press. "UConn Parades Through Hartford," ESPN.com, April 17, 2011. http://sports.espn.go.com/ncb/tournament/2011/news/story?id=6378549

Borges, Dave. "Alex Oriahki: El Capitan," New Haven Register, June 28, 2011. http://borgesblognhr.blogspot.com/2011/06/alex-oriakhi-el-capitan.html

Boyer, Zac. "Report: UConn Assistant Andre LaFleur Headed To Providence," April 16, 2011. http://www.ctpost.com/uconn/article/Calhoun-to-Obama-in-White-House-ceremony-Yes-1380987.php

"Jim Calhoun To Ring Bell At New York Stock Exchange," UConnHuskies.com, April 7, 2011. http://www.uconnhuskies.com/sports/m-baskbl/spec-rel/040711aac.html

"Kemba Walker Attends Knicks-Celtics Game With Mayor Michael Bloomberg," New Haven Register, April 24, 2011. http://www.nhregister.com/articles/2011/04/24/sports/doc4db4a8ba615c1215583294.txt

Rubin, Roger. "Kemba Walker, NCAA Tournament Star, To Throw Out First Pitch At Yankee Stadium, April 13," New York Daily News, April 7, 2011. http://articles.nydailynews.com/2011-04-07/sports/29412434_1_sack-wern-houses-yankee-stadium-bob-cousy-award

"UConn's Michael Bradley Gives Up Scholarship For Andre Drummond," SportingNews.com, September 2, 2011. http://aol.sportingnews.com/ncaa-basketball/story/2011-09-02/uconns-michael-bradley-gives-up-scholarship-for-andre-drummond

"USA Basketball: Under-19 Team Stats," USABasketball.com. http://www.usabasketball.com/mens/u19/2011_mu19_usa_cum.html

14786446R00140

Made in the USA
Lexington, KY
19 April 2012